THE DIALOGICAL THEATRE

The Dialogical Theatre

Dramatizations of the Conquest of Mexico and the Question of the Other

Max Harris

Associate Director, Center for the Study of Mind and Human Interaction,
Assistant Professor of Behavioral Medicine and Psychiatry and
Lecturer in Religious Studies, University of Virginia

St. Martin's Press

First published in Great Britain 1993 by
THE MACMILLAN PRESS LTD
Houndmills, Basingstoke, Hampshire RG21 2XS
and London
Companies and representatives
throughout the world

This book is published in Macmillan's *Studies in Literature and Religion* series
General Editor: David Jasper

A catalogue record for this book is available from the British Library.

ISBN 0–333–53450–6

Printed in Hong Kong

First published in the United States of America 1993 by
Scholarly and Reference Division,
ST. MARTIN'S PRESS, INC.,
175 Fifth Avenue,
New York, N.Y. 10010

ISBN 0–312–08562–1

Library of Congress Cataloging-in-Publication Data
Harris, Max, 1949–
The dialogical theatre: dramatizations of the conquest of Mexico
and the question of the other / Max Harris.
p. cm.
Includes bibliographical references and index.
ISBN 0–312–08562–1
1. Theater—Religious aspects—Christianity. 2. Religion and
drama. 3. Mexico—History—Conquest, 1519–1540—Literature and the
conquest. 4. Intercultural communication in literature.
5. European drama—History and criticism. I. Title.
PN2049.H26 1993
809.2'9358—dc20
92–19478
CIP

Contents

General Editor's Preface

The Dialogical Theatre is a natural sequel to Max Harris's previous book *Theatre and Incarnation*. Theologically it is very much centred on the Christian doctrine of the incarnation as 'encounter', not only between God and humanity but also between individuals and cultures. But its literary, historical and sociological horizons have expanded the discussion in a remarkable interdisciplinary exercise. From the opening pages, 'encounter' is the key word. We begin with an examination of Mikhail Bakhtin's sense of the dialogical (which he related specifically to the novel), and explore Bakhtin's sense of carnival and the creative working against repressive authority and ideology, but denying Bakhtin's contention that the theatre and drama fail to play a part in dialogic encounter and a recognition of 'otherness'.

Harris's specific dramatic subject is the conquest of Mexico. His range of examples is broad, from Dryden's now-neglected play *The Indian Emperor* (1665) to his own intense personal experiences of contemporary folk drama and festival in Mexico. His style conveys the excitement and immediacy of these performances, while never losing its grip on the tight and complex theoretical issues which underlie his thesis. For in the theatre, whether it be the formal stage of the European tradition or the immense, all-embracing spectacles of folk festival in the New World, nothing is ever straightforward or simple.

Harris demonstrates clearly how theatre speaks on a number of levels at once – religious, political, social – always in dialogue and always eluding the specific oppression of text, author, ideology or theology. Theatre has a remarkable capacity to absorb new elements – the camera-clicking tourists of today become the new version of the Spanish conquerors of the sixteenth-century in contemporary Mexican folk drama. Hence this book also speaks with a variety of related voices, just as Bakhtin himself embraces a fundamental political discussion within his explorations into literature, religion and folk culture.

The sense of alterity and 'the other' is now unavoidable in literary theory and theology. From discussions of Tzvetan Todorov and Martin Buber here, one should be led on to reckon with Emmanuel

Levinas and his vastly important programme of post-rational ethics. What excites me particularly is the expansion of the boundaries of the study of literature and religion which this book represents. In his concluding pages Harris brings the reader back very firmly into a consideration of Christian doctrine and a 'performative interpretation' of the biblical text, but the result of his argument is that this activity now must reckon with a huge range of unavoidable issues outside the cloistered pursuit of biblical criticism and theological enquiry.

The conquest of Mexico becomes here the matrix for a fresh appraisal of questions of power and domination, cultural encounter and the theology of mission. I commend this book as a learned, passionate and timely exercise in interdisciplinarity, which takes us back to theory and to the study in the awareness that our pursuits there cannot be isolated from dramatic expressions of the human spirit, complex, violent and often irreverent, against the dangers of authority and official culture and religion.

DAVID JASPER
University of Glasgow

Preface

The play, with its cast of 1500 Mexican Indian 'lords and chiefs', with its artillery battery of fireworks, and 'cannon balls' that drenched their victims on impact with 'moistened red earth', was extraordinary enough. But the realization that the villain of the piece, the Great Sultan of Babylon and Tetrarch of Jerusalem, 'was the Marqués del Valle, Hernando Cortés', is startling. For this was 1539, less than two decades after Cortés had led a band of Spanish soldiers and a growing army of indigenous allies to victory over the Aztec empire. The modern editor of the eye-witness account assures us 'that this was not Hernando Cortés in person but some one, presumably an Indian, who impersonated Cortés'. But this clarification raises a further question. Why was an Indian noble, recently converted to Christianity, playing the conqueror of Mexico playing the Sultan of Babylon?[1]

Indigenous dramatizations of the theme of conquest in Mexico contain surprising signs of dialogue between Catholic and Indian on the morality of colonization. The Sultan Cortés is, I believe, one of many such dialogical signs. But this answer (which will be elaborated further in Chapter 6) breeds still more questions. These have to do with the dialogical nature of the theatre, and with Mikhail Bakhtin's insistence, as he celebrates dialogical languages and genres, that drama is a monological genre. They concern the question of the other ànd the ethics of cross-cultural encounter, problems very much to the fore as we observe the quincentennial of the conquest of America and continue to struggle with ethnic and religious conflict in a rapidly shrinking world.

My book addresses these questions. It has three parts. In the first, after an introductory chapter focusing on the work of Bakhtin and Tzvetan Todorov, I argue, with reference to European dramatizations of the conquest of Mexico (by Dryden, 'Zárate', and Artaud),

---

1.   Toribio de Motolinía, *History of the Indians of New Spain*, ed. and trans. F. B. Steck (Washington, D.C.: Academy of American Franciscan History, 1951) pp. 159–67.

that drama is a dialogical genre. In the second, I show how the theatre served as a means of communication between conquerors and conquered in the years immediately following the conquest of Mexico, and how even today indigenous dramatizations of the theme of conquest in Mexico express the ambivalence of native Catholics towards the conquest that brought them both Christianity and foreign rule. And, in the third, I propose a dialogical model of cross-cultural encounter in general (and of Christian missions in particular) that is grounded, figuratively, in the theatrical transaction of offering one's own cherished text for independent performance by another, and of entering as a performer into the world of another's text.

This book has been a number of years in the writing, and its author owes many debts of gratitude to those who have helped him along the way. Larry Bouchard, Jim Childress, Caryl Emerson, David Gitlitz, Sheryn Gray, Ann Harris, David Little, Fernando Opere, Bob Potter, Ben Ray, Don Rice, Julia Rottman, Robert Scharlemann and Nathan Scott have read the manuscript in whole or in part, at various stages of its development, and I am grateful to them for their encouragement and suggestions for improvement. My thanks are due, too, to David Jasper, who has once again proved to be an editor of great patience and sensitivity.

I was fortunate in being able to spend the 1990–1 academic year as a Fellow of the Virginia Center for the Humanities, and as a Fellow of the Commonwealth Center for Literary and Cultural Change, at the University of Virginia. I am grateful to Robert Vaughan and to Ralph Cohen, the respective directors of these Centers, and to the staff and other fellows for the opportunity they afforded me to complete my book in an atmosphere of intellectual stimulation and warm friendship. My book is far better for the experience.

I am grateful, too, to the people of Peace Presbyterian Church in Waynesboro, Virginia, who have not only cared deeply for me and my family but have been extraordinarily patient with their pastor's habit of dividing his time, often most unevenly, between the academy and the parish.

Parts of my book first appeared in academic journals, and I am thankful to the several editors for permission to reprint and to their anonymous readers for suggested improvements. Chapter 2 appeared, in a slightly different form, in *Restoration: Studies in English Literary Culture, 1660–1700*. A version of Chapter 3 was published in

Bulletin of the Comediantes. And material from Part Two was printed, in a condensed form, in *Radical History Review* and *Journal of the American Academy of Religion*.

Translations from French and Spanish are my own, unless otherwise stated. Quotations from the Bible are ordinarily from the New International Version. I have spelled Cortés thus, except when discussing plays in which the dramatist uses the form Cortez, and I have, in the interests of consistency with those whom I quote, throughout called the Aztec ruler Montezuma.

It is appropriate, too, to express my appreciation to those who have travelled with me in Mexico on various occasions: John and Vivienne Rix, my father John Harris, and my sons Joel and Matthew. Their lively companionship made the exciting but often arduous journeys much more enjoyable than they could have been alone. My thanks are also due to the University of Virginia for two travel grants that enabled me to visit fiestas in Cuetzalán in 1988 and Huejotzingo in 1989; to my wife Ann for allowing me to take Joel to Cuetzalán and Matthew to Huejotzingo; and to my mother Betty for letting me take her place on a research trip my fáther undertook while writing a novel about Pancho Villa. What I owe to my parents, to my wife and to my children, of course, extends far beyond the scope of this book. They have given me love.

Finally, I would like to dedicate this book to the memory of my father, who died while I was completing the final draft.

M. H.

List of Plates

Part One
The Question of Drama

1

Dialogical Genres and Cultural Encounters

A monologue may be entertaining or overbearing. It may even, in the mouth of a skilled character actor, embrace a variety of voices and points of view. But, in critical circles, the term 'monological' has gained currency as a description of language that admits only one point of view. 'Dialogical', on the other hand, connotes a willingness to free the captive audience, and to meet the other as a subject speaking from an alternate perspective. 'Dialogue', according to one definition, 'means communication between simultaneous differences'.[1]

In her *Historia del teatro en México*, the Mexican scholar Yolanda Argudín calls the theatre 'the best means of communication between conquerors and conquered'[2] in the years immediately following the Spanish conquest of Mexico. I can think of no more startling claim with which to begin a study of the theatre's dialogical potential. For not only has Mikhail Bakhtin, one of the foremost opponents of monological thinking, argued that drama as a genre excludes the possibility of true dialogue between worlds. But Tzvetan Todorov, after introducing Bakhtin's dialogical principle to French scholars in 1981, in his next book offered the conquest of Mexico as a graphic illustration of the failure of the human community to reckon with otherness in its midst.[3] For a dialogical theatre to have flourished at the violent meeting-point of two such alien cultures would provide a fascinating qualification of Bakhtin and Todorov's respective theories.

More importantly, it would raise the question of whether features of the Franciscan missionary theatre, to which Argudín refers, might point us to a mode and model of fruitful intercultural dialogue in other volatile contexts. Is it possible that an understanding of theatrical form might contribute to a partial resolution of what J. H. Elliott, in reviewing Todorov's *The Conquest of America*, called 'that intractable problem of the other'?[4] Or, to put it another way, might

3

the multiplicity of voices that combine in the performance of a dramatic text provide some kind of model for human encounter in a pluralistic world? 'Given the pervasive cultural fragmentation' of our time, we are, according to Nathan Scott, 'irrevocably committed to an ethos of encounter'. And, he warns, in such a climate 'we are likely over and over to be assailed by the impulse impatiently to obliterate "dialogue" (as Bakhtin would say) by some form of "monologue" '.[5] Might the drama, despite Bakhtin's misgivings, suggest a mode of resistance to this temptation?

And, lest it be feared that a liking for dialogue breeds a tolerance of all points of view and an allegiance to none, it must be remembered that Argudín is citing an avowedly missionary theatre, whose Franciscan sponsors believed deeply in the universal claims of both the Christian gospel and the Catholic church. If a dialogical theatre could flourish under such auspices, is it possible that the theatrical form itself restrains monological pretensions without suppressing particular commitments? This would be worthy of note in a wide variety of fields. But the question it raises may certainly be posed in religious terms. Might the Christian church, without relinquishing its allegiance to the person of Jesus Christ or to the scriptures that bear witness to him, find in the figure of the theatre an unexpected guide towards a genuinely dialogical encounter with those whom Stanley Samartha has called 'neighbours of other faiths'?[6]

I do not for a moment anticipate the simple answer that theatre can always serve as a medium of cross-cultural communication. Nor do I have in mind anything so quixotic as the ordination of troupes of thespian evangelists (or politicians or cultural attachés). Rather, my questions have to do with the possibility that the theatre might provide a fruitful model (or metaphor) for the conduct of cross-cultural exchange. Might an understanding of what it is that makes the theatre dialogical enhance our ability to conduct ourselves dialogically outside the theatre?

Such questions have not, to the best of my knowledge, been asked before. Their answers therefore require careful preparation. It will be well, for example, to address Bakhtin's intrinsic objections to the concept of a dialogical theatre before venturing into the unfamiliar world of sixteenth-century Mexican missionary theatre in search of a particularly striking instance. We will consider Argudín's claim in more detail in Part Two, when our story reaches sixteenth-century Mexico. And we will tease out the religious and ethical implications of the dialogical theatre in Part Three. But our preparations begin closer to home, at least for European readers, with the work of Bakhtin and Todorov.

BAKHTIN AND LITERARY GENRES

Bakhtin is a writer of considerable complexity (and prolixity), and it is hard to do justice to his theory of dialogical genres in a few pages.[7] We can begin, however, with four essays on the novel that he wrote between 1934 and 1941. First published in Russia in 1975, they appeared in English translation in 1981 under the collective title *The Dialogic Imagination*.[8] One of the topics uniting these essays is the multiplicity of human languages. What many would see as an impediment to human communication Bakhtin celebrates as a gift that safeguards dialogue. And this, in turn, helps to shape his hierarchy of literary genres.

The Prime Minister does not, I suspect, speak the same language at the breakfast table as he does in the House of Commons. Certainly, my own family would quickly disabuse me if I used the language of the pulpit over corn flakes and coffee. We adapt our speech to suit the occasion. Bakhtin illustrates this principle by describing the linguistic facility of an illiterate Russian peasant: 'He prayed to God in one language (Church Slavonic), sang songs in another, spoke to his family in a third and, when he began to dictate petitions to the local authorities through a scribe, he tried speaking yet a fourth language (the official-literate language, "paper" language)'. Human society, according to Bakhtin, is blessed with a multitude of tongues. There are languages that generate their own dictionaries and manuals of grammar; and, within 'any single national language', there are 'social dialects, . . . professional jargons, generic languages, languages of generations and age groups, tendentious languages', bland languages, 'languages of the authorities' and of the oppressed, languages 'of various circles and of passing fashions'. This happy state Bakhtin calls 'heteroglossia'.[9]

Bakhtin welcomes such profusion because, as he sees it, each language embodies in some measure a different ideology or point of view. One person's 'freedom fighters', for example, are another's 'terrorists', *'mujahidin'*, 'holy warriors', 'martyrs', *'bandidos'*, *'guerrilleros'*, 'nationalists', 'republicans', 'Bolsheviks', or 'barbarian hordes'. The coexistence or, even better, the interanimation of different languages bears witness against the presumptions of 'mono-glossia' and guards against the imposition of a single, 'official' point of view. Whereas Michael Edwards, in his book *Towards a Christian Poetics*, interprets the biblical story of the Tower of Babel convention-ally as an account of 'the fall of language into multiplicity',[10] it becomes in Bakhtin's scheme of things the gracious gesture of a God who knows the political value of variety.[11] The multiplicity of tongues and of the points of view that they express guards against the singu-lar vision of totalitarianism.

The political conditions under which Bakhtin wrote helped to shape his thought. As Allon White puts it,

> Much of Bakhtin's work can be read as a brilliant, lightly dis-guised polemic against the process of centralization and State domination going on in Russia during the period of Stalinism. By championing the heteroglossia of the 'folk' against the imposed authority of monoglossia, he was implicitly criticizing from a populist perspective the 'dismal sacred word' of ruthless State centralization.[12]

For Stalin, too, recognized the link between language and ideology. Legislating a single literary style ('socialist realism'), he denied alter-native points of view a literary voice. Bakhtin did not attack the centralized discourse of Stalinist Russia directly. Prudently he took issue only with the approved literary languages of ancient Greece. But in the uniformity of style embraced by the 'high' classical genres (epic, lyric and tragedy) he sensed a precedent for the ideological uniformity imposed in his own day.

An epic, according to one definition, is 'a long narrative poem in elevated style recounting the deeds of a legendary or historical hero'.[13] Homer's *Odyssey* is an epic. So are the Old English *Beowulf*, the Hindu *Ramayana* and Milton's *Paradise Lost*. The language of the epic, according to Bakhtin, is 'the language of tradition'. Rhetoric, character and plot are determined by an 'impersonal and sacrosanct tradition', embodying 'a commonly held evaluation' of the nation's past and excluding 'any possibility of another approach'.[14] Epic sup-ports the official mythology of a culture. The lyric poet, on the other hand, writes of the personal and present. Sappho was a lyric poet, as were Petrarch, Wordsworth and Keats. But the lyric poet's voice is solitary, rigorously 'stripping all aspects of language of the inten-tions and accents of other people, destroying all traces of social heteroglossia and diversity of language', so as once again to offer only a single point of view.[15] Whereas the epic collapses all the voices of a culture into that of the approved bard, the lyric excludes all the voices of a culture but that of the solitary poet. Tragedy shares with the epic its liking for national myths, dramatizing an isolated epic moment with heightened emotional intensity. Sophocles' *Oedipus Rex* is a tragedy. So, arguably, are Shakespeare's *King Lear* and Racine's *Phèdre*. Although tragedy does not draw from Bakhtin the same individual attention as do the other two genres, it suffers the same censure: 'All plots, all subject and thematic material, the entire basic stock of images, expressions and intonations', have their origin in the national language and its attendant myths.[16] Tragedy, too, endorses the official voice of the culture.

But no culture can remain closed indefinitely to the surrounding clamour of other languages, however it may combine them, as the Greeks did, under the single rubric of incomprehensibility, 'barbarian'. Bakhtin discerns two moments in the history of European civilization when the power of a dominant ideology and its attendant literary forms was broken by the influx of 'a multitude of different languages'. The first was 'on the boundary between classical antiquity and Hellenism', the second, 'during the late Middle Ages and Renaissance'.[17] On each of these occasions, Bakhtin observes, a new genre emerged: the novel. Or, to paraphrase Bakhtin more carefully, the prose romances, adventures and biographies of the Hellenistic world developed a form of 'novelistic discourse', which went underground during the Middle Ages, surviving as parody and folklore, only to emerge again in robust health in the boisterous fictions of Rabelais and Cervantes.[18]

The novel flourishes under conditions of cultural and linguistic interanimation, according to Bakhtin, because unlike the classical genres it thrives on a multiplicity of languages and points of view. The novelist, Bakhtin wrote, is not like the poet. He

> does not strip away the intentions of others from the heteroglot language of his works, he does not violate those socio-ideological cultural horizons (big and little worlds) that open up behind heteroglot languages – rather, he welcomes them into his work.[19]

For the novelist may introduce characters who speak a variety of regional, social and professional dialects, a liberty denied the classical poet under the law of the separation of styles. He or she may also incorporate into the novel secondary texts – letters, speeches, legal documents, poems, aphorisms – that simultaneously represent the voice of another and, in the implicit commentary provided by their context, the author's own refracted voice. Moreover, in reported speech the voice of the speaker is filtered through that of the narrator. And, under cover of a 'direct authorial word',[20] the novelist may use the language of another with only intonational acknowledgement. Bakhtin cites, as an illustration of the latter phenomenon, the following passage from Dickens's *Little Dorrit*:

> That illustrious man and great national ornament, Mr Merdle, continued his shining course. It began to be widely understood that one who had done society the admirable service *of making so much money out of it*, could not be suffered to remain a commoner. A baronetcy was spoken of with confidence; a peerage was frequently mentioned.[21]

Grammatically, the passage is offered as if it were the objective word of its author. But its ironic tone identifies the language as that of public opinion. Only the phrase that Bakhtin italicizes directly represents the author's dissenting point of view.

In such 'double-voiced discourse', Bakhtin suggests, 'there are two voices, two meanings and two expressions. And all the while these two voices are dialogically interrelated . . . ; it is as if they actually hold a conversation with each other'.[22] The passage from Dickens is a comparatively simple instance. For novels often convey a much more complex interweaving of voices. Just as Dickens refracted the voice of public opinion through his own authorial voice, so the characters in a novel may each process one another's speech patterns (and the prejudices embedded in them) through their own words and thoughts. In this way the many speech styles filtered through the 'all-encompassing' voice of the novelist are also 'dialogized' in relation one to another. 'What is vital', according to Gary Saul Morson and Caryl Emerson, 'is that the languages be viewed from each other's perspectives, that they be "hybridized" so that an "interminable" dialogue is created among them'.[23] Moreover, since Bakhtin conceives language 'not as a system of abstract grammatical categories' but as the 'ideologically saturated' vehicle of 'a world view',[24] this internal dialogue is finally a conversation amongst the many different worlds that these voices represent.

But, it may be objected, this theory of multi-voiced dialogue ignores the real power structure of a novel. For is not the writer of fiction a kind of literary ventriloquist, whose characters have no freedom to enter into independent dialogue with their creator? Does he not invent their voices and write their script? Bakhtin's answer to this charge is the concept of 'polyphony', which he developed at length in *Problems of Dostoevsky's Poetics* (1929).[25] Although readers of Bakhtin often confuse 'polyphony' with 'heteroglossia', the two terms are 'not even roughly synonymous. . . . The latter term', as Morson and Emerson explain, 'describes the diversity of speech styles in a language, the former has to do with the position of the author in a text'.[26] In a polyphonic novel, the author's views lie in the same plane as those of his characters. For the novelist begins by creating 'personalities', not plot, and by then setting the stage for these personalities to encounter one another. The plot develops from the unforeseen responses of these personalities; it does not demand that their responses conform to its preconceived requirements. In this way, Bakhtin believed, the novelist is able to create a 'plurality of independent and unmerged voices and consciousnesses, a genuine polyphony of fully valid voices'.[27] The writer's own opinion may be expressed through one or more of these personalities, and thus placed in dialogue with others who represent different points of view. But the outcome of the dialogue is never settled in advance, for the polyphonic novelist encounters his or her characters as an equal.

Bakhtin appealed, by way of analogy, to the Judeo-Christian doctrine that God created a free people, capable of arguing with him (as Job did), and 'capable', as Morson and Emerson put it, 'of surprising him, as Dostoevsky's characters surprised their creator'.[28] But the degree of freedom enjoyed by characters in a polyphonic novel, one might argue, is quite as problematic as the degree of freedom enjoyed by human beings in the Judeo-Christian scheme of things. Strands of biblical teaching, after all, proclaim that God 'does as he pleases with the powers of heaven and the peoples of the earth' (Daniel 4: 35). One notes, therefore, the qualifying adverb that insinuates itself into Morson and Emerson's affirmation of the freedom of created characters. 'To be sure', they write, 'characters in a polyphonic work have been created by the author, but once they come into being, they *partially* escape his control and prevent him from knowing in advance how they will answer him'.[29]

Even with this qualification, however, these are large claims for the novel and, on the whole, I am content to let them pass. None the less, I want to challenge Bakhtin on what will seem at first to be a small point, but which will prove in the end to have significant implications not only for literary theory but for a wide range of human discourse. Whatever may be true of epic or lyric poetry, I believe that drama, even in its classical form, is a dialogical genre.

BAKHTIN AND DRAMA

Bakhtin does not see in drama the potential for dialogue that he discerns in the novel. In the former, for example, he finds no 'dialogized heteroglossia'. 'The system of languages in drama', he writes,

> is organized on completely different principles, and therefore its languages sound utterly different than do the languages of the novel. In drama there is no all-encompassing language that addresses itself dialogically to separate languages, there is no second all-encompassing plotless (nondramatic) dialogue.[30]

There is, in other words, no authorial voice appropriating, modifying and commenting on the speech of others, as there was in the passage from *Little Dorrit* quoted earlier. There is only the fictional dialogue of the characters within the plot. And this, for Bakhtin, is not at all the same. When characters in a dramatic text address one another, their speech is not actively engaged in a free exchange of views; it is only 'a depicted thing'. The words of the characters can never be involved in conversation with 'the word doing the depicting',[31] since in drama the author's voice is confined to the 'awkward and absurd . . . language of [the] stage directions'.[32] There can be no double-voiced discourse, simultaneously resonant with the voices of the author and of the other. Only the characters speak.

Moreover, in drama shaped according to the classical doctrine of the separation of styles, the characters speak only the dramatist's language. In a play by Sophocles, Corneille or T. S. Eliot, for example, all the characters speak a single formal poetic diction. Whatever their social or professional status, the characters' speech is uniform and therefore embodies a uniform ideology. In classical drama this is the ideology of the ruling class to which the poet belongs or which he serves. Drama, for Bakhtin, is a monological representation of dialogue between characters rather than a mode of dialogue between worlds.

Like Aristotle, Bakhtin finds in the drama an impulse to unity. But, unlike Aristotle, he describes this unity as 'monolithic'. For the unity to which classical drama aspires resists loose ends and seeks to reduce the 'messiness' of the world to a carefully contrived aesthetic whole. A unified plot proceeds without distraction from an orderly beginning to a conclusive end. The final scene resolves any apparent disparity of viewpoints. Bakhtin writes:

> In drama the world must be made from a single piece. . . . The whole concept of a dramatic action as that which resolves all dialogic oppositions, is purely monologic. A true multiplicity of levels would destroy drama, because dramatic action, relying as it does upon the unity of the world, could not link those levels together or resolve them.[33]

Bakhtin's charges are most easily sustained against classical drama. It comes as no surprise, therefore, when he acknowledges parenthetically that it is 'the drama (strictly conceived)' that is his primary target. 'It goes without saying', he explains in a footnote, 'that we continually advance as typical the extreme to which poetic genres aspire', and that it is 'pure classical drama' that expresses 'the ideal extreme of the genre'.[34] He is even willing to admit that 'contemporary realistic social drama may . . . be heteroglot and multi-languaged'. But, he insists, such heteroglossia is not intrinsic to the drama. On the contrary, he discerns the influence of the novel. 'In an era when the novel reigns supreme', Bakhtin writes, 'almost all the remaining genres are to a greater or lesser extent "novelized" '. The plays of Ibsen, Hauptmann, and the other Naturalist dramatists are a case in point.[35] Whatever dialogical tendencies the modern theatre may display are uncharacteristic; they are benefits that have accrued from living in the shadow of the novel.

Bakhtin does, however, make one concession to the stage. Laughter mocks the pretentions of official ideology, language and literary genres, and Bakhtin delights in the parodies of classical authority and of the sacred language of the church that he finds in various media, including the drama, during the Middle Ages.[36] He cites with approval Pushkin's observation that the art of the theatre was 'born in the public square' and only later appropriated by 'aristocratic society'.[37] For theatre in the public square is raucous, bawdy and uncowed, happily lacking the fastidious decorum of the classical stage. In so far, then, as drama remains in the public square or as elements of folk comedy survive on the formal stage, Bakhtin believes that the theatre retains its capacity to dispute the official world view. Thus he hears in the ancient satyr play, in the comic masks of Atellan farce and of Italian *commedia dell'arte*, in the macaronic language of certain liturgical plays, in the spectacles of the medieval carnival, in the political satire of the French *soties* and in the Shakespearean fool, a theatrical counterpoint to the official voices of their age.[38]

But parodic laughter does not make drama polyphonic. In *Problems of Dostoevsky's Poetics*, Bakhtin challenges Anatoly Lunacharsky's suggestion that the 'multi-voicedness' of Dostoevsky's fiction is akin to that of Shakespeare's plays. 'Certain . . . early buddings of polyphony', Bakhtin concedes, 'can indeed be detected in the dramas of Shakespeare'. But his is not 'a fully formed and deliberate polyphonic quality'. Bakhtin's argument at this point consists of three unsupported assertions. First, 'the drama is by its very nature alien to genuine polyphony'. Secondly, although there may be 'a plurality of fully valid voices' in Shakespeare's work as a whole, such a plurality does not exist in any individual play. Each play 'contains only one fully valid voice, the voice of the hero'. Finally, the voices in Shakespeare's plays do not represent 'points of view on the world' to the same degree as they do in Dostoevsky's novels.[39] Bakhtin's judgement is, to say the least, sweeping. He admires Shakespeare more than any other playwright. But even Shakespeare, for all his appreciation of the carnivalesque, his transgression of classical restraints and his ability to create independent voices, could not in Bakhtin's view redeem the drama from its intrinsically monological bonds. 'The drama', Bakhtin insists, 'is *by its very nature* alien to genuine polyphony'.

Bakhtin's judgement has been challenged on a number of grounds. Manfred Pfister, for example, has written persuasively of the 'comic subversion' of official discourse in a wide range of Shakespeare's plays.[40] Graham Pechey has argued that Brecht's theatre was 'dialogized . . . to the point of polyphony', with its self-conscious 'actor-narrators' offering a 'double-voiced quotation of speech and gesture', and its singers, placards and projections providing 'deliberate interruption and commentary'.[41] Helene Keyssar has discovered polyphonic qualities in the refusal of select black American and feminist dramas 'to finalize or assert dominant ideologies'.[42] And John Docker, citing Bakhtin's preference for the 'lower' forms of literature, has found a rich 'multi-consciousness' in popular melodrama.[43] Others have pointed to particular periods of theatrical history that have been more radically 'carnivalized' or to particular plays that have been more thoroughly 'novelized' than others. Michael Bristol, for example, has made such a claim for the Elizabethan theatre,[44] and Della Pollock has 'reappropriated' Brecht's *Drums in the Night* as a 'multi-voiced, multi-faceted . . . novel'.[45]

But each of these strategies proposes exceptions rather than a fundamental challenge to Bakhtin's rule. Such a challenge has been issued by Vasile Popovici. Suggesting that Bakhtin's mistake was to focus exclusively on the literary aspects of a dramatic text, Popovici argues that 'the dialogical nature of the dramatic genre is not to be found in the internal organisation of a play'. For the dramatic text, unlike the novel, is incomplete. Like a musical score, it awaits performance. And performance, according to Popovici, reveals a multi-faceted 'dialogue between the stage and the audience'. There the several voices of the playwright, director, designer and actors encounter, in the spectator, 'a questioning agent who connects and completes the fragments he is offered'. The dialogical aspect of drama, Popovici therefore concludes, 'is revealed at the level of performance'.[46]

This is a simple but telling observation. For playwrights, unlike novelists, relinquish control of their texts once they surrender them for performance. Novelists, despite the freedom they may grant their characters to speak a variety of alien languages or to take their authors by surprise, still in the end write the characters' speeches and deliver those words to the reader in a fixed form. The playwright's words (and those of her characters), by contrast, are refracted through the interpretative medium of a company of actors and their director. Whatever dialogue may or may not be in the text itself, there is inherent in the theatrical process of transferring script to stage a series of dialogues between the many independent, living voices involved in writing and production. There is also, as Popovici reminds us, the response of the audience, and the possibility of subsequent performances before different audiences and perhaps by different actors in different cultures and different epochs. It is clear, therefore, that we must look beyond the literary script for the full dimensions of a dialogical theatre. I shall argue in subsequent chapters that a dialogue between worlds may in fact be found in dramatic texts. But the main thrust of my challenge to Bakhtin's notion that the drama is a monological genre will be to insist that the dramatist's offer of his or her own text for performance by another is an inherently dialogical gambit. For once such an offer has been accepted, the dramatist's voice is no longer alone. A company of other voices at once begins to batten on the text, adding to the written word a variety of designs and intonations that simultaneously refract the author's voice and make possible theatrical performance.

TODOROV AND THE OTHER

'Otherness', according to Tzvetan Todorov, is 'the key to [Bakhtin's] whole work'.[47] Bakhtin's enthusiasm for the novel and for the carnival, for the vitality of ethnic cultures in the face of an intrusive central government, and for the ideological polyphony of Dostoevsky's fiction, is grounded in his enthusiasm for the other. For Bakhtin a multiplicity of alternative perspectives enriches both human society as a whole and individual self-understanding in particular.

Otherness has also become the focus of Todorov's recent work. After he introduced Bakhtin to French readers in 1981, Todorov brought the dialogical principle to bear on a specific historical encounter in *The Conquest of America: The Question of the Other*. Todorov defines his subject at the outset of this book as 'the discovery [that the] *self* makes of the *other*'. At once, however, he acknowledges that this is a subject 'so enormous that any general formulation soon ramifies into countless categories and directions'. Surprised by my own thoughts, emotions or behaviour, I can discover in myself a stranger, the other whom I did not know. Turning outwards, I find myself encountered by other individuals whose point of view is never quite my own. Subsuming isolation in the collective, I confine the other to social groups 'to which *we* do not belong'. These groups may be 'interior to society: women for men, the rich for the poor, the mad for the "normal" '. Or they may be 'exterior to society': the French for the English, the Arab for the Jew. Other societies may have cultural, moral and historical links to our own. Or, at the furthest margin of alterity, we may stumble across 'unknown quan-

tities, outsiders whose language and customs [we] do not understand, so foreign that in extreme instances [we are] reluctant to
admit that they belong to the same species as [our] own'. It is this
latter category, which he calls 'the exterior and remote other', that
Todorov has chosen, 'somewhat arbitrarily and because one cannot
speak of everything all at once', as the topic of his book.[48]

His mode of discourse is narrative. Persuaded by Bakhtin's meth-
odological axiom that 'it is only on a concrete historical subject that
a theoretical problem may be resolved',[49] Todorov eschews the ab-
stractions of 'logical argumentation' and opts instead 'to narrate a
history'. Specifically he directs his attention to the European discovery and conquest of Mesoamerica. For this, he insists, is 'the most
astonishing encounter of our history'. Europeans had 'never been
entirely ignorant' of the civilizations of Africa, China and India. But
when Columbus set out westwards across the Atlantic in 1492, no
one in Europe even imagined that the continent of America or the
civilizations of native America existed.[50]

Todorov is well aware of Bakhtin's enthusiasm for those moments 'when a national culture loses its sealed-off and self-sufficient
character, when it becomes conscious of itself as only one among
other cultures and languages'.[51] Eventually, the discovery of America
would have such a 'decentring' effect on European culture. But
resistance was immense. At first, Todorov observes, Europeans conceived the indigenous peoples of America as equal and identical to
themselves, assimilating the other into their own system of values
and denying all signs of difference. Or they interpreted the Indian's
difference as a mark of almost subhuman inferiority. In either case,
Todorov charges, 'the existence of a human substance truly other',
capable of both difference and equality, was denied.[52] The denial of
genuine human alterity allowed the European mind to resist almost
indefinitely the 'decentring' of its own verbal-ideological universe.
Only recently, for example, have the classical and Christian narratives begun to make room in 'the history of Western civilization'
for those of the Maya, the Aztec and the Incas.

Todorov's interest in the conquest of America is not that of a
historian but, by his own confession, that of a 'moralist'. 'The present',
he writes, 'is more important to me than the past'. His tale, therefore,
although it requires the discipline of the historian to render it 'as true
as possible', is first and foremost the inquiry of a moralist resolved
'never to lose sight of what biblical exegesis used to call [the]

tropological or ethical meaning' of a narrative. Only by telling such an 'exemplary story', he believes, can he 'answer the question, How to deal with the other?'[53]

It is not a question easily answered. Ironically, Todorov's book has itself drawn charges of insularity. Roberto González-Echevarría, for example, complains that 'Todorov stubbornly refuses to come out of himself (of his present) to understand the other',[54] be it the Spanish Christian who fails to meet post-Enlightenment standards of tolerance, or the American Indian whose multiplicity of languages and cultures Todorov tends to reduce to a single racial type. Deborah Root has also remarked on Todorov's erasure of difference amongst Indian peoples. 'Todorov', she writes, 'seems to assert an inter-changeability of "Indians," which produces an equivalence between nomadic hunter-gatherers and urban imperial peoples, Aztecs and Mayas, and so forth'. This monologized Indian is then charged by Todorov with three crucial limitations: 'a concept of time which was almost completely past-oriented; a profound social conformity; and a cultural stasis which rendered change nearly impossible'. This is, in Root's opinion, a profoundly biased account of pre-Columbian society. Moreover, it enables Todorov to advance, as Root puts it, 'a racialist explanation' for the Spanish conquest, suggesting 'that the Mexicans were defeated *because they were "Indians"* '.[55]

By way of explanation for this simplification of the sixteenth-century other, Rolena Adorno suggests that Todorov's historical narrative, like Bakhtin's literary criticism, masks a more immediate political concern.[56] Discovering in Todorov's text a number of 'parenthetical comparisons between the Christian conquest of the sixteenth-century and the communist takeovers of the twentieth', Adorno argues that Todorov's primary concern is not with 'the exterior and remote other' but with more immediate 'violations of state sovereignty and human and civil rights'. His 'unstated referent', she proposes, 'is Eastern Europe'. Todorov left his native Bulgaria for France in 1963, at the age of 24.

A number of Todorov's generalizations about the encounter between Europe and Mesoamerica take on a new significance in this light. His insistence, for example, that the Spanish were able to defeat the Indians because of an advanced semiotic technology (a mastery of writing and an ability to manipulate signs to their own advantage) has been challenged on historical grounds.[57] But it is an eloquent description of the monological apparatus of central state control. Adorno argues, however, that this very light exposes Todorov's failure to reckon with alterity. Todorov's book, she writes,

> is an ethical discussion of conduct of the self vis-à-vis the other in which, in the sixteenth-century case study, the other as subject is absent. It emerges, in reflections on the twentieth, as the self being objectified or 'othered' by the state, particularly the totalitarian regime. Where we might have expected to hear from the sixteenth-century Amerindian others, those potential subjects slip immediately from sight only to emerge, at the end of the book, as ourselves. . . . Todorov's 'other' is ultimately the 'us' persecuted by the [official] totalitarian 'we'.[58]

Such criticism is only partially warranted. We may concede that Todorov's book contains a number of historical inaccuracies and ethnographic generalizations; but the reading of history from a present, personal perspective need not impede dialogue with another's point of view. Indeed, Bakhtin and Todorov would argue that it is just this that makes dialogue possible. 'Creative understanding', Bakhtin wrote, 'does not renounce itself, its own place in time, its own culture'.[59] Bakhtin, accordingly, read the history of literary genres from the perspective of his own distaste for Stalinist Russia. And he exalted the novel because he found in it a dialogue between the novelist's 'all-encompassing' voice and the many alien voices that he or she employs. There is, in Bakhtin's mind, no question of the novelist needing to suppress her or his own point of view in order to pursue dialogue with another. Todorov, too, declares that he has

> tried to avoid two extremes. The first is the temptation to reproduce the voices of these figures 'as they really are'; to try to do away with my own presence 'for the other's sake.' The second is to subjugate the other to myself, to make him a marionette of which I pull the strings. Between the two, I have sought not a terrain of compromise but the path of dialogue.[60]

To the degree that he has 'subjugated the other' to his own purposes, he has failed. But the mere presence of his own voice, reading the other's texts in the light of his own experience, does not mean that he has silenced the other. Dialogue requires two voices, and not just that of the other.

The challenge, of course, in a genre which grants the author an 'all-encompassing' voice, is to guard the other's subordinate voice against distortion. Todorov believes that he has done so by means of 'many quotations'.[61] But, as Adorno reminds us, quoting Michel de Certeau, 'The written discourse which cites the speech of the other is not, cannot be, the discourse of the other. On the contrary, this discourse, in writing the Fable that authorizes it, alters it.'[62] Citation embeds the other's curtailed voice within the scholar's discourse and, in doing so, modifies it. To the degree that the temptation to subjugate is avoided, this is, according to Bakhtin and Todorov, 'the path of dialogue'. But other genres may walk this path more nimbly. I hope to show that the theatre, by allowing no one 'all-encompassing' voice to control the performance, cites the text of the playwright (who in turn may cite the texts of others) and protects the plurality of voices in a way that scholarly discourse or, for that matter, the novel does not.

None of these scholars disputes the magnitude of Todorov's question concerning the other, nor the appropriateness of the matrix in which he has chosen to pursue it. They would argue, however, that Todorov's book illustrates rather than resolves the problems that he raises. Even so sympathetic a critic as Jonathan Culler concludes his review of Todorov's book by admitting that 'the "question of the other" remains unsolved' and asking, somewhat hopelessly, 'Is there anywhere a method for dialogue of cultures?'[63]

It is here that my own study begins. For my inquiry into the question of the other is also conducted within the historical matrix of the Spanish conquest of Mesoamerica and, like Todorov, I have focused especially on the conquest of Mexico. However, I have added a second literary or, more precisely, theatrical matrix. The blending of European and native traditions produced an extraordinarily vibrant missionary theatre in Mexico in the decades immediately following the conquest. It is only in the last twenty years, however, that these plays, principally in Náhuatl, have begun to be studied systematically. They are proving, as Robert Potter has noted, to be 'of enormous interest and relevance' not only to anthropologists and to theatre historians but to all who are interested in 'the unique sociological circumstances of post-Conquest Mexico'.[64] The conquest of Mexico has also been the subject of a number of European theatrical texts, from Dryden's *The Indian Emperour* and 'Fernando de Zárate's' *La conquista de México* to Antonin Artaud's scenario for the Theatre of Cruelty, *La Conquête du Mexique*. And it continues to be the theme of much indigenous folk drama still performed with great vigour throughout Mexico. Some of these folk plays and dances are identified explicitly as *La conquista*. Others, although their names traditionally suggest a struggle between Moors and Christians or Santiagos and Pilatos, display unmistakable signs in performance of pitting Indian against Spaniard.

I shall discuss the European dramatizations of the conquest of Mexico in the remainder of Part One, and the missionary and folk treatments of the theme in Mexico itself in Part Two of this book. The subject of dramatizations of the conquest of Mexico will thus serve as a single matrix within which to contest Bakhtin's verdict that the theatre is a monological genre and to address Todorov's question as to the best mode of reckoning with otherness within the human community. The two concerns will prove to be intimately related. For I shall suggest in Part Three that the performance of another's text without loss of one's own perspective, and the offer of one's own text for independent performance by another, together provide both a mode and model of mutually enriching cross-cultural relationships.

2

Aztec Maidens in Satin Gowns

The best-known English dramatization of the conquest of Mexico is John Dryden's *The Indian Emperour* (1665).[1] It is not an easy play from which to argue for the dialogical nature of the theatre. For Dryden's play is written throughout in heroic couplets. All the characters – priests, soldiers, nobility, men, women, Aztecs and Spaniards – speak the same language. Every trace of popular comedy or carnivalesque disruption is excluded,[2] and, like Dryden's other heroic dramas, it reflects Dryden's conservatism in matters of political and moral theory.[3] Moreover, although it was popular in its day, it has enjoyed only a short history of subsequent interpretative performances. The most graphic indication of the difficulties involved in the search for dialogism in *The Indian Emperour*, however, may perhaps be found in a painting, William Hogarth's *The Conquest of Mexico* (1732) (see Plate 1).[4]

A SCENE FROM *THE INDIAN EMPEROUR*

A first glance at Hogarth's *The Conquest of Mexico* can be disconcerting for the uninitiated. For the painting is set in an eighteenth-century English drawing room. Family portraits and neoclassical statuary decorate the walls, and a bust of Sir Isaac Newton occupies the place of honour on the elevated mantelpiece. In the foreground, fashionably dressed members of the British aristocracy and their families engage in polite conversation and entertainment. There is no apparent sign of conquest or of Mexico.

Further data dispel the confusion but only partially ease the mind. The painting commemorates a private theatrical performance in 1732 at the house of John Conduit, the wealthy Master of the Mint. The play was Dryden's *The Indian Emperour, or The Conquest of Mexico by the Spaniards*, and Hogarth's painting is known by several titles, among them *The Conquest of Mexico* and *A Scene from 'The Indian Emperour'*. The performers were the Conduits' only child, Catherine, and three of her wellborn friends. The children can be seen on a small, raised dais to the right of the painting: a young actor, in chains, flanked by three young actresses. A curtain has been drawn to disclose the stage, and some of the audience are watching the play. Hogarth has depicted Act 4, scene 4 of Dryden's text, which takes place in 'a prison'. There Cortez is 'discovered, bound', and the Aztec princesses, Cydaria and Almeria, contend for his love. Tactfully, Hogarth has added a third princess, Alibech. Although not on stage at this point in the play, Alibech was acted by Catherine Conduit, whose father had commissioned the painting, and she could not be omitted.

But even with this explanation the painting is troubling. For Todorov has told the story of the Spanish discovery and conquest of the New World as a paradigm of our failure to reckon with alterity within the human community, and it is just this apparent denial of alterity in Hogarth's painting that is so disturbing. The New World on stage is barely distinguishable from the Old World of the audience. All the characters, whether they represent conquistador or Aztec, wear European dress. According to Frederick Antal, the children are wearing '17th-century Spanish costumes'.[5] Sixteenth-century Cortez thereby suffers only a mild anachronism. But the three Aztec princesses, in elegant satin gowns, are denied all ethnic difference. A discreet feather in the headpiece of each actress is the only token of the exotic;[6] otherwise the Indian princesses have been fully assimilated into the European world of their audience. It was apparently easier to reckon with the proximate otherness of a Spanish man than with 'the exterior and remote' alterity of the Aztec women.

Nor does Popovici's emphasis on performance offer much initial encouragement. For Hogarth's painting gives us no confidence that a dialogue between the stage and the audience was taking place in John Conduit's drawing room. Although some of the spectators face the stage, most are engaged in conversation, in hunting for a dropped fan, or simply in staring into space. This kind of behaviour was commonplace among Restoration theatre audiences. Dryden was not the only playwright who complained of 'Pratlers in the Pit' making such a noise 'that oft the Play is silenc'd by the Farce'.[7] Hogarth's painting is aptly named a 'conversation piece'.[8] The

animated voices of the spectators would seem, at the very least, to
have obscured the voices of the cast and to have suppressed any
potential dialogue between the audience and the stage.

Finally, there lurks in the shadows at the back of the stage a figure
we have not yet noted. Hidden beneath a black clerical gown and a
long wig, standing with his back to the audience and with his nose
in a text that he reads by candlelight, is the prompter. Those who
have read Jacques Derrida's collection of essays, *Writing and Difference*, will recall his contempt for this guardian of the text. In characteristic fashion, Derrida plays on the similarity of the French words
souffleur (prompter) and *souffler* (to spirit away, to steal, or to in-
spire). The prompter (*souffleur*), hidden but unavoidably present just
off stage, polices the stage on behalf of the absent author, insisting on
allegiance to the text. As an actor, Derrida writes in the first person,
I am therefore '*inspired* [*soufflé*] by an *other* voice', that of the prompter,
'that itself reads a text older than the text of my body or than the
theater of my gestures'. The other's breath [*souffle*] steals [*souffle*] my
freedom, and in 'the fecundity of the *other* breath is [my] unpower'.[9]
The performers in Hogarth's painting, it would seem, are ciphers,
their temptation to difference held in check by the furtive authority
of the prompter.

It is ironic that, for all the prompter's care, the author's carefully
preserved, single voice appears to be lost amidst the casual banter of
the audience. And it is one of those intriguing coincidences of literary history that Derrida should offer his remarks as part of a discussion of Artaud's Theatre of Cruelty. For the first production of
the Theatre of Cruelty, had sufficient funds been raised, would have
been Artaud's own scenario for *La Conquête du Mexique*.[10] Artaud's
scenario and Derrida's commentary will be the topic of Chapter 4.
For now, however, we turn from Hogarth's canvas to Dryden's
script.

THE QUESTION OF PERSPECTIVE

Dryden's Mexico, like Hogarth's, has a distinctly European flavour.
Montezuma and his court sound like European lords and ladies of
the seventeenth-century. Their notions of honour and their struggles
to balance the claims of passion and duty would not have been out
of place in the courts served by Corneille and Calderón. And

Montezuma's rationalist criticism of revealed religion prompts Anthony Pagden to remark that the Aztec lord is, in Dryden's play, 'really an English gentleman and something, too, of a sceptic'.[11] To dress Catherine Conduit and her friends in satin gowns was to respond faithfully to this aspect of Dryden's script.

But there are other aspects of Dryden's text that suggest a greater appreciation of alterity. These come to light as we focus on the question of perspective. For Dryden appears to grant that the colonizer's perspective is, in its own way, as limited as that of the colonized. To do so represents a major concession to the principles of equality and difference on which Todorov insists.[12]

Consider, for example, the juxtaposition of Guyomar's description of the Spanish ships with Cortez's initial account of the climate and people of the New World. In Act 1, scene 2, Guyomar, the younger son of Montezuma, reports his first sighting of the Spanish fleet offshore. He describes the unknown (masts, sails and hulls) in terms of the familiar (trees, birds, wings and floating palaces):

> The object I could first distinctly view
> Was tall straight trees which on the waters flew,
> Wings on their sides instead of leaves did grow,
> Which gather'd all the breath the winds could blow.
> And at their roots grew floating Palaces,
> Whose out-bow'd bellies cut the yielding Seas.

In the opening scene, the conquistadors resort to the same expedient, describing the unknown (Mexico) in terms of the familiar (European literature). Faced with the strange, new world of the Mexican landscape, they draw on the known world of classical authority. Their comparison of 'this Infant world', freshly 'brought forth' and laid 'in Natures lap', with the 'decay'd and wither'd' landscape of the Old World owes much to Lucretius's account of 'the new-born earth' in *De rerum natura*.[13] So does Cortez's praise of the temperate Mexican climate.[14] Contemporary authority is also invoked: when Vasquez observes that the land remains uncultivated and the people 'untaught', Cortez's response borrows heavily from Montaigne:

> Wild and untaught are Terms which we alone
> Invent, for fashions differing from our own:
> For all their Customs are by nature wrought,
> But we, by Art, unteach what Nature taught.[15]

For Cortez to quote Montaigne is, of course, anachronistic. But it enables Dryden to make the point, as Derek Hughes remarks, that the Spaniards 'are as blinkered in their perceptions of nature as the Indians . . . are in their perception of art'.[16] Both assimilate the unknown phenomena of the other's world into the familiar co-ordinates of their own world. Whereas the Aztec prince describes art (the Spanish fleet) in terms of nature, the Spaniards pass nature through the filter of art (the writings of Lucretius and Montaigne).

But the same Restoration audience that would have judged Guyomar's account of the Spanish fleet to be naive might have accepted Cortez's description of the New World at face value. Lucretius and Montaigne were fashionable authorities in Dryden's world. Dryden is quick, therefore, to discredit the Spanish theories of a New World paradise. The second scene begins with the announcement that 500 prisoners of war have been sacrificed to the Sun in honour of Montezuma's birthday, and continues with a public ceremony marred by misplaced passion, palace intrigues and plans of vengeance. The number of surreptitious asides alone explodes the Spanish hypothesis of a new-born world of natural innocence.[17]

Nor is the audience free to admire Spanish virtues. The issue of just conquest, central to Todorov's critique of European 'egocentrism'[18] in the New World, provides the occasion for Dryden to dismantle Spanish pretensions to honour. In the first scene, Vasquez questions both the practical wisdom and the theoretical justice of attacking Montezuma's army:

> Rashly to arm against so great a King
> I hold not safe, nor is it just to bring
> A War, without a fair defiance made.

Pizarro's rejoinder is 'blunt and cynical'.[19] 'Declare we first our quarrel', he counsels, 'then Invade'. Cortez demurs:

> By noble ways we Conquest will prepare,
> First offer peace, and that refus'd make war.

Nobility, however, here consists only of a specious offer of peace intended to justify the war that follows.

This was the Spanish *modus operandi* at the time. Royal decree mandated that a legal document, known as the *Requerimiento*, should be read to Indians before hostilities were launched. The *Requerimiento* announced the jurisdiction of the Pope over the whole earth and his 'donation' of the New World to the King and Queen of Spain. The Indians were 'required' to yield voluntary submission to the Spanish crown and to listen to the preaching of Christian priests. Should they do so, they would be left in all other respects 'free without servitude'. Should they refuse, the Spanish forces would press their claims by warfare.[20]

Dryden may have learned of the *Requerimiento* from Montaigne.[21] In Act 1, scene 2, while Cortez courts Cydaria, Pizarro informs Montezuma of the Spanish claim:

The Soveraign Priest, – – –
Who represents on Earth the pow'r of Heaven,
Has this your Empire to our Monarch given.

Montezuma challenges the papal donation with sentiments that Dryden borrowed from the French essayist:

Ill does he represent the powers above,
Who nourishes debate not Preaches love;
Besides what greater folly can be shown?
He gives another what is not his own.[22]

Just as Guyomar draws on Mexican sights to describe the Spanish ships, to the Spanish depend on European theories to negotiate their encounter with the New World and its inhabitants. The one is no more reliable than the other.

Another indication of the limits of both Old and New World perspectives occurs earlier in the same scene. When Cortez appeals to the authority of 'Charles the Fifth, the World's most Potent King', Montezuma questions the title. From the Indian Emperor's point of view, the Spanish monarch appears to be no more than 'some petty Prince, and one of little fame. For to this hour', Montezuma adds,

I never heard his name:
The two great Empires of the World I know,
That of Peru and that of Mexico;
And since the earth none larger does afford,
This Charles is some poor Tributary Lord.

'You speak of that small part of earth you know', Cortez retorts. But Cortez's judgement falls equally on the Spaniards' limited perspective: Vasquez continues to insist that 'all the Nations of the Earth' do, in fact, submit to Charles.

Dryden, it is true, gives no more accurate an account of the details of the other's world than does the fictional Cortez in his play. His discovery, as Michael Alssid puts it, of 'numerous similarities . . . between the primitive and civilized minds' tends to blind him to any significant difference between the two cultures.[23] And his critique of Catholic Spain does no more than reflect the general bias of northern Europe at the time. But his recognition that the European viewpoint is no more privileged than that of the Indian moves beyond mere nationalism. Faintly it 'heralds', to use Todorov's terms, the 'perspectivism' that characterizes our own age.[24]

THE BACKGROUND OF HETEROGLOSSIA

Moreover, the fact that Dryden calls into question the words of Lucretius and Montaigne spoken by his characters implies an internal dialogue between worlds that Bakhtin had not anticipated in the drama 'strictly conceived'. It is not a dialogue between the Old and New Worlds represented. Nor is it rendered in a variety of languages. Rather, it is a dialogue in which certain fashionably authoritative voices, refracted through the playwright's uniform language of heroic couplets, are subjected to dramatic interrogation. Bakhtin writes of the novel:

> The incorporated languages and socio-ideological belief systems, while of course utilized to refract the author's intentions, are unmasked and destroyed as something false, hypocritical, greedy, limited.[25]

This is a fair description of Dryden's dramatic stance towards both the *Requerimiento* and the passages from Lucretius's *De rerum natura* appropriated by the conquistadors in the play's opening scene.

It might also describe Dryden's attitude to the world of heroic romance from which he borrows freely. The code of conduct espoused by Dryden's 'heroes' has, as several scholars have noted, 'much in common with that celebrated by La Calprenède, Scudéry,

and others'.[26] Specific details of plot and discourse 'at times extend
almost to word for word translation'.[27] Whereas it used to be thought
that Dryden's heroes were intended to invite unmixed admiration,
recent criticism[28] has sensed a suspicion on Dryden's part that, in his
use of heroic materials, he was dealing, to use Bakhtin's phrase, with
'something false [and] hypocritical'.

Cortez's nobility, as we have seen, is rendered suspect in the
opening scene. In Act 2, scene 2, his commitment to the heroic code
of honour is also called into question. Honour, he insists, requires
him not to question but to obey his 'Princes orders' to make war on
the Indians. Moreover, he adds, 'Honour once lost is never to be
found'. Shortly afterwards, however, overcome by his love for
Cydaria, he calls off the Spanish attack:

> Honour be gone, what art thou but a breath?
> I'le live, proud of my infamy and shame,
> Grac'd with no Triumph but a Lovers name;
> Men can but say Love did his reason blind.

Passion triumphs over reason, personal interest over loyalty to the
King. Twentieth-century readers may sympathize, but the continental guardians of honour would have disapproved. Although some
scholars discern substantial improvement in Cortez's moral stance
during the course of the play, it is probably fair to conclude with
J. M. Armistead that the Spanish 'hero' is 'educable, though flawed'.[29]

Dryden's attitude to his Aztec 'heroes' Montezuma and Guyomar
is similarly ambivalent. Claims for Montezuma's nobility are generally based on his spirited defence of natural religion against the
narrower 'revealed' religion of the Christian Priest in Act 5, scene 2.[30]
Certainly the immediate dramatic context of this scene is heavily
weighted in favour of the Indian. Because Pizarro wishes to discover
more of the Emperor's gold and the Priest intends to convert him by
force as well as argument, Montezuma is being stretched on the rack.
There he displays both heroic fortitude and a rational defence of his
religion. The scene is borrowed in part from Montaigne,[31] and the
views expressed by Montezuma can be found in Montaigne, Hooker,
Grotius and Lord Herbert of Cherbury, among others.[32]

But Dryden interrupts our admiration of the noble primitive. As
Cortez enters the prison, he bestows on it, in Derek Hughes's phrase,
'a startlingly unwarranted consecration': ' 'Tis sacred here to Beauty
and to Love'.[33] Unaware as yet of the torture being carried out

within, Cortez intends to recall the declarations of love he had exchanged, while a prisoner there himself, with Cydaria. Dryden, however, may intend us to remember a moment of jarring incongruity earlier in the play. In Act 1, scene 2, immediately after announcing the sacrifice of 'five hundred Captives' in honour of Montezuma's birthday, the Aztec High Priest proclaimed Montezuma 'the peaceful power that governs love'. The singing of a 'beauteous quire' then heralded the arrival of the Emperor. Cortez's remark in the torture chamber echoes this prior juxtaposition of cruelty and the rhetoric of love and beauty. We are thus reminded that the natural religion espoused so eloquently by Montezuma on the rack can embrace civility and human sacrifice alike. The fashionable authority of natural religion in Dryden's world is called into question.

Montezuma has other flaws besides. As John Winterbottom remarks, the Indian ruler 'is the helpless victim of an ignoble love for the daughter of a woman he has wronged, and in the heat of passion he is capable of the grossest neglect of his responsibilities as emperor'.[34] Winterbottom therefore proposes that Guyomar be regarded as the real hero of the play. Guyomar, he observes, consistently chooses the path of duty over that of passion. But Anne Barbeau's supportive assertion that Guyomar 'is at first a model of calm and exact virtue' is at odds with Montezuma's rebuke of the 'unseemly discord' which quickly erupts between Guyomar and his brother Odmar over the hand of Alibech.[35] Nor is it self-evident that Dryden regarded Guyomar's voluntary exile at the close of the play as honourable rather than, as one critic has suggested, the sign of a primitive incapacity to 'advance with history'.[36] The lack of any clear hero in a play that so readily invokes the heroic code bespeaks a dissenting authorial voice in dialogue with the characters' invocation of the world of heroic romance.

Bakhtin's concept of 'heteroglossia as a background' may help us to understand the nature of Dryden's dialogue with the voices of La Calprenède, Scudéry, Lucretius and Montaigne. For these voices are cited, as it were, in translation in the uniform language of heroic couplets and might seem, therefore, to be drained of their capacity for dialogue. But in one of the essays in *The Dialogic Imagination*, Bakhtin draws a distinction between what he calls the novel's First and Second Lines. He prefers the Second (more recent) Line, because this 'incorporates heteroglossia *into* a novel's composition', representing directly a diversity of human languages. But he is not willing to abandon the First Line to the charge of monologism. For, although this adopts a single, 'idealizing' style, which 'leaves heteroglossia outside itself, that is, outside the language of the novel, . . . even *its* perception presumes heteroglossia as a background, and even it interacts dialogically with various aspects of this heteroglossia'. 'Such stylization', he concludes, 'involves a sideways glance at others' languages, at other points of view and other conceptual systems, each with its own set of objects and meanings'.[37] The multiplicity of voices recalled and relativized by the dramatic poetry of *The Indian Emperour* suggests that Dryden intended the background of heteroglossia to be clearly heard.

Other voices of classical and contemporary authority, audible in the background of *The Indian Emperour,* include those of Virgil, Henry More, Joseph Glanvill and Thomas Hobbes. A brief reference to each will illustrate the scope of Dryden's orchestration of heteroglot voices. In Act 2, scene 1, the ghost of the Indian Queen describes her experience of the afterlife in language resonant with echoes of Virgil's narrative of the 'mournful fields' in Book 6 of *The Aeneid*.[38] Dryden thereby establishes a link between the pagan world of Mexico and that of the ancient Mediterranean, and the subsequent action of the play suggests that the triumph of Christianity over the ancient world is being providentially replicated in the victory of Christianity in the New World.

In the same scene the Aztec High Priest conjures up an 'Earthy Spirit' which, to the priest's dismay, foretells the victory of 'a God more strong' than the Aztec pantheon. Both the early church, in its encounter with the classical world, and the Spanish church, in its encounter with the New World, regarded such spirits as demonic. Ironically, the Aztec priest recalls this judgement in his frustrated rejection of the unco-operative spirit as 'black and envious'. But this spirit speaks truth, and such veracity is hardly consonant with the traditional Christian view of the demonic. It reflects instead what Armistead calls 'the redeemed demonology' of Christian neo-Platonists such as Henry More and Joseph Glanvill. These contemporaries of Dryden suggested that although departed spirits, angels and 'daemons' could all appear to advise or inform the living, they could do so only to further the beneficial designs of Providence. By conforming the world of Mexican ghosts and spirits to the theories of contemporary neo-Platonism, Dryden was proposing, according to Armistead, that 'the Christianizing of the Indian Spirit world [was] a less radical conversion than the one experienced in the world of Greco-Roman mythology'.[39]

Perhaps it is because Dryden is inclined to minimize religious difference that he is in principle willing to accept it. Here he differs from Thomas Hobbes, for Hobbes advocated, in the interests of political order, a single national religion: whatever faith individual citizens may espouse in the privacy of their conscience, they must adhere in public to the religion of their sovereign. Dryden discredits such ideas of forced conversion by placing them in the mouths of the greedy Pizarro and the violent Spanish Priest. Moreover, Cortez offers at the end of the play to rule Mexico jointly with a still-pagan Guyomar. Although Guyomar declines Cortez's offer, this does not, in Barbeau's view, weaken Dryden's implicit criticism of a politically motivated religious uniformity.[40]

THE PRESENCE OF THE AUDIENCE

Such is Dryden's way with his sources. The voices of contemporary debate are given articulate expression on stage and then interrogated by the dramatic action. The characters, of course, are oblivious to this interrogation. The real dialogue is being conducted, as Jocelyn Powell puts it, 'over the characters' heads'.[41] Dryden and the actors who speak his words are inviting the audience to see in a fresh light sentiments expressed by the characters but drawn from the fashionable world of the audience. Despite the first impression created by Hogarth's painting, there is after all a dialogue being proposed between stage and auditorium.

Indeed, on re-examination certain aspects of the painting testify to such a dialogue. Caroline Lennox, playing the role of Cydaria in white satin, addresses the audience rather than her companions on stage. This stance, conventional in the Restoration theatre,[42] deliberately offers Cydaria's speech to the audience for its consideration. The actress acknowledges that she is being watched, and this, according to Powell,

> is the key to the Restoration style, to the dialogue between the actor and the audience that was its life-blood. . . . The actor did not live his roles. He shared his author's idea of their nature with his audience.[43]

The contemporary costumes, too, although they may suppress the alterity of the characters, further the dialogue between stage and audience. The audience is being entertained by a historical romance and is being asked to consider matters of contemporary debate. The costumes make emblematic reference to the historical setting, and guard against complete absorption in it. Dryden 'is wanting the worlds to clash', Powell observes, 'because he is using history as an emblem to throw modern behaviour into relief', and so to sustain 'the dialogue between fiction and contemporary life that was so crucial to the Restoration style'.[44]

Much of this, as Powell notes, anticipates Brecht's theory of *verfremdungseffekt*. Even the lively discussion amongst the members of the audience might be defended on Brechtian grounds. For Brecht advocated a theatre in which the spectators did not 'hand in . . . their normal behaviour . . . at the cloakroom'. He wanted his audience instead to smoke cigars, to engage in 'free discussion', and 'to cast [a] vote' in response to the issues raised on stage.[45] Some of the audience in Hogarth's painting – the Duke of Richmond in the rear, leaning over his wife's chair, and the little girl with the fan in the front row – are gazing at the stage in rapt attention. Others are engaged in conversation. Whether Hogarth thought of them as discussing the play is, of course, impossible to tell. But, given the similarities between the theatre of Brecht and that of the Restoration, it is not improbable. In any case, it is clear from Dryden's handling of his sources that he at least, like Brecht, wanted to initiate a dialogue with his audience.

Finally, once more there is the prompter. It is odd that Derrida should have expressed such fear of 'the dictatorship of the text'[46] while writing of Artaud. Artaud, of course, shared that fear. But Artaud, more than any other writer on the theatre, was aware of the signs that surface only in performance and which cannot be controlled by a pre-existent script. Although a text may specify the words to be spoken, 'music, dance, plastic art, pantomime, mimicry, gesticulation, intonation, architecture, lighting, and scenery',[47] to use one of Artaud's lists, are added in performance and can, as Brecht put it, 'adopt an attitude' to the words spoken.[48] The actor's gesture and tone of voice, for example, can endorse or undermine the authority of a character's point of view. They can do so in keeping with or contrary to the perspective of the author.

Unfortunately, we know too few details of subsequent performances of *The Indian Emperour* to guess the attitude adopted by successive companies to Dryden's text.[49] Jack Lindsay does suggest that, in Hogarth's painting and perhaps therefore in the performance it commemorates, 'the heroic is mocked . . . by being enacted by children in doll-like poses'.[50] This may have been unintentional on the part of the cast at the Conduits'. But it does indicate that even the most careful protection of the text by the prompter cannot guarantee the tenor of the performance. Unfortunately, too, there have been no modern revivals of *The Indian Emperour*.[51] Subsequent generations inevitably bring different concerns to a dramatic text and enter into dialogue with it from widely divergent points of view. One only has to think of the recent stage history of another play with a colonial theme, Shakespeare's *The Tempest*, to recognize the varied productions that a single text can generate.[52]

The prompter, even in Derrida's nightmares, concerns himself only with the words spoken. He protects, if you will, the author's part in the dialogue. But the director, designer and cast are free, even if, as rarely happens, they play the text in its entirety, to respond to the author's voice through the signs exclusive to performance. This dialogue between the author and the several members of the company is then extended, as Popovici suggests, to include a succession of audiences. Subsequent performances enlarge the circle of participants in the dialogue. Some plays find interlocutors well beyond the political, cultural and epochal boundaries of their original production. *The Indian Emperour* has not been one of these. But even this play gives evidence of being fired by the same dialogical imagination that Bakhtin claimed could be found only in the novel. The drama 'strictly conceived' is a dialogical genre after all.

Finally, although Dryden was more interested in his own world than in that of the Aztecs, this is not enough to convict him of a denial of alterity. Like Brecht, he used a distant setting to advance an alternative perspective on a present debate. Even Todorov frankly admits that the present is more important to him than the past, and that he tells 'an exemplary story' from the past in order to answer a present moral question.[53] Dryden's dramatic poem captures very little of the genuine otherness of the Mexican world. But it does acknowledge the existence of multiple perspectives and, in some measure, call into question the universal authority of any particular perspective. There is, it would seem, more dialogue between worlds and a greater awareness of alterity in a performance of *The Indian Emperour* than first meets the eye of the viewer of Hogarth's painting.

3

A Marrano in
Montezuma's Court

In *The Indian Emperour* Dryden openly engages his audience in dialogue with texts drawn from authorities of high current reputation, and refracted through the action and characters of his play. Matters were not so simple in contemporary Spain, the colonial power responsible for the conquest and administration of Mexico. For, according to Catherine Swietlicki, seventeenth-century Spain may be compared in some respects to 'the Stalinist Russia of Bakhtin's time'. 'There are', she observes, 'certain similarities between the two powers' preoccupations with establishing unified ideologies and eradicating forces opposed to the dominant culture and its philosophy'. Not least of these similarities, she suggests, is the role played by the Spanish Inquisition and the Russian secret police in 'enforcing . . . monolithic dogma'.[1]

Under such circumstances, a dramatist writing for the public stage may cite authoritative voices not to question them, as Dryden did, but for the protective aura of orthodoxy they afford. This can give rise to a different form of dialogism, in which the playwright's voice is split in two. A first, orthodox authorial voice endorses acceptable dogma in words that conceal a second, dissenting authorial voice. The dissenting voice is not easily heard. Such is the case with the play to which we now turn. For *La conquista de México* guards its dissent under what seems at first to be an unqualified endorsement of the voice of authority. Even the dramatist's name is a matter of dispute and probable disguise, shielding him from the intrusive eye and monological voice of the Inquisition. The question of authorship and the authority of the Inquisition therefore provide a single point of entry into the world of the play.

ZÁRATE AND ENRÍQUEZ GÓMEZ

On 13 April 1660, eight years before *La conquista de México* was first printed in Madrid, a spectacular *auto de fe* was held in Seville.[2] Among those condemned were 78 *judaizantes*, professed Christians of Jewish heritage accused of surreptitiously practising the religion of their forebears. The Jew (and the Moor) were the internal others in Spanish society, as much a threat to the singularity of the Spanish Christian world as were the external Indian others in the New World. For nearly 300 years, intermittent persecution had forced many Iberian Jews to submit to exile or to Christian baptism. But the very nature of such conversions rendered the 'New' Christians suspect in the minds of the 'Old' Christian majority. Legal challenge successfully barred the *conversos* and their descendants from offices open only to Christians. Proven Christian ancestry therefore became a matter of vital social and professional importance. Moreover, the suspicion that Jews who had refused baptism and survived were guilty of encouraging New Christians to revert to Judaism heightened anti-Semitic feelings. Royal edict finally ordered all Jews expelled from Spain in 1492 and from Portugal in 1497. Rather than leave, many chose to be baptized; others were compelled to stay and were baptized by force. These reluctant converts swelled the numbers of the already problematic *converso* community. Those who maintained a private Jewish faith behind a public Christian façade were known as *marranos* or *judaizantes*. Their discovery and eradication became a primary goal of the Inquisition.[3]

One of the New Christians condemned in Seville in 1660 was Antonio Enríquez Gómez. Enríquez Gómez was a Marrano playwright and poet of considerable repute who, fearing for his life, had fled to France in 1636. Among the works he wrote in exile were some openly sympathetic to Judaism. Many were highly critical of the Inquisition.[4] Wanting the status that would accrue from holding a large scale *auto general*, the Inquisitors in Seville cast their nets as wide as possible. Enríquez Gómez, believed by the Inquisitors still to be abroad, was sentenced *in absentia* and burned in effigy.[5]

All was not, however, quite as it seemed. Living in Seville at the time was the playwright Fernando de Zárate, an elderly gentleman with an impeccable Old Christian name. Most recent biographers imagine him in the crowd at the *auto de fe*, and he may even have followed the procession to the *quemadero* to watch the effigy of

Enríquez Gómez burn. Zárate had good reason to be interested in the fate of the *converso* dramatist. For a year later Zárate was himself arrested by the Inquisition, and charged with judaizing. Enríquez Gómez, it turns out, had been living and writing in Seville since 1649 under the assumed name of Fernando de Zárate y Castronovo. Enríquez Gómez died in jail in 1663, having received the last rites of the Roman Church. Among his confiscated effects was a bundle of plays that were sold by the Inquisition and subsequently published under the Zárate pseudonym.[6] Some 28 plays by 'Zárate' survive, all of them apparently characterized by a fervent Christianity. *La conquista de México* appeared in 1668.[7]

The identity of Enríquez Gómez and Zárate was lost to literary historians for nearly 200 years. Their plays were known, but only a meagre and often fictitious biography clung to the name of Enríquez Gómez, and 'Zárate' remained a complete mystery. The first modern suggestion that the two were one and the same person was made by Adolfo de Castro in 1857.[8] Castro based his claim on an entry he discovered in an eighteenth-century index of forbidden books. A play attributed to Zárate was banned, with the parenthetical explanation, 'He is Antonio Enríquez Gómez'.

But Castro's hypothesis generated a storm of rebuttal. The critics' principal objection had to do with the apparently irreconcilable religious beliefs of the 'two' playwrights. Ramón de Mesonero y Romanos, for example, reminded his readers that Enríquez Gómez's plays betray a suspicious 'predilection for ancient Jewish history', and that their author was known to have fled Spain under threat of persecution as a judaizer. Zárate, on the other hand, wrote plays 'which reveal the intimate Christian faith of their author'.[9] Old prejudice dies hard: Zárate's work was pronounced far superior to that of Enríquez Gómez, and Castro's theory was, in Glen Dille's phrase, 'relegated to the footnotes' for a hundred years.[10]

In 1962, however, I. S. Révah published the results of his patient archival research into the life of Enríquez Gómez.[11] He established beyond doubt that the dramatist was of Marrano heritage. Enríquez Gómez's father and paternal grandfather had both been arrested by the Inquisition for secretly holding to their ancestral faith. It was Révah, too, who discovered that Enríquez Gómez had secretly returned from voluntary exile in France in 1649 and had settled in Seville under the pseudonym 'Zárate'. By 1988 Glen Dille could write confidently that 'all scholars have come around to accept [Révah's] discovery as to Zárate's true identity'.[12]

But scholars remain puzzled by the apparent discrepancy between Enríquez Gómez's avowedly Jewish writings and 'the flag-
waving Christianity of his Zárate plays'.[13] *La conquista de México* has
been cited as an example of the latter. Although many scholars share
the view of J. A. Cid that the dramatist's Jewish faith 'held firm until
the end',[14] Dille offers *La conquista de México* as evidence that Enríquez
Gómez at last embraced 'a loving and accommodating Christianity'.[15] Winston Reynolds, too, remarks that the play was written 'in
the spirit of a holy crusade'.[16] I hope to show instead that, in *La
conquista de México*, 'Zárate's' official Christian voice engaged in
dialogue with the concealed Marrano voice of Enríquez Gómez, and
that the play yields a reading critical of Christian imperialism and
sympathetic to the Marrano predicament.[17]

LOPE DE VEGA

My task is complicated by the suggestion of Carlos Romero Muñoz
that *La conquista de México* is not by 'Zárate' at all. It is, he proposes,
a lost play of Lope de Vega, *La conquista de Cortés*, written between
1597 and 1599 and published erroneously under the Zárate pseudonym.[18] Romero's argument for Lope's authorship of *La conquista de
México* is based on a careful stylistic analysis of the published text. In
the dramatist's mode of versification, as well as in the presence of
allegory and the absence of a *gracioso* (fool), Romero finds little
resemblance to other plays published under the names of Zárate and
Enríquez Gómez. He discovers, however, an uncanny likeness to
comedias written by Lope de Vega during the period in question.

Romero's evidence is persuasive and would perhaps settle the
issue of authorship, were it not for the double-voiced nature of the
play, to which he also draws attention:

> The whole work is permeated with an evident Christian and
> Spanish nationalist providentialism. At first sight, the adherence
> of the author to what his words say is total, although it is fair to
> say that *these same words* can convey very different things. One
> can, then, read [*La conquista de México*] in a straight or literal
> manner, and also in an oblique and even inverted manner.

Tantalizingly, Romero declines to conduct such an experiment in 'oblique' reading, and passes directly to his stylistic analysis.[19]

In an earlier article, however, Romero had given a clue as to the form that such a reading might take. At the time, he thought that 'Zárate' had borrowed passages from two of Lope's surviving New World plays, and that these recognizable allusions to the older playwright's text served as a kind of 'lightning conductor' or 'alibi', designed to protect 'Zárate' from the 'vigilantes' of the Inquisition.[20] Whereas Enríquez Gómez was hunted and finally imprisoned by the Inquisition, Lope was, as Romero points out, 'a lay official [*familiar*] of the Holy Office'. In using Lope's material, Romero suggests, 'Zárate' might have hoped to consolidate his Old Christian disguise by a literary association with certified orthodoxy.

Romero goes on to propose that 'Zárate' transformed Lope's theme and material into 'metaphors for other matters'. In *La conquista de México*, he writes, the dramatist 'wishes to be understood as "Zárate" and, at the same time, as Enríquez Gómez'. The Marrano playwright, he concludes, 'seeded' his plays with 'signs which, in the end, unequivocally, brilliantly, bring us to the point of reading them as he wished them to be read: in great part, in contradiction to what they seem to express'.[21] Romero identifies neither the signs nor the significance that he finds in them. But it is clear that he hears two distinct voices in *La conquista de México*, and that one quietly contradicts what the other fervently professes. There is much to be said for his initial suggestion that the public Christianity of 'Zárate' and the private Judaism of Enríquez Gómez both found expression in this way within a single text.

Romero's concept of an oblique reading, however, is hard to reconcile with his conclusion that Lope de Vega wrote *La conquista de México*, for religious ambiguity is not characteristic of Lope's plays. On the contrary, Lope was long regarded as an uncritical spokesman for the conservative ideals of his age.[22] Although several scholars have now challenged this assumption, and have discovered in his plays occasional discreet dissent from the official mythology of Golden Age Spain,[23] none has questioned his commitment to Christianity. Even those who have found sympathetic *converso* characters[24] are quick to point out the anomalous nature of these 'rare exceptions'.[25]

Double-voiced religious discourse is, however, increasingly regarded as a feature of the Zárate plays. Glen Dille, for example, discovers in the sensitive portrayal of the *morisco* Don Pedro in

El valiente Campuzano a veiled criticism of Old Christian prejudice. For *moriscos* – New Christians of Moorish ancestry – were subject to the same indignities as those of Jewish lineage. The blustering Old Christian *hidalgo* Campuzano, as the title of the play suggests, is the official hero, and it is he who triumphs in terms of the plot. The swashbuckling braggart prevents his sister from marrying Don Pedro, killing the tainted *morisco* in a concluding duel. But it is Don Pedro who displays the greater virtue. The play, writes Dille, is 'to be understood in two ways'. Officially, 'it would seem to uphold the status quo'. Behind the safety of the conventional plot, however, lies 'a cleverly presented exposition of the injustices' to which *conversos*, whether of Moorish or Jewish heritage, were subject.[26]

Even in *Las misas de San Vicente Ferrer*, a play so drenched in Catholic hagiography that Timothy Oelman could not imagine the Marrano Enríquez Gómez having written it,[27] there is discreet sympathy for the ethnic and religious outsider. One of the chief characters of the play, Muley, is a black man born and raised in the Congo and transported to the white man's world by Spanish slavetraders. Shipwrecked, both literally and figuratively, he is unable to find his religious place in the new world of the Mediterranean. Alternately pagan, *converso* and Moor, he is finally, in accordance with Old Christian prejudices, the villain of the piece. But for much of the play, as David Gitlitz points out, it is Muley's 'intolerable circumstance of being black in a white world' that most interests 'Zárate'. Although Gitlitz doubted the identity of Zárate and Enríquez Gómez, he was so struck by the dramatist's ability to focus the problem 'from a minority point of view' that he suspected Zárate, too, of being a New Christian, depicting his own anguish in the guise of a black *converso*.[28] Once again, although the voice of the plot speaks with an impeccable Old Christian accent, it is placed in dialogue with a voice that speaks softly from the outsider's perspective.

If Romero is correct, therefore, *La conquista de México* bears traces both of Lope's literary style and of Enríquez Gómez/Zárate's double-voiced religious discourse. While any explanation of this phenomenon remains speculative, it is not unreasonable to suppose that Enríquez Gómez reworked and renamed Lope's now missing *La conquista de Cortés*, retaining Lope's distinctive style but adding a qualifying, dialogical voice. The specific contribution of this second voice will become clearer as we try Romero's experiment in reading *La conquista de México* obliquely. But Romero was, I believe, substantially correct when he imagined Enríquez Gómez embarking on 'a passionate adventure of designification and subsequent resignification of another's text'.[29]

The question remains, however, as to why Enríquez Gómez would have been attracted to the theme of Spanish conquest in the New World. David Gitlitz provides a clue. Following his suggestion that Zárate's sympathetic portrayal of the black Muley involved a disguised portrait of the *converso* predicament, Gitlitz remarks that such 'substitution' may have been 'habitual' with Zárate. By way of precedent, he points to the case of another *converso* playwright, Miguel de Carvajal. Although Gitlitz does not mention *La conquista de México* in this context, his reference to Carvajal is most suggestive. For Carvajal's *Las cortes de la muerte* (1557) includes a scene in which New World Indians complain that, despite their sincere conversion to Christianity, they are still mistreated by Spaniards coveting their gold. The Indians insist that their conversion was genuine, being the effect of 'preaching alone' and not of force. They recall and apply to their own situation Christ's Parable of the Labourers in the Vineyard (Matthew 20: 1–16), in which those who enter the master's service at 'the eleventh hour' receive no less blessing than those who have worked for him all day. And they invoke the saying of Christ (Matthew 22: 37–40) that the Law and the Prophets depend on humanity's twin obligations to love God and not harm one's neighbour, a duty the Spanish Christians are patently neglecting. Their complaints are upheld by Death, in whose court the Indians have made their appeal, and by the church fathers who have joined him on the judicial bench. Carvajal, Gitlitz suggests, has 'sublimated his own situation in that of a substitute: . . . Indians in place of *conversos*'.[30]

It may have been this same opportunity for substitution that attracted Enríquez Gómez to Lope's text. To dramatize the triumph of Catholic Spain in the New World meant also to depict the fate of those at whose expense her victory was won. 'Zárate's' defeated Indians could at times recall Enríquez Gómez's oppressed Marranos. C. H. Rose and Timothy Oelman remark:

Enríquez Gómez often wrote for three audiences simultaneously: for a Christian audience, for a *converso*/Marrano audience accustomed to looking for cryptic clues, and for himself, for the ironic pleasure which he felt in his ability to convey multiple meanings.[31]

An Old Christian audience would have seen in *La conquista de México*
a celebration of Spanish expansion in the New World. A Marrano
audience may have found the key to an alternative reading in the
kinship between Indian and Marrano. Even the change in title may
contain a cryptic clue. Lope's title, *La conquista de Cortés*, celebrates
the conqueror. 'Zárate's' title shifts attention to the conquered. Moreover, 'Zárate' substitutes a word that, in its syllabic count and in its
first and last letters, recalls the heritage of Enríquez Gómez. 'México'
bears traces of 'Marrano'. As we shall see, however, Enríquez Gómez's
narrative of substitution does not end, like Carvajal's, in vindication
for the ill-treated *converso*, but in anguish over the Marrano failure to
withstand the violent imposition of Christianity.

LA CONQUISTA DE MÉXICO

We should not expect an oblique reading of *La conquista de México* to
yield a fully developed alternative narrative. For 'Zárate' proceeds
by way of occasional analogy rather than sustained allegory, and not
every sign in *La conquista de México* has dual referents. On the contrary, the play's Christian narrative is only partially 'seeded', to use
Romero's term, with signs of a Marrano presence. Such signs, sparse
at first, increase in density as the play progresses.

Initially, the narrative gives rise to a matter of sanctioned public
debate: the contrast between the ideals of Spanish imperialism, represented by Cortés, and its regrettable materialism, displayed by his
followers. Disembarking on the island of 'Azucamiel' (Cozumel) at
the head of a squadron of soldiers bearing banners and harquebuses,
Cortés voices his impression that he has landed in a 'friendly new
world'. His soldiers are therefore to harm no Indian; nor are they to
steal or even to request gold. For his sole intent, he proclaims, is
missionary:

> la Fe de Christo professo,
> esta ensalçar imagino,
> esta adoro, esta confiesso.

> [The faith of Christ I profess,
> This I intend to propagate,
> This I adore, this I confess.] (229)[32]

Aside, two of his captains, Añasco and Tapia, protest their own loyalty to 'the Faith and the Cross', but admit that it is the lure of gold that has drawn them to 'this barbarous land'. Tapia is confident that Cortés's attitude will change when he actually sees gold, and Añusco declares,

> oro deseo, oro quiero,
> por esto las armas tomo,
> con el oro duermo, y como.

> [Gold I desire, gold I want,
> For this I bear arms,
> I eat and sleep gold.]

After all, he says, is not God 'the Eternal Creator of gold and silver', and did he not create these gifts 'for man' (230a)?

This opening portrait of the mixed motives of the conquistadors is not found in the play's historical source, the account of the conquest by López de Gómara.[33] Enríquez Gómez may have added it in order to draw an analogy with the Inquisition, whose mixed motives had already cost him dearly. For the Holy Office, too, professed loyalty to the faith of Christ while enriching itself with the confiscated property of its victims. Chief among these, as Henry Kamen notes, were 'the *conversos*, whose notorious wealth must have stirred many an orthodox spirit'.[34] As a young man, Enríquez Gómez had himself lost his patrimony to the Inquisition,[35] and in his *Política angélica* (1647), he devotes several pages to the contradiction between the Inquisition's covetousness and its professed concern with matters of the soul. Adopting a self-consciously Christian voice, he cites at one point Matthew 10: 6–10. When Jesus sends his disciples 'to save the lost sheep of the House of Israel', he is reported to have added, 'Own neither gold nor silver, and accept no money in your pouches'.[36] Enríquez Gómez comments:

> Ministers of God, if you want to subdue the House of Israel, avail yourselves of the teaching of Christ, give freely what has been freely given to you; convert, subdue, and save; but let it be in such a way that, if the Gospel is found in your mouth, gold is not found in your purses; for the Apostles did not give salvation for silver, nor faith for coins; they gave faith for faith, and grace for grace; and if you deny this, you will have neither grace here nor glory yonder.[37]

The attitude of 'Zárate's' conquistadors recalls that of the Christian
'ministers' whom Enríquez Gómez admonished.

The Spaniards' first encounter with the inhabitants of the New
World follows. Three Indian men flee before the 'harquebus, drum
and trumpet' of the Spaniards. Cortés describes them in pastoral
language as 'fearful sheep', who by their flight demonstrate that
they are 'people of peace'. The Indians' wives are less timid, and are
greeted by Cortés as 'daughters of Christ'. Assuring the Indians of
his peaceful intentions, Cortés places great stress on the fact that he
and his men are 'Christians' (230a–231a), as if the term were synonymous with 'peaceable'. The Spaniards leave to unload cannon from
their ship ('although we come in peace'), while the Indian women
persuade their husbands to come out of hiding. The men examine,
with some confusion, the mirrors given to their wives, and then
approach a cross the Spaniards have erected. They are puzzled by its
significance, until a dove encircled by a halo of gold and accompanied by the music of flutes miraculously alights on it. The Indians
then fall prostrate before the cross, mistaking it for a sacred symbol
of the sun's grandeur extending to all four points of the compass:

> O señal sagrada,
> alta, heroyca, y eminente,
> ô tu angulo divino,
> ô palos puesto de modo,
> que cubris el mundo todo,
> tan grandes os imagino,
> pues con essas quatro puntas,
> su circulo dividis,
> y en el vuestro descubris
> del Sol las grandezas juntas.

> [O sacred sign,
> high, heroic, and eminent,
> O you divine angle,
> O poles set such
> that you cover the whole world,
> I regard you as so great,
> since with these four points
> you divide its circle,
> and in yours you reveal
> the united grandeurs of the Sun.] (233b)

Parts of this scene at the cross are demonstrably indebted to an extant play by Lope de Vega, *El Nuevo Mundo descubierto por Cristóbal Colón.*[38] But in Lope's play the Indians worship the cross in terms that anticipate its Christian significance. They see it as the powerful instrument of a God as yet unknown, as a worthy resting place for the phoenix (a common emblem of Christ) to consummate its death and resurrection, and as the source of a liquid capable of healing wounds and raising the dead (1846–82). The introduction of New World cosmology to the corresponding scene in *La conquista de México* transforms incipient Christianity into pagan idolatry. Since Jews regard God himself as the only proper object of worship, one wonders if Enríquez Gómez is not implicitly condemning all adoration of the cross. One can only speculate. But there is no doubt that the author of *La conquista de México* stripped Lope's scene of much of its aura of proto-Christian sanctity.

Thus far we have heard, at best, uncertain intimations of a Marrano voice. But the next incident surely bears intentional irony. A company of Spanish guards ensconces itself at the foot of the cross and, as the dialogue makes clear, begins to gamble:

ALV[ARADO]. Iugaremos, Alferez? ALF[ÉREZ]. Ponga mesa.
SOLD[ADO]. La caxa no està aqui? ALF[ÉREZ]. Llega la caxa.
SOLD[ADO]. De no traer aqui vn millon me pesa.
AÑASC[O]. Echa essos huessos, y la mano baxa.
ALF[ÉREZ]. A diez. AÑ[ASCO]. Digo. SOLD[ADO]. Mi suerte sola es essa.
ALV[ARADO]. Y yo la paro con mayor ventaja.

[ALVARADO. Shall we play, Lieutenant? LIEUTENANT. Set up a table.
SOLDIER: Isn't there a drum [box?] here? LIEUTENANT. The drum will do.
SOLDIER. I'm sorry I didn't bring a million [pesos].
AÑASCO. Throw these bones [dice], and lay down your hand.
LIEUTENANT. Ten. AÑASCO. Right. SOLDIER. That's all my luck.
ALVARADO. And I'm going to stop for greater profit.] (234)

Neither Lope's *El Nuevo Mundo descubierto* nor Gómara's chronicle mention gambling soldiers. The ironic allusion to the gospel account of Roman soldiers casting lots during Christ's crucifixion (John 19: 23–4) seems therefore to be deliberate and inescapable. What is less quickly apparent is that if the Spaniards are thus cast as Roman soldiers of occupation, the Indians, whose land has been invaded, are cast as Jews. The author of *La conquista de México* is quietly establishing the terms of his dialogue between worlds.

The first act continues with Cortés instructing the Indians in the Christian faith, giving an orthodox account of the Trinity, the incarnation and the atonement, and emphasizing, as the Indians in Carvajal's play did, the twin pegs on which the 'Law of Christ' hangs:

> amanle de coraçon,
> y al proximo como a ti.

> [Love God with your heart,
> And your neighbour as yourself.] (236b)

Aguilar, a Spaniard shipwrecked on the coast of Yucatán some years ago, then joins the conquistadors, and his knowledge of the local Indian language is hailed by the suddenly pious Alvarado, Cortés's second-in-command, as a 'miracle', without which the Spaniards would have failed in their mission of 'conquest' (237b). Cortés meanwhile erects a cross in an Indian temple. The displaced idol collapses, and the demons who had inhabited it protest, threatening to travel to the Old World if they are driven from the New (238a). Act I concludes with Aguilar's story of the 'barbarous' Mayans among whom he has lived, dwelling especially on their bloody human sacrifices and cannibalism, and ending with his confident assertion that Spanish arms 'will conquer this world for Carlos, King of Spain'. The closing note of the first act is thus one of triumphant imperialism, justified by the barbarity of the inhabitants of the New World. Here the official Old Christian voice predominates. But it has not been alone in the first act. A second dissenting voice has discreetly questioned it.

Both the voice of dissent and the dual identity of the characters become more marked in the short second act. The act begins with an exemplary debate between Idolatry and the Christian Religion, and continues with the first battle between Indians and Christians. The Spaniards, aided by their patron saint Santiago, gain the victory, but there is no explanation of why the Spanish assurances of peace have dissolved into acts of war. A new group of Indians are even more convinced that the Spaniards have come in search of gold, and their suspicions are confirmed when the Spaniards 'snatch with great haste . . . some small ingots of gold' proffered by the Indians (242b). Cortés reprimands his soldiers for this display of greed, but it is not long before he is himself asking Montezuma's ambassador for gold 'to cure my people of their sickness' (245b). This entails for Cortés a retreat from his initial idealistic prohibition of such requests. Cortés's credibility is further undermined when he secretly orders that the Spanish fleet be scuttled to prevent retreat. Publicly he denies responsibility, and announces the loss of the fleet as a sign of God's will that the army should advance on Montezuma's capital (248). Sinking the ships may have been, as Gómara and other Spanish chroniclers believed, the tactic of a military genius.[39] But assigning responsibility to God would seem to be the dramatist's addition to Gómara's account, and, in the economy of the play, it shows Cortés to be a man who misuses the name of God to mask his own desires. The balance between the missionary ideals and the materialistic greed of Spanish imperialism is lost. The representative of the former is implicitly discredited.

It is in this act, too, that the shipwrecked Spaniard Aguilar is given the newly converted Indian Mariana in marriage. Significantly, he calls her 'my beautiful new Christian [*mi nueva Christiana hermosa*]' (244a). When, shortly afterwards, Cortés addresses his soldiers as 'well-born Spanish noblemen [*Españoles hidalgos, bien nacidos*]' (246), the dramatic identity of the Spaniards as Old Christians and the Indian converts as New Christians is unmistakable. That this identification should be made in the context of a marriage between members of the two parties is an implicit challenge to the premium placed in the Old World on purity of blood.

In the third act, the Christian and Marrano voices of the play speak radically different lines. In terms of the plot, the Christian hero Cortés triumphs unequivocally over Aztec paganism. But the other voice in the dialogue offers Montezuma as a veiled portrait of Marrano confusion in the face of Christian imperialism. Although the horrors of Montezuma's Aztec religion are stressed by the official Christian voice, the concealed voice depicts the emperor as a wealthy Marrano at a loss to know how best to respond to the demands of an armed Christianity that will tolerate neither his riches nor his faith.

Early in the act, Montezuma consults a concealed household idol, whose gilded features and halo of golden rays identify it as the Sun (249). It may be coincidental that the Old Testament once represents the patriarch Israel as the sun and his wife Rachel as the moon (Genesis 37: 9–10). But when, later in the third act, Montezuma is advised to decorate himself and his palanquin with emblems of the sun and moon (255b), one cannot help wondering if the playwright wants temporarily to suggest an alternative Jewish identity for

Montezuma's god.[40] For, although Montezuma's idol demands multiple human sacrifice in keeping with its official pagan identity, it also startles the reader with language that speaks directly to the Marrano predicament. Tempted to embrace Christianity, a Marrano might well have imagined such a reproof from the God of Israel:

> como, que a vn Dios antiguo, y conocido,
> dexais por vn Christiano de oy venido?
> yo no os he dado luz todos los dias?
> yo no os he dado el agua conveniente
> para vuestro maiz? pues que ossadias
> mueuen a despreciarme aquesta gente?
> yo no os he dado de las manos mias
> ricos tesoros abundantemente?
> pues porque me dexais, y estos dorados
> rayos, por vnos palos mal cruzados?
> yo no puedo morir, su Dios fue muerto;
> un muerto puede ser Dios que dê vida?
> bolved, bolved, que es graue desconcierto.

> [How can you leave an ancient, known God
> For a Christian God who has arrived only today?
> Have I not always given you light?
> Have I not given you timely water
> For your corn? What boldness
> Moves this people to despise me?
> Have I not given you from my hands
> Rich treasures in abundance?
> Why then do you leave me, and these golden
> Rays, for some poorly crossed sticks?
> I cannot die, their God was put to death;
> Can a corpse be God who gives life?
> Turn, turn from this grave disorder.] (250)

Such words are not out of place in the mouth of the Aztec deity. But they may also serve as a coded but still poignant reminder to the Marrano community of the antiquity, faithfulness and vitality of the God of Israel. For they draw attention to the comparative novelty and helpless death of the Christian God. They recall, like the Exodus story and the commemorative Jewish Feasts of Passover and Tabernacles, the older God's faithful provision of light, water and bread (*maiz*).[41] And they remember, too, the wealth this God has given his people.

As Cortés advances closer to the capital of Mexico, Montezuma resorts to various protective strategies adopted by the Marrano community. Complaining of Spanish covetousness wrapped in 'a cloak of religion' (254a), he sends gold to Cortés, as the Marranos did to the Pope,[42] in an attempt to buy freedom from Christian harassment (254b–255a). Arrested by Cortés ('In my own country', he says in astonishment), he offers for his freedom 'so large a ransom that your ships could not carry the gold'. Finally, like many an Iberian Jew who did not welcome martyrdom, he 'volunteers' to become a Christian and a subject of Spain:

Cortes, yo quiero ser Christiano luego,
y de Carlos tu Rey serê vassallo.

[Cortés, I want soon to be a Christian,
And a vassal of Carlos your King.] (257)

Montezuma's capitulation does not save him. Temporarily released from prison, he is killed by a stone thrown by one of his own people.

Clearly, Montezuma is not a Marrano *hero*. Rather, I believe, he offers us an anguished portrait of Marrano capitulation before the surrounding forces of the Christian world. Enríquez Gómez admired the bolder path of fidelity to the ancestral religion even at the cost of martyrdom. In exile, he had sung its praises in his *Romance al divín mártir, Judá Creyente*. But it was not a course that Enríquez Goméz was himself able to take. If he wrote *La conquista de México*, he did so while pretending to be the Old Christian Zárate. A few years later he would persuade the Inquisition of his reconciliation with Christianity rather than face the stake. The character of Montezuma may be a veiled portrayal of Enríquez Gómez's own predicament, planted for safety within Lope's text and then assigned for further protection to the Zárate pseudonym.

Fittingly, it is the Old Christian voice that has the last and triumphant word. The play ends with the spectacular defeat of Mexico and the triumph of Christianity. The final stage direction reads:

Acometan al muro disparando los arcabuces, y los Indios tirando flechas, traigan escalas y con rodelas suban, denles en ellas los Indios muchos alcanciazos, vayan subiendo y andando hasta entrar

dentro, y salga vn carro en que venga la religion Christiana
triunfando, y traiga a sus pies a la Idolatria, y por la puerta de la
Ciudad venga Cortes con su gente en orden, despues de auer
publicado vitoria, y llegue al carro de la Religion y ella le pone vn
laurel en la cabeça.

[[The Spaniards] attack the walls [of the city], firing their
harquebuses, while the Indians shoot arrows; they bring scaling
ladders, and climb up with their bucklers, on which the Indians
drop many earthenware missiles; they continue climbing and
advancing until they enter [the city], from which a carriage comes
out, bearing the Christian religion in triumph, Idolatry at her feet;
and through the gate of the city comes Cortés with his followers
in order, having pronounced victory; when he arrives at Religion's carriage, she places a laurel wreath on his head.]   (259)

The triumph of armed Christianity concludes both narratives. For
'Zárate's' celebration of the expansion of Catholic Spain and Enríquez
Gómez's anguish over Marrano capitulation both hinge on the suppression of alterity within the Spanish Christian world. It is a conclusion that would have generated very different emotions in its
respective Christian and Marrano audiences.
    Any attempt to read the work of a dramatist who, to protect
himself from the Inquisition, concealed all communication with his
Marrano audience beneath a heavy gloss of Old Christian
providentialism, is fraught with difficulty. The fact that it took literary scholars 300 years to penetrate 'Zárate's' disguise and to begin to
re-read his plays in light of his Jewish heritage, is some indication of
the difficulty involved. The problem is further complicated, in the
case of *La conquista de México*, by the probability that Enríquez Gómez
was adding his own voice, and that of his Old Christian persona
'Zárate', to the borrowed voice of Lope de Vega. The discovery of
Lope's original text would certainly make it easier to disentangle the
several voices of the play. In its absence, however, I have tried to
understand *La conquista de México* 'in two ways', reading 'Zárate's'
text so as to hear Enríquez Gómez's voice.

4

Aspiring Tyrants and Theatrical Defiance

It will be remembered that I am addressing Bakhtin's reluctance to acknowledge in the theatre the same potential for dialogue between worlds that he finds in the novel, and Todorov's observations concerning the failure of the human community to reckon with otherness in its midst. And I am doing so within the single matrix of dramatizations of the conquest of Mexico.

I began by discovering a literary dialogue between worlds in what was, from Bakhtin's perspective, a most unlikely setting: a neoclassical poetic drama of aristocratic provenance. Dryden's *The Indian Emperour*, moreover, did not confine its multi-voiced discourse to the text, as a novel must, but in performance invited its audiences to participate in the dialogue as questioning agents. For all its reference to exotic peoples and its debate with classical authority, however, the dialogical performance of *The Indian Emperour* was always something of a debate among friends. Broadly speaking, neither Dryden nor his audiences belonged to a world apart from that in which the play was written and performed.

But now, from the even more unlikely setting of a Golden Age *comedia* believed for centuries to be a model of Old Christian orthodoxy, I have retrieved a theatrical dialogue between worlds in which the voice of the other was not merely represented but spoke for itself. Necessarily it did so most guardedly. Enríquez Gómez, as an internal other within a world committed to his eradication, was not in a position to question directly the voices of current authority in so public a medium as the theatre. But, if my analysis of *La conquista de México* is correct, the concealed Enríquez Gómez was executing a subtle counterpoint to the fervent and distracting Christian conversation in which 'Zárate' engaged his Old Christian audience. Enríquez Gómez wrote in two worlds, in a way that Dryden, when he composed *The Indian Emperour*, did not. As we shall see in Part Two, Mexican Indian performers who address the question of conquest

49

also act in two worlds and often resort to a similar strategy of simultaneous, contrasting voices. In their case, however, the concealed voice is not embedded in the text but revealed in performance. Having focused in the previous two chapters primarily on dialogue within the text, therefore, we now turn to the question of the relationship between text and performance.

The dimension of performance considerably extends the dialogical range of the theatre. For performance adds to the voices of the text not only the questions of the audience but the intonational and gestural commentary of the performers,[1] the visual eloquence of the costume and the stage designers, and the mediated discourse of the director. Subsequent performances multiply points of view, as successive generations of actors, designers, directors and redactors add their voices to the ongoing dialogue, challenging, subverting, expanding and illuminating the voices of the original text. The stage ought therefore to be the meeting place of many voices.

Some have felt, however, that the alternative perspectives that these voices bring to the theatrical dialogue are irretrievably suppressed by the presence of an authoritative text. Just as the agenda generated by a religious or political text may be said to suppress the voices of a people colonized in its name, so also it is said that the prescribed speech of the dramatist's script robs all those who stage it of their creative freedom. Derrida properly cites Artaud as the most influential voice in the twentieth-century attempt to establish a 'theater which is no longer a colony' of the playwright's text.[2] Peter Brook, Robert Wilson and Peter Stein are just a few of the many contemporary directors whose reluctance to be bound by a preexistent text displays the influence of Artaud. A balanced understanding of the relationship between dramatic text and theatrical performance is therefore crucial to my argument that the offer of cherished text for independent performance by another is an inherently dialogical gambit and a mode and model of fruitful crosscultural relationships.

LA CONQUÊTE DU MEXIQUE

The colonization of the New World by the Old World and the colonization of performance by a pre-existent text were for Artaud mutual symbols of one another. The First Manifesto for his proposed Theatre of Cruelty, published in October 1932, declared, 'It is essential to put an end to the subjugation of the theater to the text'. The second Manifesto, issued six months later, announced that the first spectacle of the Theatre of Cruelty would be *La Conquête du Mexique*.[3] Ironically, *La Conquête du Mexique* was never staged and survives only in the form of a scenario. We cannot, therefore, give an account of its performance. But we can describe the soirée at which the scenario was first read, and this, too, as we shall see, reveals something of a clash of worlds.

Late in the afternoon of 6 January 1934, as darkness settled over Paris and the street lights began to warm the winter air, a group of wealthy guests, bankers and executives well-disposed to the arts in general and to theatre in particular, began to arrive at the home of Paul and Lise Deharme on the Quai Voltaire. The setting, linking the traditional and the experimental, the familiar and the esoteric, seemed auspicious. The Palais du Louvre, housing one of the world's great art collections, could be seen on the far bank of the Seine, and the soirée was to open with the reading of an acknowledged masterpiece, Shakespeare's *Richard II*. But the promise of the avant-garde was also in the air. Paul Deharme was a successful director with Radio Paris and had championed the surrealistic potential of the new medium, citing its capacity to work directly on the subconscious of the listener and so to create 'a theatre analogous to the theatre of the dream'.[4] Lise was an experimental novelist and poet, fascinated by the fashionable world of faery. Their guests had been invited to witness a performance by Artaud and to underwrite his projected Theatre of Cruelty. The date, the Feast of Epiphany, had no doubt been chosen by Artaud for its associations with the magi from the East. For he regarded 'the legend of the Three Magi Kings' as of greater importance than the nativity to which it had been attached by Christians.[5] He did not broach this theme, however, on the invitation sent to his prospective patrons.[6]

Artaud's mother and sister, visibly moved, were also present. And among the guests invited not for their wealth but for their friendship with the Deharmes were Robert and Youki Desnos. Robert was a surrealist poet working at the time for Paul Deharme at Radio Paris. Youki, born Lucie Badoud, had achieved a certain notoriety as the model for a nude exhibited by the Japanese painter Foujita at the 1924 Autumn Salon. Both model and painting had been given the name Youki, meaning in Japanese 'pale pink snow'. Youki had married Desnos in 1932,[7] and describes the soirée at the Deharmes' in her *Confidences*:

> Flattered at being invited by [Lise] to an artistic treat of which she did not usually consider them worthy, [the wealthy guests] came full of good intentions. The atmosphere was set fair. The cheque-books wanted only to be pulled from their pockets. Lise was content. Artaud gave a reading of Shakespeare's *Richard II*, playing all the roles.[8]

It must have been a strange performance. Artaud 'read, played, and mimed' all the parts, despite the fact that his acting style was generally considered to be best suited to 'special' roles, such as 'angels or archangels, surrealistic demons, apocalyptic monsters, fantastic people'.[9] While his movements and his facial expressions were exaggerated, his voice was doggedly monotonous. Charles Dullin, who directed Artaud on a number of occasions, wrote:

> Whenever Artaud had to move he tensed his muscles, he arched his body and his pale face turned hard with fiery eyes; like this he would advance using arms and hands as well as legs; he would zig-zag, stretching out his arms and legs and tracing wild arabesques in the air.[10]

The body of the actor, Artaud thought, should appear to be 'in trance, stiffened by the tide of cosmic forces which besiege it', and his voice should deliver language in 'the form of Incantation'.[11] It was an effect that Artaud himself never quite mastered. Janet Flanner, who saw Artaud act in one of Dullin's productions, remembers 'a deep voice that sounded as if he were deaf it was so unmodulated'.[12]

None the less, Artaud's one-man rendition of *Richard II* passed without incident. It was what followed that alienated his audience of potential investors. Artaud began to explain, according to Youki Desnos,

> how he would arrange his 'Theater of Cruelty'. The chairs would have to be uncomfortable, even if necessary pulled from beneath the seated spectators so as to prevent them becoming drowsy. Bad smells would be projected into the auditorium, etc., etc. And since

one would not be concerned with vain material contingencies, money would be spent extravagantly, and that was that. The faces of the potential sleeping partners became gloomy. . . . They had not come to be told by Artaud that he considered them pigs, boors, and that he was offering them a unique occasion to rehabilitate themselves by financing an enterprise of which they were not worthy.

'It was', Youki concludes, 'the first time that I had seen anyone ask for money in these terms. The results were not very dazzling'.[13]

By way of further illustration of his plans for the Theatre of Cruelty, Artaud treated his audience to 'the first hearing of an unpublished theatrical scenario, *La Conquête du Mexique*'.[14] 'This subject has been chosen', Artaud announced, 'because of its immediacy and all the allusions it permits to problems of vital interest for Europe and the world'. First, and 'from the historical point of view, *La Conquête du Mexique* poses the question of colonization'. For a moment Artaud sounded like a precursor of Todorov:

By broaching the alarmingly immediate question of colonization and the right one continent thinks it has to enslave another, this subject questions the real superiority of certain races over others and shows the inmost filiation that binds the genius of a race to particular forms of civilization.

But Artaud's motive was not so much to enter into dialogue with 'the exterior and remote' other as it was to hurl invective at the interior and proximate other. *La Conquête du Mexique*, he told his Parisian audience, 'revives in a brutal and implacable way the ever active fatuousness of Europe. It permits her idea of her own superiority to be deflated'. For it compares the ancient texts and papal decrees of European Christianity with 'the splendor and forever immediate poetry' of the 'natural religions' of the New World. And 'it contrasts the tyrannical anarchy of the colonizers to the profound moral harmony of the as yet uncolonized'.

Artaud's scenario, however, is more complex than his introduction might suggest. For Mexico, too, has its ancient codes and guardian priests governing contemporary performance, and Montezuma is oppressed by these no less than by the invading army of Cortez. The power of the governing text is therefore represented in Artaud's scenario both by the colonizing pretensions of Catholic Europe and by the hidebound court of Montezuma. Like the plague, to whose disruptive power Artaud compared the Theatre of Cruelty,[15] 'the brutal force' released by the clash of Aztecs and conquistadors frees and exhausts the passions ordinarily held in check by another's words. Artaud's Europe is a culture of reason and the written word, his Mexico a realm in which repressive decrees, whatever their source, can be overthrown in 'cruel' performance.

Artaud had also chosen his subject because of the spectacular conflicts it would generate on the stage. 'There are, first of all', he announced, 'the inner struggles of Montezuma', in whom 'one can distinguish two characters'. The one 'obeys almost religiously the orders of destiny' issued by the stars; the other, once the rites have been dutifully performed, 'wonders . . . if, by chance, he is not mistaken'. Montezuma's dilemma, however, would not be concealed by superficial speech prescribed by a literary playwright, but 'shown in an objective pictorial fashion' in 'dances, pantomimes and scenic objectifications of all sorts'. Signs drawn from the dictionary of phenomena would, in the manner of the Symbolists, be crafted into a composite sensory image of an invisible psychological state. Other conflicts generated by Artaud's subject and to be given spectacular expression in the theatre would involve

> the crowd, the different social strata, the revolt of the people against destiny as represented by Montezuma, the clamoring of the unbelievers, the quibbling of the philosophers and priests, the lamentations of the poets, the treachery of the merchants and the bourgeoisie, the duplicity and the profligacy of the women.

The scenario itself is divided into four acts. The first, called 'Warning Signs', offers 'a tableau of Mexico in anticipation'. The landscape was to be 'evoked by means of lighting' and symbolic objects. Not the appearance but the apprehension of the land was to fill the theatre. For this is 'a landscape which senses the coming storm', and in its evocation 'everything trembles and groans, like a shop-window in a hurricane':

> Objects, music, stuffs, lost dresses, shadows of wild horses pass through the air like distant meteors, like lightning on the horizon brimming with mirages as the wind pitches wildly along the ground in a lighting prophecying torrential, violent storms.

As the lights change, the focus shifts from the landscape to the populace. 'The bawling conversations, the disputes between all the echoes of the population' are answered by 'the mute, concentrated, terrorized meetings of Montezuma with his formally assembled priests, with the signs of the zodiac, the austere forms of the firmament'.

Meanwhile, elsewhere in the theatre, Cortez and his fleet are visible. For *La Conquête du Mexique* was not to be staged behind a conventional proscenium arch, in which scenes must necessarily follow one another. On the contrary, 'the spectacle will be extended, by elimination of the stage, to the entire hall of the theater and will scale the walls from the ground up on light catwalks, will physically envelop the spectator and immerse him in a constant bath of light, images, movements, and noises'.[16] As a counterpart to the scene on land, there would be a simultaneous '*mise en scène* of sea and tiny battered ships', accompanied by 'Cortez and his men larger than the ships and firm as rocks'.

Act II is sketched only briefly in Artaud's scenario and is called, somewhat obscurely, 'Confession'. The subject once again is Mexico, but 'seen this time by Cortez'. The conquistadors have landed between the acts and now march inland. Outwardly Cortez is still firm – there is to be 'silence concerning all his secret struggles' – but what he sees is unnerving: 'apparent stagnation and everywhere magic, magic of a motionless, unheard-of spectacle, with cities like ramparts of light, palaces on canals of stagnant water'. He hears 'a heavy melody'. The oppressive atmosphere, sustained almost unbearably, spreads to every corner of the theatre. Suddenly, 'on a single sharp and piercing note, heads crown the walls' of the city. There is 'a muffled rumbling full of threats' and 'an impression of terrible solemnity'. The audience, inhabiting for a moment Cortez's consciousness, is surrounded by row upon row of strangely painted and ornately feathered heads peering down from the catwalks. Slowly, 'Montezuma advances all alone' towards Cortez.

In Act III, 'Convulsions', the opposing forces collide and roil. Mexico is under siege, and 'revolt' breaks out 'at every level of the country' and 'of Montezuma's consciousness'. Artaud describes first 'the battleground in the mind of Montezuma'. With a gesture of unparalleled violence, the Aztec ruler 'cuts the living space, rips it open like the sex of a woman in order to cause the invisible to spring forth'. Repressed passions and spiritual forces are given theatrical form. Against a stage wall 'stuffed unevenly with heads [and] throats',

and accompanied by 'cracked [and] oddly broken melodies',
Montezuma appears 'split in two, divided; with some parts of himself in half-light, others dazzling; with many hands coming out of his
dress, with expressions painted on his body like a multiple portrait
of consciousness'. The beasts of the zodiac, whose oppressive decrees Montezuma debates, cease their roaring in his mind and exter-
nalize themselves as 'a group of human passions made incarnate by
the learned heads of the official spokesmen brilliant at disputation'.
Fate's script imposes itself through the advice of scholars.

Meanwhile, battle rages throughout Mexico. In one part of the
theatre, 'the real warriors make their sabers whine, whetting them
on the houses'. Elsewhere, 'flying ships cross a Pacific of purplish
indigo', some fleeing, 'laden with the riches of fugitives', and others
hastening to the carnage, packed with 'contraband weapons'. As the
siege intensifies, the theatre is filled with images of horror. In one
corner, 'an emaciated man eats soup as fast as he can'. Everywhere,

> space is stuffed with whirling gestures, horrible faces, dying eyes,
> clenched fists, manes, breastplates, and from all levels of the scene
> fall limbs, breastplates, heads, stomachs like a hailstorm bom-
> barding the earth with supernatural explosions.

The fourth and final act begins with and is named after 'the
abdication of Montezuma'. The resignation of the Aztec ruler 'results in a strange and almost malevolent loss of assurance on the part
of Cortez and his fighters'. Quarrels flare up over the discovery of
treasure, which, by means of mirrors, may be 'seen like illusions in
the corners of the stage'. The 'brutal force' which, like the plague, has
wrought its cruel therapy, is almost spent:

> Lights and sounds produce an impression of dissolving, unravel-
> ling, and squashing – like watery fruits splashing on the ground.
> Strange couples appear, Spaniard with Indian, horribly enlarged,
> swollen and black, swaying back and forth like carts about to
> overturn.

Cortez, like Montezuma in the previous act, is riven by doubt, ap-
pearing simultaneously in several manifestations. 'The funeral rites
of Montezuma' are conducted amidst a 'crowd of natives whose
steps sound like a scorpion's jaws'. Lust and disease spread through
the theatre. Foul-smelling 'miasmas', projected into the auditorium,

encounter 'noses swollen with the stink'. From this diseased lull, there bursts 'like a tidal wave' the last revolt of the conquered people. As 'the sharp spasms of battle' once again fill the theatre, the audience is left with a final image of European defeat, 'the foam of the heads of the cornered Spaniards who are squashed like blood against the ramparts that are turning green again'.

Artaud ends his scenario with images recalling the ignominious Spanish retreat on the Night of Sorrows.[17] Deliberately, he makes no mention of Cortez's subsequent return and capture of the Aztec capital. Contemptuous of European culture, he has found a way to pay lip-service to the historical record while planning a theatrical victory for the colonized. Every power that, in Artaud's view, is suppressed by the fixed voice of textual authority shares that victory.

La Conquête du Mexique was never staged. Although Artaud raised, in the end, approximately $3000 towards its production, the sum proved inadequate for the kind of spectacle he had in mind and the project was abandoned.[18] Nor has anyone since tried to realize his scenario in the theatre.[19] Perhaps this is fitting. For a performance aiming at fidelity to a text now more than 50 years old would contravene the very principle invoked by *La Conquête du Mexique*. Artaud had called for the overthrow of textual 'authority' and of 'the exclusive dictatorship of speech', and had demanded 'an independent and autonomous' theatre, free from subservience to written dialogue.[20] His scenario for *La Conquête du Mexique* contained no stipulated dialogue and was written, as he noted in his invitation to the Deharmes' soirée, 'for direct realization on the stage'.[21]

ARTAUD AND DERRIDA

In two essays on Artaud included in *Writing and Difference*, Derrida makes much of Artaud's metaphor of liberation. 'Artaud', he writes, 'desired the conflagration of the stage upon which . . . the body was under the rule of a foreign text' and subject to the jurisdiction of the author's furtive viceroy, the prompter. He resisted 'the imperialism of the letter' and wanted 'to overthrow the tyranny of the text'. In the conventional theatre the director is no more than a 'slave', subject to 'the dictatorship of the writer'; director and actors are 'interpretive slaves who faithfully execute the providential designs of the "master" '. What Artaud longed for was a theatre 'liberated from diction, withdrawn from the dictatorship of the text', 'no longer enslaved to a writing more ancient than itself'; or, to put it in terms of pre-conquest innocence, 'a stage whose clamor has not yet been pacified into words'.[22]

The director, robbed of his own voice by the inscribed voice of an absent other, is for Derrida an image of humanity under the authority of the word. And the playwright who imposes his words on another's stage is, like the sixteenth-century colonist who invaded the New World, an image of the European God. 'The Other, the Thief, the great Furtive One', according to Derrida, 'has a proper name: God'.[23] It is this that attracts Derrida to Artaud. For Derrida writes, 'The theater of cruelty expulses God from the stage'. It is not that this kind of theatre, in some crass fashion, gives 'atheism a platform'. Instead, 'the theatrical practice of cruelty, in its action and structure inhabits or rather *produces* a nontheological space'. 'The stage', Derrida writes, 'is theological for as long as it is dominated by speech, by a will to speech, by the layout of a primary logos which does not belong to the theatrical site and governs it from a distance'. Artaud's vision, as Derrida understands it, was therefore a theatre emancipated from such divine oppression. 'The origin of a theater such as it must be restored, is the hand lifted against the abusive wielder of the logos, against the father, against the God of a stage subjugated to the power of speech and text'.[24]

We shall return, in Chapter 10, to the relationship between 'the word of God' and human performance. For the time being we remain with the theatre, where Artaud's demands can be rendered in more simple terms. Theatre, he believed, is a matter of performance. Dramatic text belongs to the domain of literature. All too often, theatrical performance is regarded as no more than the decorative illustration of a literary text. But, as Artaud rightly points out, there are many other elements in performance besides the spoken word. There are, for example, 'music, dance, plastic art, pantomime, mimicry, gesticulation, intonation, architecture, lighting, and scenery'. It was from these raw materials that Artaud wished to create a 'pure theatrical language', independent of the literary medium of prescribed speech.[25] Such a language, he hoped, would allow the theatre to develop as an autonomous art, able to express directly, without the rationalizing intervention of words, the passions at loose in the psyche and the mysterious 'forces' of the unseen world.

In his efforts to minimize the influence of the playwright, Artaud drew attention to the many different sign systems that operate in the theatre beyond the spoken word encoded in the text. But he withstood the possibility of dialogue implicit in this multiplicity of sign systems (or, as Bakhtin might call them, 'languages'). Instead, Artaud suppressed dialogue, insisting that all the sign systems of the theatre, including the live actors, speak in his own voice and that the voice of the other in the text be silenced. Like Derrida, he feared that the other's voice, breathing in the text, would stifle his own.

Readers of *The Theater and its Double* are sometimes surprised to discover that Artaud, once he has pronounced the theatre free from any obligation to a pre-existent text, is eager to compile a retrospective text, 'fixed in its least details',[26] that will serve as a record of performance. He had told his audience at the Quai Voltaire that the creative activity of rehearsing *La Conquête du Mexique* would in the end generate specific text: 'These images, movements, dances, rites, these fragmented melodies and sudden turns of dialogue', discovered in rehearsal,

> will be carefully recorded and described as far as possible with words, especially for the portions of the spectacle not in dialogue, the principle here being to record in codes, as on a musical score, what cannot be described in words.[27]

Determined to liberate the theatre from the tyranny of the playwright, he remained unwilling to hand it over to the anarchy of the actors. 'My plays', he wrote in a letter to Jean Paulhan, are not 'left to the caprice of the wild and thoughtless inspiration of the actor, especially the modern actor who, once cut off from the text, plunges in without any idea of what he is doing. I would not care to leave the fate of my plays and of the theater to that kind of chance. No.'[28]

Artaud's use of the first-person singular possessive pronoun is telling. They are, he insists, 'my plays'. 'In my view', he writes, 'no one has the right to call himself author, that is to say creator, except the person who controls the direct handling of the stage'. Having wrested control from the playwright, Artaud is determined to retain it. As director, he is to be neither the slave of the playwright nor the servant of the cast, but 'a kind of manager of magic, a master of sacred ceremonies',[29] exercising, as Derrida puts it, a 'totalitarian'[30] control over the stage. He is, in other words, like so many revolutionaries, interested in stripping tyrants of their power not to share it but to vest it in himself.

Artaud shares another trait with many a revolutionary. He must seize power for the good of the people. Although his audience may at first be small, he will in the end convoke 'mass spectacle[s]' where he will 'free the repressed unconscious', drain the collective 'abscesses' and 'impose on the assembled collectivity an attitude that is both difficult and heroic'.[31] Amidst the language of liberation one finds the language of imposition. Artaud will be like a surgeon to whose 'cruelty' the patient who wishes to be healed must first submit.[32] He will 'treat the spectators like the snakecharmer's subjects', producing by means of a rigorously and centrally controlled theatrical language 'a more or less hallucinatory state and impelling the sensibility and mind alike to a kind of organic alteration'.[33]

The rhetoric of totalitarianism, once it has been noticed, can be found throughout *The Theater and its Double*. Artaud wonders, for example, whether 'there can be found a nucleus of men capable of imposing this superior notion of the theater'.[34] He delights in Balinese dances in which he professes to see 'the absolute preponderance of the director' and a theatre in which 'everything . . . is calculated with an enchanting mathematical meticulousness' and 'nothing is left to chance or to personal initiative'.[35] Like the Soviet censors under Stalin, he calls for an end to 'personal' art: 'This empiricism, randomness, individualism, and anarchy must cease. Enough of personal poems, benefitting those who create them much more than those who read them. Once and for all, enough of this closed, egoistic, and personal art.' In a burst of chilling honesty, he adds, 'We are not free. . . . And the theater has been created to teach us that first of all'.[36]

Indeed, having expelled, in Derrida's terms, the logocentric God from the stage, Artaud aspires to a kind of divinity of his own. Not only is he a 'manager of magic', manipulating the sleeping forces of the universe. He will be 'a sort of unique Creator' (the upper case C is Artaud's own),[37] combining in himself the powers of author, director, stage manager and technician, and quelling any impulse to independence on the part of actors and audience alike. Paradoxically, in a world in which 'we are not free', Artaud aspires to a position of total control. It was, perhaps, not necessity but preference that disposed him to act every part in *Richard II*.

We may conclude, therefore, that for all Artaud's interest in other cultures he was never attracted to the kind of dialogism proposed by Bakhtin and embraced by Todorov. Other cultures and individuals were, one suspects, little more to him than entities to be colonized to his own advantage. Mexico was a symbol of his own alienation from

European values rather than an independent culture having its own plurality of voices. When actually confronted by primitive Mexico during his visit to the Tarahumara Indians of northern Mexico in 1936, Artaud doggedly assimilated Tarahumara customs into his own eclectic amalgam of Western occult traditions.[38] Closer to home, Artaud treated the guests of the Deharmes to a contemptuous monologue, hoping none the less to mine their bank accounts in support of his own projects. In the theatre, actors and audience alike were to be controlled and entranced but never engaged in a relationship of mutuality. And although, in Derrida's words, Artaud may have called for a 'theater which is no longer a colony' of the playwright, it was partly in order to render the playwright's text a colony of the director, to be stripped of whatever resources it might offer and then discarded.[39]

A DIALOGICAL MEDIUM

To exile the author, therefore, is not to liberate the stage. It may be to surrender it to the colonial pretensions of what the British playwright Arnold Wesker has called, somewhat truculently, 'the director as fascist'.[40] But I am persuaded that both Artaud and Wesker have overestimated the other's power to render the stage a monological space. The author's voice need not be suppressed for the several voices of the cast, the designers and the director to be heard. And the company need not deny its own points of view in order for the author's voice to reach the stage. The preparation of a dramatic text for live performance necessarily entails a dialogue between the world of the playwright and that of the performers. For dramatic script, as Artaud so diligently pointed out, supplies only the words to be spoken. All the other sign systems of the stage, including gesture, intonation, movement, lighting, costume and scenic design, may be suggested but cannot be defined by stage directions. Dramatic script imposes its vision on performance far less efficiently than a musical score or an architectural blueprint.

The first public performance of a playwright's script extends the dialogue begun in rehearsal to an audience at a specific time and place. Subsequent performances and revivals of the play renew the dialogue under different circumstances, interacting not only with prior appropriations of the text but with fresh cultural insights and conditions. To take just one example of a 'classic' play text, Shake-speare's *The Tempest* has been seen as an affirmation of Jacobean theories of kingship and, in the Dryden–D'Avenant–Shadwell version, as both a popular spectacle and a profound exploration of Restoration politics.[41] It has been played as an illustration of the theory of evolution,[42] the benefits of British imperialism,[43] a critical meditation on the psychology of colonialism,[44] a 'charming pastoral for children',[45] and an experiment, indebted to Artaud, in releasing the forces of 'rape, murder, conspiracy and violence' hidden in the text.[46] And these are but a few of the points of view brought to bear on Shakespeare's text. But in every case, however the text may have been 'revised', the performance has been recognizably an engagement with Shakespeare's *The Tempest*, rather than, let us say, *King Lear* or Agatha Christie's *The Mousetrap*. Shakespeare's voice is heard, but it is never heard alone. The voices of successive generations of actors and directors, interacting with Shakespeare's text and addressing particular audiences from fresh perspectives, are also heard.

The playwright initiates the theatrical dialogue by offering text for performance. He or she can do no more. A company of actors and their director accept that invitation when they undertake to perform a particular text. They may challenge but they can never wholly suppress the author's voice. Members of an audience, however fleetingly, participate in the dialogue when they attend a performance. Whether or not those involved are happy with the restrictions it may place on their authoritarian pretensions, live theatre entails the offer of cherished text for independent performance by another, and a performance shaped in some measure by another's text. In the theatre, as in any cross-cultural encounter, dialogue can be resisted by a 'colonist' who demands that performance be governed only by his text, or by performers who refuse any engagement with another's text. But the theatre, in practice if not in the theories of men like Artaud and Wesker, resists such resistance. It is an inherently dialogical medium.

With this in mind, we can turn now from European dramatizations of the conquest of Mexico to dramatizations of the theme of conquest in Mexico itself. For there, according to Yolanda Argudín, we find that theatre was, in the years immediately following the Spanish conquest, 'the best means of communication between conquerors and conquered'. There, too, we find a delicately balanced dialogue between Spanish text and indigenous performance.

Part Two
The Drama in Mexico

Part Two
The Diaspora in Mexico

5

Flower Wars and Battle Plays

Fray Toribio de Motolinía, in his *History of the Indians of New Spain*, reports that in Tlaxcala, for the feast of Corpus Christi 1539, there was staged a most extraordinary play.[1] Some 1500 Nahua Indians[2] who, twenty years before, had never heard the name of Jesus Christ and who had known nothing of the aspirations of European Christendom, enacted 'a prediction'. In the dusty main square of the city, before an audience of 'Pope, cardinals [and] bishops, all impersonated', the armies of Catholic Europe and the New World, in earnest and raucous play, liberated Jerusalem from the Turks. Fireworks simulated artillery. Cannon-balls were made of 'mud dried in the sun' and 'filled with moistened red earth, so that the one who was struck by them seemed badly wounded and covered with blood'. Patron saints galloped in on horseback to lead the Christian armies into battle, and the Archangel Michael, by means of ropes and pulleys hidden behind painted clouds,[3] appeared on the central tower of Jerusalem to persuade the Turks to trust in God and to recognize Carlos V, Holy Roman Emperor and King of Spain, as 'his captain on earth'. For the play's finale, visionary pretence merged with sacramental reality: many of the defeated Turks, played by 'adult Indians, who had been designedly prepared for Baptism', asked for reception into the church and 'were actually baptized'.

Motolinía was the Franciscan guardian of Tlaxcala from 1536 to 1542.[4] He may also have been the author of *The Conquest of Jerusalem*.[5] Like many of his fellow Franciscans, he believed that the recent conquest and ongoing conversion of the New World presaged the imminent triumph of Christianity in the Old World. Spain would lead the Indians of the New World across the Atlantic and through the Mediterranean to join forces with the Catholic armies of Europe in a successful last crusade against the remaining infidels of the Old World. *The Conquest of Jerusalem* staged in Tlaxcala thus embodied, according to Motolinía, 'a prediction which, we pray, God may fulfil in our day'.[6]

But beneath the confident millenarianism of *The Conquest of Jeru-salem* another voice may be heard. It is easily missed. In passing, and without further comment, we are told that 'the Great Sultan of Babylon and Tetrarch of Jerusalem', leader of the infidels defeated by the Indian army of New Spain, 'was the Marqués del Valle, Hernando Cortés'. Later it is mentioned, again without explanation, that the Captain General of the Turks 'was . . . Don Pedro de Alvarado', Cortés's second-in-command during the conquest of Mexico.[7] There is no question of Cortés and Alvarado themselves acting these roles. Alvarado was in Honduras at the time and Cortés, although in Mexico, was nursing an injured foot and preparing for his final return to Spain.[8]

Commentators have therefore puzzled over these references.[9] García Icazbalceta could not understand why 'the friars, authors of all these fiestas, should have offended the conquistadors by placing them in the party of the infidels'.[10] Georges Baudot insists that 'there could not have been the least intention of offence'. Rather, it was nothing more than 'a mischievous joke that the proven friendship of Fray Toribio for the conquistadors fully authorized, as everyone surely understood'.[11] Roland Baumann wonders if the Tlaxcaltecas were swaying with the current political winds. Cortés and Alvarado were embroiled in controversy with Antonio de Mendoza, the Vice-roy of New Spain at the time, and, in *The Conquest of Jerusalem*, Mendoza is assigned the role of Captain General of the victorious Indian army of New Spain. Perhaps, Baumann suggests, 'the Tlaxcalans ridiculed the two conquistadors because they felt it could not displease the viceroy'.[12] These explanations, however, do not satisfy Fernando Horcasitas. 'Could it be', he asks, 'that the Indians found satisfaction in seeing their own conqueror routed by a native army?' Answering his own question affirmatively, he continues, 'Only in this way can one explain the mysterious role in which he was made to appear in the Tlaxcalan play'.[13] Othón Arroníz is of the same opinion, finding in 'the incredible audacity' of making Cortés chief of the Muslim infidels 'clear indication . . . of a natural resent-ment in the conquered people, which could only rise to the surface at moments of festivity and under theatrical guise'.[14]

'To hear those faint long-ago Indian voices', requires, as Inga Clendinnen remarks, not only 'patience and perseverance' but 'from both reader and author a tolerance of ambiguities, and of inherently contestable judgements'.[15] We need, therefore, to approach *The Con-*

quest of Jerusalem with care. In this chapter, we shall consider the play's antecedents in both Europe and Mexico before the conquest, and in early missionary drama in Mexico after the conquest. We shall close the chapter by looking in some detail at a companion piece, *The Conquest of Rhodes*, performed in Mexico City earlier in 1539. Then, in Chapter 6, we shall return to *The Conquest of Jerusalem* itself. There I shall argue that the Indian actors of *The Conquest of Jerusalem* were playing parts with dual and simultaneous referents, each referent yielding a different reading of the play. A European reading would have seen Christians defeating Turks in the Holy Land. A Mexican reading would have seen Indians defeating conquistadors in the New World.

THEATRICAL ANTECEDENTS BEFORE THE CONQUEST

Elaborate battle plays, many of them dramatizing the triumph of Christians over infidels, were part and parcel of both courtly and popular entertainment in medieval Europe. *The Play of Antichrist*, probably performed at the German imperial court of Frederick Barbarossa about 1160, is one of the earliest examples.[16] Coincidentally, it too dramatizes prospectively the final liberation of Jerusalem from the Turks by the Holy Roman Emperor. Because the stage directions specify that the formal speeches be 'sung' in Latin, the play is sometimes mistakenly defined as liturgical drama.[17] But the stage directions also speak of armies being marshalled, advancing to battle, rushing together to fight, and attacking Jerusalem. The play may therefore owe more to the tournament mêlée than it does to church liturgy.

Certainly, later battle plays involved fierce hand-to-hand combat and elaborate scenic properties. A *Siege of Jerusalem*, for example, recounting the triumphant history of the First Crusade in 1099, entertained those assembled for a royal banquet in Paris in 1378. Christian knights, arriving in 'a well-made . . . sailing ship', propelled on wheels 'by people secretly hidden inside' so that 'it seemed it was . . . floating on water', besieged 'a float made to look like the city of Jerusalem'. The city was defended by 'Saracens'. Ship, castle and 'pavillon' were used in a *Siege of Troy* performed in the same hall in 1389. The 'castle' representing Troy, we are told, was '40 feet high,

20 feet long and 20 feet wide', having a large central tower and a smaller turret at each corner. It was 'moved on four wheels that turned very ingeniously'.[18]

An almost identical device, described as 'a castle on wheels, moved by men inside it, having five towers, one at each corner and one in the middle', was used during the festivities accompanying the coronation of Fernando el Honesto at Zaragoza in 1414. The king also saw, on leaving the cathedral after his coronation,

> a town made of wood, likewise set on wheels, and moved from within, that was so realistically made that it seemed as if there were really houses and roofs and towers inside it. A little further on were two castles with armed men inside them who fought a battle against the town, using siege-engines which shot missiles made of leather stuffed with wadding, as big as a boy's head. The men in the town defended themselves, letting off fireworks to simulate gunfire.

This performance, we are told, commemorated the Siege of Balaguer.[19]

These battle plays could at times expand to monstrous proportions. The commemorative *Siege of Orleans*, staged in that city on a number of occasions in the fifteenth-century, lasted a number of weeks, separate episodes drawing vast crowds on each successive day.[20] The very full stage directions specify the movement of armies of 2000 men,[21] of eight separate battles in the open and no less than thirteen attacks on towns, towers, fortresses, bridges or other scenic units, many of these assaults involving missiles, scaling ladders, cannon and simulated gunfire.

Glynne Wickham has demonstrated that the scenic units used in England for such performances were made of painted canvas wrapped around a wooden frame mounted on wheels and capable of being dismantled for purposes of storage.[22] There is no reason to doubt that the mode of construction was the same on the Continent, and that from there it passed to Mexico. Thomas Gage, living in Chiapa de los Indios from 1625 to 1627, described the battle plays he saw there:

> This town lieth upon a great river, to which belong many boats and canoes, wherein those Indians have been taught to act sea-fights with great dexterity. . . . They will arm with their boats a siege against the town, fighting against it with such courage till

they make it yield. . . . . They will erect towers and castles made of wood and painted cloth, and from them fight either with the boats or one against another, with squibs, darts, and many strange fireworks.[23]

Such plays, now known generically as *fiestas de moros y cristianos*, are still popular in parts of Spain. Some involve naval battles; most are fought on foot and on horseback in a town's central square and surrounding streets. As many as 2500 citizens, divided into squadrons of 'Moors' and 'Christians', take part. Armed with ancient muskets and accompanied by martial music, they battle noisily for possession of a strategic 'castle', the Moors finally being defeated and sometimes accepting Christianity.[24] The best known of these takes place every April in Alcoy, in the province of Alicante.[25]

Although, in terms of theme and mode of staging, the European tradition provides some precedent for the Tlaxcala *Conquest of Jerusalem*, Fernando Horcasitas has argued that the Franciscan theatre in Mexico was, in another respect, the first of its kind. For the audience in Tlaxcala was only recently converted to Christianity. 'I do not know', Horcasitas asserts, 'of a single case in which the theatre had [previously] served as a means of proselytism. The drama which existed in Europe during the Middle Ages did not have the goal of converting pagan tribes, but of reinforcing the faith of nations that had been Christian for many generations'.[26] This is true on the whole, but not entirely. As early as 1204 at Riga on the Baltic, a battle play was performed to instruct 'neophytes and pagans . . . in the rudiments of the Christian faith'. The chronicle reports:

> That summer there was given a very elaborate prophet play such as the Latins call a *commedia*, in the centre of Riga, in order that the heathen might learn the rudiments of the Christian faith by visible demonstration. The substance of this play or comedy was diligently explained to the neophytes and pagans who had been brought there by means of an interpreter. When, however, the army of Gideon fought with the Philistines, the pagans, fearing that they were about to be killed, started to run away and had to be called gently back.[27]

Riga, like Tlaxcala, was the site of recent military conquest and evangelization.[28]

There are, however, important differences between the Riga and Tlaxcala plays. The Riga play was acted by the conquerors in Latin, having to be 'interpreted' for the 'neophytes and pagans who had been brought there'. *The Conquest of Jerusalem* was acted by the Indians in their own language and in their own community. 'All sources agree', writes Robert Ricard, of the Mexican missionary theatre as a whole, 'that the participants, the actors proper, the supernumaries, singers, and dancers, were Indian, and that everything spoken or sung was in the native language, most frequently Náhuatl'.[29] In many cases, too, the plays were directed by the Indians. Bartolomé de Las Casas, the most vocal missionary champion of Indian rights, visited Tlaxcala in 1538. There he saw an *auto* featuring Our Lady and the Apostles:

> The Apostles or those who represented them, were Indians, as was the case in all the *autos* that they had previously performed (and it must be taken for granted that no Spaniard takes charge of nor meddles in the *autos* that they put on with them), and the one who represented Our Lady was Indian, as were all those who took charge of the play.[30]

In all probability, Motolinía had a hand in preparing the script or at least in suggesting the topic of *The Conquest of Jerusalem*. But the performance itself seems to have been entirely under the control of the Indians. In this respect, then, we can affirm Horcasitas's claim for the originality of the Mexican plays. For they were the first catechetical plays to be performed by the evangelized community, in its own tongue, and under its own direction.

The Nahua Indians, of course, had possessed a vibrant theatrical tradition of their own long before their encounter with Europeans. Miguel Leon-Portilla describes four kinds of prehispanic drama.[31] The first, 'a perpetual cycle of religious drama', encompassed 'the various festivals and sacrifices in which the Náhuatl-speaking people honored their gods'.[32] These religious rituals contained a variety of 'dramatic elements'. Marilyn Ravicz has found in them narrative content, music, dance, rudimentary plots, elaborate costumes, staging and sound effects, monologues, dialogues and colloquies to support the dramatic action, and spectacle involving both the audience and the performers.[33] A second, comic theatre acted as a counterpoint to the somber rituals. José de Acosta, for example, in his *Historia natural y moral de las Indias*, mentions a 'humerous interlude' performed as part of the festival of Quetzalcoatl at Cholula. Actors 'pretending to be deaf, ill with colds, lame, blind and one-armed' approached the idol in hopes of healing. 'Those with colds came coughing and sneezing', the lame limped and complained loudly, and the deaf answered the god 'nonsensically', all of which 'made the people laugh uproariously'.[34] There is also evidence, in the form of fragmentary dramatic texts, of two other kinds of theatre: marketplace re-enactments of popular mythology by small groups of entertainers, and domestic interludes 'emancipated', in Leon-Portilla's phrase, 'from strictly religious themes'.[35]

But the prehispanic spectacle that most closely resembled *The Conquest of Jerusalem* was the *xochiyaoyotl* or 'flower war'. This was a kind of tournament, fought at regular intervals between warriors from Tenochtitlán and its allies on the one hand, and Tlaxcala, Huejotzingo and their allies, on the other. The goal was not to kill but to capture and so replenish the supply of sacrificial victims for gods whose life was thought to be sustained by human blood.[36] Each of the cities had on its borders a field set aside for use in the flower wars. The opposing armies, broken into small companies representing the different cities involved, would approach the battlefield in procession, led by a priest bearing an idol. After an initial courteous exchange of greetings, the contest would begin. At first, 'only a limited number of knights were sent in, perhaps two hundred in all, while the rest watched and admired. But as the fury and carnage increased others were fed in until all were committed'.[37] Warriors in full military regalia, sporting multi-coloured shields and voluminous feathered head-dresses, hacked at each other with obsidian-edged, wooden swords called *maquahuitl*.[38] Although the stated purpose was to take captives, it was not uncommon, when political tension between the opposing armies ran high, for some of the combatants to be killed in battle.[39]

Prehispanic Náhuatl theatre and tournament were thus closely tied to a form of religion that the missionary orders found deeply repugnant. It may seem surprising, therefore, that Motolinía would grant the Indians of Tlaxcala such freedom in the staging of a Christian narrative. Not all the orders were willing to do so. As Ricard notes, 'the genre [of indigenous missionary drama] appears to [have been] almost exclusively Franciscan'.[40] Horcasitas, too, remarks on the 'extraordinary liberty' granted by the Franciscans to indigenous artists in Mexico. Comparing two examples of native sculpture in mission churches, he finds on the façade of an Augustinian church 'sculpture prepared and directed by Europeans, . . . the art of the Old World transplanted', but in the processional chapels of a Franciscan friary he sees sculpture that 'shows the still vigorous hand of the conquered people'. The Franciscans, he comments, 'permitted certain liberties'. Theatre, unlike sculpture, is a medium notably resistant to external control, and Horcasitas suggests that the Dominicans and Augustinians were generally unwilling to risk the 'irreverence and even heresy' that might result from placing theatre in the hands of 'neophytes'. The Franciscans, by contrast, 'in their simplicity and in their desire to get close to the Indians', provided the kind of freedom in which an indigenous Christian theatre could flourish.[41]

This is a phenomenon worthy of note. For Spain has been charged, even by historians sympathetic to her cause, with having founded in Mexico 'a colonial church' modelled on the patterns of the mother country and governed exclusively by Europeans, 'a foreign framework applied to the native community'.[42] This may well have been true generally and in the end. But to offer a text shaped by the perspective of one world for uncensored performance by the members of another, as Motolinía seems to have done in Tlaxcala, is, at the very least, to let the reins of cultural hegemony hang slack. Such a venture risks ambivalence, or, as Mikhail Bakhtin positively conceives it, it makes possible 'communication between simultaneous differences'.

EARLY MISSIONARY THEATRE IN MEXICO

The Conquest of Jerusalem was not the first battle play performed in Mexico after the conquest. A *moros y cristianos* was staged in honour of Cortés, during his long march to Honduras in the winter of 1524–5, in the gulf community of Coatzacoalcos.[43] Nor was *The Conquest of Jerusalem* the earliest example of Franciscan missionary theatre in Mexico. Some form of catechetical drama was probably included in the 'invenciones . . . y danzas' that accompanied the consecration of the first church in Mexico City in 1525. Plays involving a measure of spectacle were often called 'invenciones',[44] and Gerónimo de Mendieta, in his *Historia eclesiástica indiana*, mentions the edifying effect that the festivities of 1525 had on 'the natives of the country'. 'Many', he writes, 'were converted and asked for holy baptism'.[45]

In neither of these brief references do we find any evidence of a Christian scenario being modified to accommodate an indigenous voice. But John Cornyn alludes to a Náhuatl dramatization of *The Conversion of St Paul* which may be susceptible of dual readings. This was performed by Indians outside the parish church of Mexico City in 1530.[46] According to the biblical narrative, prior to his conversion Paul 'consented to the death' of the first Christian martyr, St Stephen (San Esteban) (Acts 7: 59–8: 1). But in the Náhuatl play he is asked by the Lord God, 'Why did you kill San Sebastian? He builds my houses for me and he sweeps the road to heaven so that my people may come straight to my home here'.[47] The substitution of the later martyr Sebastian for the New Testament martyr Esteban involves, according to Marilyn Ravicz, a surreptitious reference to Quetzalcoatl:

> Shrines to St Sebastian were often built over places where Quetzalcoatl had been worshipped. Quetzalcoatl had been the one who swept clean the road to the gates of Dawn, over which the dead warriors travelled on their way to the Sun.[48]

The first missionary ethnologist in Mexico, Fray Bernardino de Sahagún, referred to Quetzalcoatl, in his role as god of the winds, 'sweeping the roads to the rain gods'.[49] And a more recent anthropologist, Victoria Bricker, has noticed a connection between Quetzalcoatl and San Sebastian in twentieth-century Indian dramatizations of conquest in Chiapas.[50] Ravicz would appear to be correct, therefore, in reading Sebastian as a coded reference to the Aztec deity.

This being the case, we may hear in *The Conversion of St Paul* two distinct voices assessing, from different perspectives, the ideology of evangelism. A Spanish Christian voice celebrates the conversion of the great apostle to the Gentiles and the beginning of that worldwide Christian mission which has now reached the New World. A dissenting Mexican voice suggests that the suppression of indigenous Mexican religion (especially the worship of Quetzalcoatl) by the Spaniards resembles the persecution of the early Church by the Jews. The Christians, declares the Spanish voice, are bringing good news to the Nahua, as the apostle Paul brought good news to the Gentiles. The Christians, responds the Mexican voice, are persecuting the Nahua, as Paul persecuted the Christians before his conversion.

Another performance that may have embraced dialogical voices took place on 26 December 1531. Two weeks earlier an Indian convert named Juan Diego had seen a vision of the Virgin Mary on the hill of Tepeyac, where the Indians had for many years worshipped their goddess Tonantzin. Shortly afterwards, he had discovered a painting of the Virgin miraculously imprinted on his cloak. On the day after Christmas the Indians of Tepeyac celebrated the arrival in their church of the miraculous painting of the Virgin of Guadalupe by staging a mock battle between 'mexicanos' (Aztecs) and 'chichimecas'.[51] The Spaniards may have read this theatrical defeat of northern Chichimecas by Christianized Aztecs as a 'prediction' of the further expansion of Spanish Christianity. For them, Mary 'represented the triumph of the Conquest'.[52] But the Indians may have seen the performance in a different light, for the Indians of central Mexico at times linked the 'barbarian' Chichimeca with the invading Spaniards. In 1586, for example, Tarascan Indians greeted the Franciscan *comisario general* with a battle play, during which they drew gales of laughter from their compatriots in the crowd for their depiction of 'savage' Chichimecas 'burlesquing . . . Spanish horsemen'.[53] The Tepeyac play, therefore, while it openly celebrated the prowess of Aztec warriors, may also have discreetly dramatized the defeat of 'chichimeca' conquistadors, under the patronage of the Indian Virgin.

In 1531 a Náhuatl *Last Judgement*, possibly written by the Franciscan Andrés de Olmos, was performed in Tlatelolco.[54] There are scattered references to other performances in the years that follow, including a probable revival of *The Last Judgement* in Mexico City in 1535, and a Passion Play in Cuernavaca in the same year.[55] But it is from Tlaxcala in 1538[56] that there comes a sudden abundance of information. Las Casas's reference to an *auto* involving Our Lady and the Apostles and directed by Indians has already been mentioned. This, he estimated, was performed before an audience of 'more than eighty thousand persons'.[57] Motolinía gives details of five other plays.[58] These clearly have an Indian flavour. Concerned with neither conquest nor evangelism, however, they seem to voice no Indian dissent.

The first of these five plays, *The Fall of our First Parents*, was performed on the Wednesday following Easter and was notable for the luxuriance of the Garden of Eden. A profusion of trees and flowers, some natural and others 'made of feathers and gold', filled the stage. There was also a multitude of animals and birds. Many of these were alive; some, as in the case of two ocelots, were tethered for safety. Other animals were 'artificial, . . . all well simulated, with some boys inside them'. 'For making a thing look natural', Motolinía remarked, 'these Indians have a singular talent'. So beautiful was this Paradise and so 'well presented' the play that, according to Motolinía, 'all who witnessed' the expulsion of Adam and Eve 'wept freely'.

Four more plays were performed on the Monday following Corpus Christi. Each lasted 'about an hour' and, since it was the feast day of St John the Baptist, each was based on material in the first chapter of the Gospel of Luke. The first, *The Annunciation of the Birth of St John the Baptist*, ended with '*un gentil motete en canto de organo*'.[59] This was followed 'on another stage' by *The Annunciation of Our Lady*. Then all 'marched in procession to the Church of St John', where, in the patio, 'on another platform, . . . gracefully . . . adorned and embellished', *The Visitation of Our Lady with St Elizabeth* was staged. Finally, after Mass, *The Birth of St John* was played. Here the Indians took advantage of the comic potential of the episode. In Luke's Gospel we are told that 'the neighbours and kinsfolk' of Elizabeth 'made signs' to Zechariah, who then 'asked for a writing tablet' on which to inscribe the name of his son (Luke 1: 58–63). Since Zechariah had previously been struck dumb and not deaf by the angel Gabriel (Luke 1: 20–2), it must have seemed more likely to the Tlaxcaltecas that Zechariah would have been the one to make signs. In their play, accordingly, Zechariah's silent efforts to be understood occasioned confusion among the 'neighbors and kinsfolk' and laughter among the audience. 'It was amusing', Motolinía recalls, 'to see the things they handed mute Zachary before giving him the slates which he had asked for, acting as if they had not understood him.'[60]

As in *The Conquest of Jerusalem*, the play encompassed a real baptism. 'In place of the Circumcision [of the infant John the Baptist]', Motolinía tells us, 'the Sacrament of Baptism was conferred on a child, nine days old, whom they named John'. Then 'the relations and neighbors of Zachary' brought 'presents and food of all kinds'. Since it was time to eat, all joined in a communal meal in simultaneous celebration of the birth of John the Baptist and the baptism of his Indian namesake. Such 'integration of the theatre and real life'[61] was a characteristic feature of missionary drama in Tlaxcala.

THE CONQUEST OF RHODES

These plays no doubt prepared the way for the more elaborate Corpus Christi celebrations of the following year. But the immediate precedent was a *Conquest of Rhodes* staged in Mexico City in 1539. This in turn was occasioned by political developments in Europe. Although the Moors had been driven from Spain in 1492, the eastern borders of Christendom, for which the Holy Roman Emperor, Carlos V of Spain, was responsible, had never been less secure. The armies of the Ottoman Empire, led by Süleyman the Magnificent, had reached the gates of Vienna in 1529, and a Europe already wracked by the internal dissensions of the Reformation looked to many as if it were about to disintegrate. The situation was not helped by the rivalry, erupting from time to time into open warfare, between Carlos V of Spain and Francis I of France. In 1538, however, the Pope, 'anxious to free [Carlos] for an attack on the Turks or the Lutherans', persuaded Emperor and King to meet with him – in jealously separate rooms – at Nice', and, on June 17, 'to sign a ten-year truce'. A month later, the two rulers met face to face at Aigues-Mortes, on the south coast of France, where, in the words of Will Durant, 'they ceased to be royal and became human', embracing one another's children and attending Mass together.[62] Catholic Europe breathed a collective sigh of relief. The news of peace reached Mexico 'a few days before Lent' in 1539,[63] and at once plans were laid for elaborate celebrations in which theatrical spectacle was to play a major role.

The people of Oaxaca organized bullfights, *juegos de cañas* (reed-spear tournaments), and a battle between 'Moors and Christians' over 'a wooden fortress' in the main square.[64] As part of the festivities in Mexico City, 'the Spaniards and Mexicans [Aztecs]'[65] in the capital decided to stage *The Conquest of Rhodes*, a large-scale dramatization, like its subsequent counterpart in Tlaxcala, of a Franciscan 'prediction'. The island of Rhodes, off the coast of Turkey, had been a frontier bastion of European Christendom since its capture by crusaders in 1309. In 1522 it had fallen to the 'infidel' armies of the Ottoman Empire. While Süleyman's army ravaged Austria, his navy advanced through the Mediterranean, capturing Algiers in 1529 and Tunis five years later. However, in 1535 the Turks suffered a minor reversal: Carlos V sacked Tunis. To the Franciscans, custodians by papal appointment of the holy places of Christendom, this small triumph seemed to be the first stepping-stone on the return journey to Jerusalem. One by one, they believed, the Mediterranean islands, including Rhodes, would fall before the forces of Christendom, culminating in a final, triumphant liberation of Jerusalem and the conversion of vast numbers of Jews, Muslims and Gentiles.[66] Encouraged by the Franciscans, the inhabitants of Mexico

City played *The Conquest of Rhodes*. The Tlaxcaltecas were to go one better and stage *The Conquest of Jerusalem* itself.

The Conquest of Rhodes was a sumptuous affair. Las Casas remembers in the main square of Mexico City a number of multi-level 'theatres' 'as high as towers', each having several distinct stages. On each of these could be seen and heard an Indian choir and orchestra playing a variety of wind instruments and drums. All told, according to Las Casas, there must have been 'more than a thousand Indian musicians and singers'.[67] Among the other scenic units were a number of 'castillos' (castles or, more simply, floats)[68] and, resplendent in the centre of the plaza, 'a city of wood' representing Rhodes. This was, no doubt, like its many European predecessors, made of painted canvas wrapped around wooden frames and mounted on wheels for the sake of mobility. Bernal Díaz, whose *Historia verdadera de la conquista de la Nueva España* is the most complete eye-witness account of the conquest and its consolidation, admired the realism of the canvas city's many towers, merlons and embrasures.[69] There were also a number of artificial woods, meadows and mountains, serving both to embellish the government buildings that edged the square and, in all likelihood, to identify specific locations around Rhodes.

In the square itself, surrounding Rhodes, the Christian army mustered. Some of the troops were on horseback and armed with lances and shields, others were on foot and armed with harquebuses. They were led by a hundred commanders, whose badges of rank were richly fashioned in gold and pearls. The army was soon joined by four large sailing ships that circled the plaza three times, as cannon on board fired and trumpets blared.[70] Mounted on wheels and propelled by men hidden within, these seemed to Las Casas to move over the ground 'as if they were on water'. Bernal Díaz tells us that the Captain General of the Christian forces 'was the Marquis Cortés'. In this instance, it is likely that Cortés himself played the role.[71] We know that he was injured in the foot while taking part in a *juego de cañas* later in the festivities.[72] In this case, however, there was no ambivalence. Cortés led the Christians, not the infidels, and he led them to victory.

The opening skirmish involved two companies of mounted Turks who were adorned with 'much gold' and dressed in silk, fine scarlet cloth and pointed hoods. They ambushed some shepherds, carrying off both men and sheep. But one of the shepherds escaped and fled to Cortés for help. At this, the Christian armies advanced to battle, freeing shepherds and sheep and taking 'many of the Turks' captive. Bulls were then released to 'disperse' the remaining infidels. This skirmish, involving the protection of Christian shepherds (*pastores*) and the flocks under their care, no doubt had symbolic import, and served as an appropriate prelude to the conquest of Rhodes itself. Although Bernal Díaz gives no details of the siege that followed, Las Casas mentions that the 'wooden city' was 'attacked by Indians from without and defended by those within'.

It is hard at first to discern a dissenting voice in *The Conquest of Rhodes*. Performed under European direction and with the conqueror, Cortés, in the leading role, it appears to have been uniformly Spanish in its point of view. But *The Conquest of Rhodes* was preceded by an elaborate 'invención', *La batalla de los salvajes*, which may have shed a dialogical light on the triumphalist drama that followed. Bernal Díaz describes the preparation of an artificial forest in the main square. As well as standing trees, draped with various kinds of moss and creeper, there were others that looked as if they were long fallen and already rotting. In the forest were many birds and animals, the smaller ones flying and running free, the more dangerous ones (two pumas and four small jaguars) enclosed for the time being in pens. Elsewhere in the plaza were two smaller glades in each of which was hidden a squadron of 'savages' (*salvajes*), some armed with 'clubs [made of] knotted and twisted [rope]',[73] others with bows and arrows. When the pens in the central forest were opened, the two squadrons advanced and a real hunt began. Once the animals had been killed the two groups of *salvajes* quarrelled and a battle broke out between them, ending with mutual retreat to their respective glades.

Then 'more than fifty *negros y negras*' on horseback entered, escorting their king and queen. All were sumptuously dressed and bejewelled. The diversity of their masks impressed Bernal Díaz, as did the way in which the women gave suck to their *negritos* and all paid homage to the queen. The black cortège also quarrelled with the 'savages' and, although Díaz is not explicit on this point, presumably fought with them.

'The origins of this spectacle', Horcasitas admits, 'are mysterious', and may lie in some prehispanic hunting rite or in a historical battle between rival tribes that the play commemorates.[74] No doubt the artificial woods, which never failed to astonish European observers, were inherited from Nahua ritual. 'Dances, interludes and games' in honour of the god Tlaloc had been performed in an artificial 'forest' erected on the temple patio in Tenochtitlán; dances to the goddess Xochiquetzal had also taken place in a 'house of flowers and . . . artificial trees'.[75] Moreover, actors disguised as 'savages' had appeared in prehispanic festivals.[76]

But the spectacle may also have Spanish roots. A glance at the index of Shergold's *History of the Spanish Stage* shows that *salvajes* or, as he translates it, 'wild men' were a common feature of medieval plays and festivities in Spain.[77] In 1399, for example, at the coronation banquet of Martin I in Zaragoza, an artificial rock (*roca*) was wheeled in, on top of which was crouched 'a great tawny lioness'. The lioness was artificial, but the wildlife which emerged from the rock was not. The chronicler describes wild boars and 'rabbits, hares, partridges, doves, and other birds that flew around the courtyard in which the banquet was being held'. 'Armed men' then attacked the lioness, but 'many men dressed as "salvajes" appeared from the rock and sought to defend her. The "salvajes" beat the armed men'. According to the chronicler, the performance was 'in imitation' of similar 'games' in ancient Rome.[78] Significantly, Bernal Díaz, immediately before describing the battle of the *salvajes* in Mexico City, also recalls the Roman games and mentions that the 'inventor' of the Mexican festivities was a Roman gentleman, proud of his descent from the great Roman patricians. Probably *La batalla de los salvajes* combined elements of both Spanish (or Roman) and Indian pedigree.

The entry of the black cortège, however, introduced an African voice to the proceedings.[79] There were about 10,000 blacks in Mexico in 1539, the largest number being employed, then as later, in the capital city. Many of these belonged to black *cofradías*, Catholic mutual-aid societies, which 'fostered a spirit of camaraderie among the slaves' and provided a framework for their participation in processions and other public festivities.[80] In some parts of the New World, the *cofradías* were thought of as 'nations', ruled by elected kings and queens. Coronation rituals were conducted at black churches, and each 'nation' sent its diplomatic representatives to the coronation.[81] This practice seems to be reflected in the participation of a black 'king and queen' in the performance in Mexico City.

The *cofradías* also became, as Colin Palmer notes , 'the cloak under which the members plotted rebellion in Mexico City'.[82] Less then two years earlier, on 24 September 1537, Viceroy Mendoza had uncovered the first slave rebellion in Mexico. 'I was warned', Mendoza writes, 'that the blacks had chosen a king, and had conspired to kill all the Spaniards, and to rise up and take the land, and that the Indians were also involved'. Incredulous at first, Mendoza corroborated the rumour, and then moved swiftly to arrest and execute the black king and the other leaders of the rebellion.[83] Although Mendoza does not mention the election of a queen on this occasion, it is possible that this took place but did not come to light. Certainly, in a later abortive rebellion in 1608 it is known that 'election of a king and queen was the first procedural business' at the clandestine gathering of conspirators. This was followed by an elaborate coronation of the new monarchs. Similar elections preceded failed slave rebellions in 1611 and 1612.[84] The 'king and queen' who led the black cortège into the main square of Mexico City in 1539 may well have been elected in a similar fashion. It is possible, too, that the blacks were discreetly celebrating their own resistance to Spanish rule much as the Indians in Tlaxcala were to do a few months later.

But why did a black *cofradía* take this particular role in the festivities? Why did the blacks fight with the *salvajes*? Why were they on horseback, a mode of transport one supposes was usually reserved for Spaniards? And why were they wearing fine costumes and masks? Clearly, the blacks were not simply participants in a festive display but were engaged in some kind of mimetic activity. Jerome Williams offers an intriguing explanation. He wonders whether these richly caparisoned 'black riders, with their masks and exaggerated uniforms, could have been satirizing or imitating the conquistadors, the *caballeros* and their ladies, present at the festivities'.[85] Such dramatized mockery of Spanish *caballeros* was not unknown in Mexico, as the example cited earlier of Tarascan Indians 'burlesquing . . . Spanish horsemen' shows.

If Williams's hypothesis is correct, an interesting connection between *La batalla de los salvajes* and the subsequent *Conquest of Rhodes* suggests itself. Might the battle between the two groups of *salvajes*, Williams asks, have referred to intertribal warfare before the conquest, and might that between the *salvajes* and the blacks dressed as conquistadors have referred, somewhat derisively, to the Spanish arrival in Mexico? Although a victory for the blacks (as Spaniards) would have affirmed an official Spanish reading of the play, the assignment of the heroic 'Spanish' roles to black slaves would have mocked Spanish assumptions of natural superiority and pretensions to grandeur.

If Williams is right, these first two mock battles would then have formed a trilogy with *The Conquest of Rhodes* that followed. The first battle would have dramatized past conflicts in native Mexico; the second would have recalled the recent military victory of Spain; and the third would have anticipated the future triumph of the combined Christian armies of the Old and New Worlds over the infidel Turks. Williams's hypothesis suggests, therefore, the possibility of a dialogical reading of *La batalla de los salvajes* that would reverberate throughout the subsequent performance of *The Conquest of Rhodes*. Cortés and his commanders, sumptuously attired, mounted and armed, would, according to the Spanish reading of the play, win a magnificent victory in fine style. But an Indian (or black) audience would remember the way in which that very style had been burlesqued by the *negros y negras* and would still be able, surreptitiously, to laugh at Spanish pretensions. This performance, too, like *The Conquest of Jerusalem*, seems to have been the meeting place for a plurality of ethnic and cultural voices.

6

Hernán Cortés, Sultan of Babylon

A group of Tlaxcaltecas may have travelled to Mexico City to see *The Conquest of Rhodes*.[1] Hoping perhaps to surpass their former enemies in the Aztec capital, they decided to stage *The Conquest of Jerusalem* in their own city and, 'to make the play more solemn, . . . to postpone it to the Feast of Corpus Christi'.[2]

A few of the Indians also had first-hand experience of the European politics embedded in the play. A delegation of five Tlaxcaltecas had travelled to Spain with Cortés in 1527. A second delegation had left for Europe in 1534, gaining an audience with Carlos V and winning, among other privileges, a Spanish coat of arms and the guarantee of royal protection for the city.[3] The colonial city of Tlaxcala may have been a consequence of this successful embassy. For a decision had been made to build a new provincial capital, distinct from the numerous Indian settlements that collectively bore the same name, on a previously unoccupied site on the south bank of the River Zahuapán.

By 1539 the church and monastery were almost completed, the plaza had been surveyed and the first government buildings, intended to house the Indian *cabildo*, or town council, were in process of construction along the north-west side of the square.[4] It was in this still unfinished but none the less, according to Motolinía, 'large and pleasant plaza' that *The Conquest of Jerusalem* was played.[5]

THE CONQUEST OF JERUSALEM

Six scenic units were prepared for the performance (see Figure 6.1).[6] One made innovative use of on-site material: the houses being erected for the *cabildo* were levelled off to a height of six and a half feet ('*un estado*') and filled with earth. On top, presumably with an earthen ramp leading up to its gates, was built Jerusalem, a five-towered

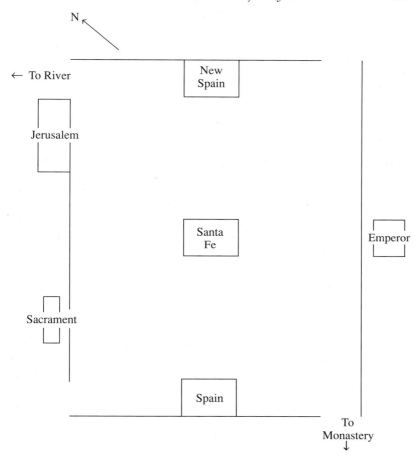

FIGURE 6.1   *Possible ground-plan for* The Conquest of Jerusalem

scenic city, complete with ramparts and merlons, and 'all covered with roses and flowers'. The upper storey was, in all likelihood, made of painted cloth wrapped around a wooden frame. This was certainly the case with four more units, 'surrounded by walls, on the outside of which were paintings that very realistically simulated mason-work'. Unlike Jerusalem, these may have been mobile. In one of these, placed beyond the south-east margin of the square,[7] the Emperor was lodged prior to his entry on to the battlefield. Two more, to the right and left of Jerusalem, represented the military camps of the armies of Spain and New Spain. A fourth, in the centre of the square, was named Santa Fe. Here the Emperor would lodge during his assault on Jerusalem. Santa Fe, one supposes, was named after the impromptu city built by Carlos's grandparents, Ferdinand and Isabella, as their base for the successful Siege of Granada in 1492.[8] A final unit, a decorated platform on which the consecrated host was to be displayed, was 'located near Jerusalem, in order that all the festivities might be enacted before the Most Holy Sacrament'.

The plot, according to the European reading of the play, would be fairly simple. Three times the armies of Spain and New Spain, led successively by Spanish dignitaries, by the Emperor Carlos V, and by the patron saints of Spain and New Spain, Santiago and Hippolytus, would assault Jerusalem. Despite initial successes they would fail to capture the city. Only the appearance of the Archangel Michael on top of the central tower of Jerusalem would finally persuade the Turks that they were fighting against 'God and his saints and angels', and that further resistance would be foolish. By God's grace, Jerusalem and its inhabitants would bear once more the name of Christ. The Mexican reading, as one might expect, is harder to retrieve. Nevertheless, I will try to suggest those moments in Motolinía's account from which a Mexican reading of the performance may partially emerge.

The play began when the Corpus Christi procession reached the square. After the sacrament and its attendant 'Pope, cardinals [and] bishops, all impersonated', had been settled on their platform, hundreds of Indians marched in 'in excellent order', playing trumpets, fifes and drums. This was 'the army of Spain'. In a flattering piece of fiction, the army was led by an Indian actor representing Don Antonio Pimentel, Count of Benavente. The Count had been a substantial benefactor of the Franciscans both in Spain and in the New World, and was the patron to whom Motolinía, a native of Benavente, would dedicate his *History of the Indians of New Spain*. Immediately behind Pimentel were troops from the kingdom of Castile and León, to which the county of Benavente belonged. Then came soldiers from several other Spanish provinces and, finally, troops from 'Germany, Rome and the Italians', countries theoretically subject to the Holy Roman Emperor. All, however, were dressed 'as Spanish soldiers'.

Motolinía explains this uniformity in terms of Indian ignorance: 'Not having seen European soldiers, the Indians do not know how each group dresses, and hence they are not wont to differentiate'.

But it is also possible that the Indians were establishing a contrast between the comparatively bland uniforms of the Spanish army and the much more impressive and variegated dress of the Indian army of New Spain that followed. Indigenous sympathies are often signalled aesthetically in Mexican folk drama. In the *danza de las plumas* from the state of Oaxaca, for example, the textually victorious Spaniards wear drab, blue uniforms, while Montezuma and his warriors dance their exuberant way to official defeat in multicoloured costumes and high, feathered head-dresses.[9] Perhaps the lack of variety in the Spanish costumes in Tlaxcala was due not to Indian ignorance but to Indian opinion. Whereas the *negros* in *La batalla de los salvajes* may have mocked the ostentation of the Spaniards, the 'European' soldiers in *The Conquest of Jerusalem* seem to have aimed at a different effect, serving as a foil for the splendour of the Tlaxcalteca warriors.

The entry of the army of New Spain, from the opposite side of the square, was much more impressive, both in number and in dress. It was divided into ten companies, 'each attired in keeping with the costume that they wear in war. . . . All wore their richest plumage, emblems and shields, for those who took part in the play were lords and chiefs'. Bernal Díaz's eye-witness account of the Tlaxcalan army arriving in Texcoco in 1521 affords us a vivid impression of such a spectacle:

> They approached in fine order, all very brilliant with great devices, each regiment by itself with its banners unfurled, and the white bird, like an eagle with its wings outstretched, which is their badge. The ensigns waved their banners and standards, and all carried their bows and arrows, two handed swords, javelins and spear throwers; some carried macanas [obsidian-edged swords] and great lances and others small lances. Adorned with their feather headdresses, and moving in good order and uttering shouts, cries, and whistles, . . . they took more than three hours entering Texcoco.[10]

In the vanguard of the army of New Spain in *The Conquest of Jerusalem* were warriors from Tlaxcala and Mexico. These were followed, also marching 'in good formation and very much admired', by actors representing tribal armies from various regions of New Spain, South America and the Caribbean islands. The Captain General of this continental army of Indians was an actor representing Don Antonio de Mendoza, the current Viceroy of New Spain.

Meanwhile, an army of Moors and Jews, led by the Sultan Cortés and distinguished by Moorish headpieces, had ensconced itself inside Jerusalem. Moors and Jews, until their expulsion from Spain in 1492, had been the internal infidels threatening Spanish Christendom. Those of their heirs who professed Christianity but secretly practised their ancestral religion were still sought by the Inquisition. Turks, as the enemy troops are called later in the play, were the external infidels and actual possessors of Jerusalem. This triple identity of the enemy is part of the European reading.

But assigning leadership of the army of unbelievers to Cortés and Alvarado is part of the Mexican reading. Horcasitas, it will be remembered, suggested that 'the Indians found satisfaction in seeing their own conqueror routed by a native army'. Arroníz, too, wrote of 'a natural resentment in the conquered people, which could only rise to the surface at moments of festivity and under theatrical guise'. I am inclined to agree. For we have already found similar traces of dissent in *The Conversion of St Paul*, *La batalla de los salvajes* and, perhaps, in the Tepeyac battle between 'mexicanos' and 'chichimecas'. We must remember, too, that the Tlaxcalans had fought against Cortés only twenty years before and that, according to Cortés's sixteenth-century biographer, López de Gómara, they were proud of the war they had waged against him. Moreover, Gómara reports, 'when they have fiestas or welcome a viceroy, sixty or seventy thousand of them come out to skirmish and to fight, *as if they were fighting against Cortés*'.[11]

Baumann discounts Gómara's report on the grounds that, in official accounts of their history, the Tlaxcalans minimized their resistance and stressed instead their ready acceptance of the Christian faith and their subsequent military alliance with Cortés.[12] But, as Bakhtin reminds us in *Rabelais and his World*, official acceptance of the status quo does not preclude unofficial opposition in carnival festivities and 'marketplace spectacles'.[13] It is therefore quite consistent that Gómara's report of Indians pretending to fight against Cortés should follow his account of an official Tlaxcalan speech in praise of Cortés.

The Mexican voice in *The Conquest of Jerusalem*, it would seem, celebrates past resistance. But it also dreams of future liberation. For the assignment of Cortés and Alvarado to the head of an army that was, from the Franciscan point of view, illegally occupying the Christian territory of Jerusalem and would soon be driven out, allowed the Indians to enact their own 'prediction' of reconquest. Conceding the claims of Christianity to Jerusalem, the Tlaxcaltecas appear to have asked: If the Turks have no right to hold Jerusalem, by what right do the Spanish now hold Mexico? From the perspective of a Tlaxcalteca Christian, the liberation of Jerusalem (as the friars would have put it) from illicit Turkish occupation, and the liberation of Mexico (as the Indian might have expressed it) from illicit Spanish occupation, may not have seemed so very different.

It is striking, too, that whereas the European army is referred to as 'the Spaniards', the Indian army is consistently designated 'the Christians'. The friars often compared the piety of the Indians with the 'infidelity of the countless nominal Catholics' who had come from Spain,[14] and the Tlaxcalan performers seem to have incorporated that perception into their dramatized argument for an indigenous Christian reconquest of Mexico. If, as the play insists, God helps Christian armies, the question of who are now the true Christians becomes a matter of real significance.

This Tlaxcalan appropriation and reversal of Spanish rhetoric conforms to a broad pattern of what Charles Gibson has called 'disguised reconciliations' between Indian and Spaniard at this period of Tlaxcalan history. 'Situations occurred' in Tlaxcala, Gibson writes,

> in which Indians accepted one aspect of Spanish colonization in order to facilitate their rejection of another. . . . Spanish colonization was such that Indians were able to range with some freedom between attitudes of affirmation and attitudes of dissent. In certain instances they came close to fulfilling the most idealistic expectations of Hispanic imperial theorists. At other times Indians seemed almost to be exploiting Spaniards, so effectively were they able to take advantage of the humanistic colonization.[15]

The Conquest of Jerusalem, although he does not cite it as such, would appear to be a splendid theatrical illustration of the kind of cultural and political manoeuvre that Gibson has in mind.

We should not suppose, however, that the Franciscans were lacking in sympathy for the Indian point of view. Gibson warns against too simple a division of colonial Mexican society into 'Spanish and Indian elements', reminding us that 'both groups were disunified'.[16] Although the friars regarded Cortés himself as a friend, they vehemently opposed the abuses to which the conquistadors and their successors had subjected the Indians. Motolinía had on a number of occasions sided with the Indians against the civil authorities in Mexico City. Indeed, so greatly had he angered the corrupt First Audiencia, under the presidency of Nuño de Guzmán, that in 1529 he had been charged with planning 'a conspiracy with the Indians to overthrow the civil government in Mexico, slay its officials, and send the Spanish soldiers and settlers back to Spain'. The government's chief witness later recanted.[17] But Motolinía's reputation as a friend of the Indians so impressed the Franciscan chapter that in 1530 he was given his first appointment to the region of Tlaxcala as a kind of 'itinerant missionary, charged with winning back dissatisfied tribes' and healing wounds inflicted during the Guzmán regime.[18] One need not suggest that Motolinía endorsed the implicit equation of Cortés and Alvarado with the rapacious Süleyman in order to grant that he was willing to hear the Indian point of view expressed theatrically.

THE DEFEAT OF CORTÉS

The fighting began in *The Conquest of Jerusalem* when the Spanish squadrons advanced on the city and the Sultan Cortés led out his troops to meet them. Some of the Moors were taken prisoner and others left lying on the field, 'although', as Motolinía notes with some relief, 'no one was wounded'. Motolinía's concern for the safety of the actors reflects the ferocity with which these mock battles were fought. The army of New Spain also took the field and inflicted casualties. But when reinforcements, bearing both food and ammunition, were sent to Jerusalem from the surrounding countries, the fortunes of battle shifted. The Spaniards were driven back, and the Count of Benavente sent a message to Carlos V, singling out the bravery of the soldiers of León, but also reporting the losses.

While in one corner of the plaza messengers ran to and fro between the Spanish camp and the Emperor's lodging, in the opposite corner the army of New Spain engaged the Moors in battle. All the Indians, we are told, 'fought valiantly', with the exception of the company from the Caribbean islands. The Caribbean natives, 'since they neither were adept in the use of arms nor had defensive weapons nor knew how to invoke the help of God', were completely wiped out, bringing 'great shame on all the army'. Jerome Williams is puzzled by this, calling it a 'textual enigma'.[19] But Horcasitas suggests that it may be understood as 'a parody of the historical reality of the Spanish conquest of the New World'. For the primitive Indians of the Antilles, unlike their counterparts on the mainland, had offered no effective resistance to the conquistadors. Their immediate defeat in *The Conquest of Jerusalem*, therefore, 'shows a certain scorn on the part of the Indians of New Spain and of the Europeans towards the Caribs, perhaps for their more simple culture and for their easy extinction at the hands of the first conquistadors'.[20] If Horcasitas is correct, this incident too forms part of the Mexican reading of the play, in which only those who resist and finally overcome the conquistadors are celebrated.

Moreover, it reminds us that Indians no less than Spaniards looked with disdain on others whom they regarded as weak and uncivilized. For this would not be the first time that 'primitive' tribes had been mocked in Nahua theatre. Commenting on Durán's inclusion of 'Huaxtecs' and 'savages' among the disguises adopted by prehispanic Nahua actors, Horcasitas and Heyden report that 'the Aztecs of . . . Tenochtitlán poked fun at the neighbouring Huaxtec people . . . in crude but comical skits of a phallic nature', and that 'farces in which "hunters" or "savages" appeared . . . ridiculed the Chichimecs or nonagricultural peoples of northern Mexico'.[21] The early demise of the Caribs in *The Conquest of Jerusalem* would appear to fit this pattern.

The Viceroy of New Spain also sent a messenger to the Emperor, receiving in reply assurance 'that our help will come from above, from heaven', and a promise that the Emperor himself would reach Jerusalem by daybreak. Carlos arrived shortly, accompanied by 'the King of France and the King of Hungary, all wearing crowns'. The former represented Francis I, now formally at peace with, but in this play carefully subservient to, the Emperor. The latter denoted Carlos's younger brother, Fernando, ruler of Hungary and Bohemia and active in the war against the Ottoman Empire. The imperial army was greeted 'with much rejoicing and with great pomp', the salute of artillery being imitated by the discharge of 'many skyrockets'. Carlos and his allies were led to Santa Fe, and the Moors, displaying 'signs of being in great fear', retreated within the walls of Jerusalem.

All three Christian armies now besieged the city, but 'the Moors', we are told, 'defended themselves very well'. Some captives were freed, however. 'The camp-master, who was Andrés de Tapia, had gone with a squadron to reconnoiter in the rear of Jerusalem, where he set fire to a place, and then through the center of the plaza led a herd of sheep which he had taken'. The liberation of the sheep recalls the similar episode in *The Conquest of Rhodes*. Why Andrés de Tapia, who had accompanied Cortés during the conquest of Mexico, should be assigned to the Christians while Cortés and Alvarado are placed among the infidels is not clear.

At this point the besieging armies began to falter. The Spanish camp was surrounded by Moors, the Emperor sent to the Pope for help, and all within the Spanish camp and on the papal platform fell to their knees facing the sacrament. In response, an angel appeared above the camp and told them that their hardships were a test of their 'constancy and bravery'. They need not fear defeat: Santiago, patron saint of Spain, was on his way. To loud cheers, an Indian playing Santiago rode into the square, dressed 'as they are wont to represent him' and riding a horse 'as white as snow'.[22] The Moors retreated, and 'Santiago on his horse, always turning up in all parts', led the Spanish armies in a more determined attack on Jerusalem. While inflicting great losses, the army of Spain nevertheless failed to enter the city.

'The Nahuales or people of New Spain' were also surrounded and also resorted to prayer. An angel appeared above their camp, which we now called 'the camp of the Christians'. 'God', the angel declared, 'has been pleased to . . . allow you to be conquered, in order that you might know that without his help you can do little'. It was a common ploy of missionaries to argue the supremacy of the Christian God over pagan idols by pointing out that 'the true and omnipotent God had allowed his faithful servants, the Spaniards, to conquer Mexico'.[23] Do we hear an echo of that argument here, and do the Indian performers reply that theirs is now the true 'camp of the Christians'? The Indians may have reasoned that the God who had defeated their idols might now help them, as Christians, to drive out the infidel Spaniards. Certainly, the angel's next remark may be read as a reminder both that the Spaniards needed the support of their Tlaxcalan allies to conquer Mexico in the first place, and that, if the missionary argument were to hold, continued possession of the land would also be contingent on piety, not nationality. 'St Hippolytus', the angel announces, 'on whose feast day the Spaniards *with you Tlaxcaltecas* gained Mexico', would come to the aid of the new '*Christians*'.[24] Soon, an Indian representing St Hippolytus galloped in 'on a brown horse' to lead 'the army of the Nahuales' in its war on the Sultan Cortés.

All three armies now renewed the assault, led by the exalted triumvirate of Santiago, Hippolytus and Carlos V. Every attempt was made to ensure the battle's realism. A house of reeds had been built at the rear of Jerusalem and was now set on fire so as to give the appearance that parts of the city itself were burning. 'Large balls made of reeds were discharged', together with others made of dried mud and filled with wet red earth to create the grisly effect of bloodshed. 'Red prickly pears' were used to the same end. The archers, too, 'had fastened to their arrowheads little pockets filled with red earth, so that it seemed to draw blood whenever they struck'.

In the midst of this final battle, supernatural intervention settled the outcome. The sudden appearance of the Archangel Michael on the main tower of Jerusalem filled both Moors and Christians with fear and all fell silent. The Archangel advised the Moors that their 'evil deeds and sins' warranted divine retribution, but 'because [they] showed reverence for the Holy Places', God had mercifully allowed them time to repent and to 'believe in his dearest Son Jesus Christ'. Now was the time for the Moors (or, in terms of the Mexican reading, the conquistadors) to repent and truly turn to Christ. With a quick manipulation of the ropes, pulleys and painted cloudwork, 'St Michael disappeared'. Impressed, the Sultan Cortés addressed his troops: 'So far we thought we were fighting with men. But now we see that we have been fighting with God and his saints and angels.' Resistance, he observed, is impossible and an appeal to God's mercy would be wise. The Moorish Captain General, Don Pedro de Alvarado, concurred and, together with all the soldiers, asked the Sultan to sue both for peace and for baptism into the church. The Sultan sent a letter to the 'Roman Emperor' admitting, in terms that only a miracle would have wrenched from the historical Süleyman, 'You alone are captain of God's armies', and we are your 'natural vassals'.

This confession is an extraordinarily sophisticated example of theatrical dialogism. For the language of natural slavery, borrowed from Aristotle, was used often by the Spaniards to justify their conquest of Mexican 'barbarians'.[25] Here the charge of natural slavery is also applied, in terms of the European reading of the play, to the Turks. We might even say that it is deflected from the Indians to the Turks. But, in terms of the Mexican reading, the European language of natural slavery is used by the Indians to suggest an even more radical idea. Cortés surrenders to an army of Indians, played in great part by Nahua 'lords and chiefs', and declares himself and his troops to be their 'natural vassals'. The Indians, proud of their heritage, have appropriated their conquerors' Aristotelian ideology and reversed its Eurocentric application.

The penitent Sultan Cortés then left Jerusalem 'with a great retinue'. He was greeted warmly by the Emperor, and led to the Pope, who received him 'with great affection'. Here, the integration of apocalyptic missionary theatre and the real sacramental life of the church became complete. 'The Sultan', we are told,

> brought also many Turks, or adult Indians, who had been designedly prepared for Baptism. They publicly asked the Pope that they be baptized. The Pope immediately directed a priest to baptize them; whereupon they were actually baptized.

ILLICIT BAPTISMS AND THREE GOOD MYSTERY PLAYS

The baptisms were also an act of political and ecclesiastical defiance. For some years conflict had simmered in Mexico over whether it was proper to abbreviate the ceremony of baptism in view of the shortage of priests and the large number of Indians requesting baptism. Motolinía himself estimates the number of Indians baptized between 1524 and 1536 at five million, a figure which Ricard considers 'not inadmissable'.[26] Faced at times with baptizing 'two or three thousand Indians . . . in the course of one day', many of the Franciscans resorted to reading the ritual of baptism over a crowd of candidates, applying the full ceremony, including 'the anointing with the sign of the cross, the breathing, the salt, the saliva and the white cloth' to a few, and then baptizing the rest with water alone.[27] The other orders objected to what they considered to be too hasty an approach.

So great was the acrimony that the dispute reached Rome, and in 1537 Pope Paul III issued a bull, recognizing the Franciscans' good intentions but instructing that in future the full ceremony be used in all cases but those of 'urgent necessity'.[28] On 27 April 1539, a synod of bishops and heads of orders in Mexico issued a specific definition of 'urgent necessity'. They also demanded that the full ceremony be used whenever possible and that the baptism of adults ordinarily be confined to the Easter season. Since this had just passed,[29] the decree meant the effective suspension of adult baptism, other than that of the old and infirm, for a full year. For 'three or four months', according to Motolinía, the prohibition held. But then, in Quecholac, Puebla, 'the friars resolved to baptize all who applied for the Sacrament, regardless of what the bishops had directed'. Motolinía, who was visiting Quecholac at the time, was one of the two friars involved. Over a period of five days he and the resident friar baptized 'Indians numbering by actual count 14,200 or so'. They were careful to observe the full ritual, though 'it proved quite a job'.[30]

The Conquest of Jerusalem, with its concluding baptism of 'many . . . adult Indians', took place less than six weeks after the episcopal announcement, during the feast of Corpus Christi.[31] If Motolinía's chronology is correct, therefore, it anticipated the mass baptisms at Quecholac by a month or more, and constituted a first calculated act of defiance. Arroníz considers *The Conquest of Jerusalem* to have been 'a defiance . . . of the colonial authorities' and 'a deliberate act of support for the sacrament of baptism such as it was administered by the Franciscans'. It dramatized, he suggests, a 'triumphant' reading of the papal bull, interpreting it as a vindication of the Franciscan eagerness to baptize.[32] It was, after all, an actor representing Pope Paul III who ordered the play's baptisms. Apparently the Indians in Tlaxcala were not the only ones willing to use the drama for subversive purposes.

After the baptism of the Turks, the Corpus Christi procession reformed. The 'entire road' over which it passed was 'strewn with many fragrant herbs and roses' and straddled by 'ten large triumphal arches' and 'more than fourteen hundred' smaller arches, 'entirely covered with roses and flowers'. At intervals beside the road were 'three artificial hills' on which 'three good mystery plays' were performed.[33]

The first, *The Temptation of Our Lord*, began with a 'consultation' among many demons 'to decide how Christ should be tempted and who should be the tempter'. Lucifer, being chosen, disguised himself as a hermit, finding it difficult, however, to hide his two horns and the lengthy claws on his fingers and toes. For the third temptation he offered Christ all the natural wealth and crafted merchandise of the Old and New Worlds, including 'many kinds of excellent wine'. 'All the Indians', Motolinía observes, 'would die for our wines'. Christ resisted this potent temptation, however, and Lucifer 'collapsed' into hell.

A saint's play, based on incidents from the life of St Francis, followed. Francis preached to the birds, 'who seemed to ask his blessing', and tamed a 'wild beast . . . so ugly that those who saw [it] about to attack became frightened'. During a subsequent sermon to a human audience, Francis was interrupted by an Indian, feigning drunkenness and singing 'what the Indians sing when they are drunk'. This no doubt occasioned much amusement among the audience; but the drunkard was finally carried off by 'very ugly' demons, shouting loudly, to 'a fierce and fearful hell which was nearby'. So were some 'well-simulated sorcerers', offering 'potions concocted in this land [that] very easily cause pregnant women to miscarry'. Other 'vices' followed. No doubt all engaged in banter with the spectators, encouraging them to join in ribald songs, purchase abortives, and pay no attention to Francis's sermon. Each vice in turn was carried away by the demons. Unbeknownst to the audience, 'the simulated hell had a secret door through which those who were inside could come out'. So when hell was set on fire at the close of the play and 'burned frightfully', to the accompaniment of vicious and demonic shrieking, it caused 'great horror', for 'no one seemed to have escaped'. Even those in the know were deeply affected.

It being by now late in the afternoon, the third play, *The Sacrifice of Abraham*, although 'very well staged', was shortened. Motolinía gives no further details,[34] except to add that after it the procession finally returned to the church. It had been a full day.

7
Santiago, the Sun King

At the beginning of October 1585 news reached Alonso Ponce, the *comisario general* of the Franciscan order in New Spain, that the fleet bearing the new viceroy and his family had docked in Vera Cruz. Ponce decided to meet the viceregal party, on its slow progress from the coast to Mexico City, in Tlaxcala. In the meantime he continued his visitation of Franciscan convents. Finally, on Thursday 24 October, in Cholula, he heard that the viceroy would enter Tlaxcala amidst elaborate celebrations the following Sunday. Leaving early on Saturday, Ponce arrived in Tlaxcala in time to eat in the convent that evening.[1]

Ponce was accompanied at all times by a friar who kept a daily account of his superior's travels. The spectacle prepared for the viceroy is described in this diary. It offers a revealing contrast to the earlier *Conquest of Jerusalem,* and it affords an opportunity, before we consider modern folk dramatizations of conquest in Mexico, to introduce Bakhtin's distinction between official and unofficial feasts.

A SPECIAL KIND OF DOCUMENT

On the Sunday of the viceroy's arrival, according to Ponce's diarist, the Indians of Tlaxcala planned to greet the viceregal party with a battle play. They had built 'a wooden castle of two or three storeys, with many windows and alcoves'. Here, a combined army of Tlaxcalteca warriors and Spanish soldiers, all played by Indian actors, intended to fight against a second army of Indians dressed as Chichimecas.

The Chichimeca Indians constituted one of the gravest threats to Spanish dominance in Mexico during the second half of the sixteenth-century. Despised and feared both by the Spaniards and by the more sophisticated Indians of central Mexico, the Chichimeca waged a fierce guerrilla war against northern settlements and convoys, frustrating Spanish expansion in the region for nearly 50 years. Final pacification was due, in part, to the voluntary settlement of some 400 Tlaxcalan families in the area of San Luis Potosí as 'colonizers' intended to have a civilizing influence on the wild Chichimecas. Although the first settlers did not leave Tlaxcala until 1591, the plan was very much in the air in 1585.[2]

The viceroy never saw the battle play. Between midday and one o'clock in the afternoon the castle caught fire and, despite all efforts to save it, was soon completely destroyed. 'It was', comments the friar, 'the mercy of God that there was no wind at the time, so that no house in the vicinity caught fire, the flames going straight upwards and climbing to the clouds'. The Indians were understandably distressed.

An hour or so before sunset, the new viceroy, Alonso Manrique de Zúñiga, Marqués de Villamanrique, finally entered the city. He was greeted by four old Indians, dressed as the Tlaxcalteca 'kings' who had led their people to victory with Cortés in the conquest of Mexico. The old men delivered the keys of the city to the viceroy and recited sonnets in Spanish, asking the viceroy to preserve the privileges granted the city by Carlos V. Then a squadron of Indian warriors, some dressed 'in their own way', others in Spanish uniform, assembled in front of the viceroy. 'All well adorned' and some armed with 'false pikes', they were, one supposes, actors from the now-abandoned battle play. Amidst 'a great multitude of Indians', they escorted the Viceroy and his family to the convent, where he was met by the *comisario general*.[3]

Gibson sees signs of 'social deterioration' in these festivities: 'a tendency toward nostalgia and pleading is evident in the Indians' attitude toward the viceroy; the four crowned kings suggest dependence upon an antiquated or artificial lore'. This in turn, he believes, was symptomatic of a general 'decline in patriotism at the end of the sixteenth-century', a decline 'marked by population decrease, new social relations, and a general relinquishment of Indian values'.[4] The waning 'patriotism', of course, was one that had involved allegiance to the native province of Tlaxcala.

The opinion that there is no dialogical voice in an indigenous performance of this kind in colonial Mexico needs to be ventured cautiously. Ponce's diarist mentions other fiestas from the same period in which Indians dressed as Spaniards and Chichimecas fought one another and in which the 'Spanish' success was equivocal at best. The Tarascan Indians from the region of Tzintzuntzan, who acted as Chichimecas burlesquing Spanish horsemen, have already been mentioned. In a second village, Indians 'dressed as Chichimecas' seemed to mock others 'dressed as Spaniards' by their ability to outrun the mounted Spaniards and so elude capture. Later, the Chichimecas danced on top of 'a large rock and wooden castle' that they had built in the *plaza*, while the Spaniards galloped ineffectually around it.[5] And, as we shall see in Chapter 8, 'Chichimecas' still appear in Mexican carnivals as figures of indigenous resistance to Spanish rule. It is possible that the Chichimecas in the abandoned Tlaxcala play would have signalled a similar dialogical reading.

But in this instance I am inclined to think not. The evidence we have seems to suggest that Gibson is correct, and that Tlaxcalan theatre had become, in Bakhtin's terms, part of the official culture. 'The official feasts of the Middle Ages', Bakhtin wrote,

> whether ecclesiastical, feudal, or sponsored by the state, did not lead the people out of the existing world order and created no second life. On the contrary, they sanctioned the existing pattern of things and reinforced it. The link with time became formal; changes and moments of crisis were relegated to the past. Actually, the official feast looked back at the past and used the past to consecrate the present. Unlike the earlier and purer feast, the official feast asserted all that was stable, unchanging, perennial: the existing hierarchy, the existing religious, political, and moral values, norms, and prohibitions. It was the triumph of a truth already established.[6]

In 1585 the festivities speak of Tlaxcala's submission to the heir of Carlos V and to his viceroy. The ceremonial delivery of the keys of the city, the sonnets recited in Spanish rather than Náhuatl, the plea for the continuation of privileges granted by Carlos V, and the protective escort offered the viceroy, all bespeak acceptance of 'the existing hierarchy'. Although the four old men recall the glories of Tlaxcala's past independence, they also endorse her present status: they represent, the friar records, the chiefs who 'became vassals of the most invincible emperor Carlos V and of the other kings of Spain, his successors'. Crisis has been 'relegated to the past'. Even the battle play, it seems, was not to have pitted the indigenous Chichimeca against the invading Spaniard, in the manner of the

Tarascan fiestas, but to have celebrated Tlaxcalteca support for Spanish expansion into the regions of the Chichimeca.

The Conquest of Jerusalem in 1539, by contrast, called into question 'the existing hierarchy'. Accepting the Christianity of the friars, it none the less challenged the government of the conquistadors. Celebrating at once the feast of Corpus Christi and the liberation of Tlaxcala, it existed on the borderline between official and unofficial culture. None of that tension seems to survive in the viceregal reception of 1585.[7]

But the weight of official ceremonial, according to Bakhtin, can never suffocate 'the true nature of human festivity'. This is to challenge the status quo, to deflate with laughter the pretensions of the rulers and to create, albeit temporarily, 'a utopian realm of community, freedom, equality, and abundance'. Such an impulse is, in Bakhtin's view, 'indestructible'. In the Middle Ages, therefore, 'it had to be tolerated and even legalized outside the official sphere and had to be turned over to the popular sphere of the marketplace'.[8] The medieval carnival was, for Bakhtin, the paradigm of unofficial folk celebration. Grotesque, often obscene, celebrating the passage of vast quantities of food and drink through the human body, carnival inverted the ascetic tendencies of official religion. Hiding social identity behind masks and elaborate disguises, mocking the pretensions of rulers, carnival created a 'second life' for the people, free of the bonds of hierarchical authority. Carnival, for Bakhtin, was 'a political drama without footlights':[9] political because it relativized the status quo, without footlights because it acknowledged no distinction between actors and spectators.

Bakhtin's conception of the folk may be, as Clark and Holquist intimate, highly 'idealized'.[10] But his theory of 'unofficial' folk performance and carnivalesque resistance is pertinent to our study of dialogical theatre. For it suggests that the challenge to conquest voiced by the Indians in *The Conquest of Jerusalem* may have found an alternative avenue of expression, once the theatre of public ceremonial was appropriated by the official culture.

It comes as no surprise, therefore, that Nathan Wachtel, in his effort to retrieve 'the vision of the vanquished', should draw attention to what he calls 'a special kind of document'. He writes:

The trauma of the Conquest still reaches the Indians of the twentieth-century; the past remains deeply imprinted on present mental structures. The persistence in the collective consciousness of a shock felt more than four hundred years ago is demonstrated by present-day Indian folklore.[11]

Specifically, Wachtel has in mind folk dramatizations of the Spanish conquest of the New World. Citing examples from Mexico, Guatemala, Peru and Bolivia, he points to the widespread popularity of dance-dramas that openly identify the Spanish conquest as their historical referent. There are others whose overt reference may be to medieval tales of chivalry, to crusades against Moors or Turks in Europe or to French imperial pretensions in Mexico, but whose real concern is still rooted in the trauma of the Spanish conquest. My own fieldwork in Mexico shows that it is not only the theme of conquest that has survived. The theatrical practice of engaging the conqueror's official discourse in a dialogue that becomes evident only in performance has also persisted.

We shall consider, in this chapter and the one that follows, two folk performances that I saw on recent visits to Mexico. On the feast day of St Francis, 4 October 1988, I watched a version of *la danza de los santiagos* in Cuetzalán, Puebla. Described by Frances Toor as 'the dance of St James, fighting the heathen on his white horse', *la danza de los santiagos* is one of many Mexican folk dramas in which Christians battle with infidels, 'the Christians winning and making the heathen ruler accept Christianity'. It is, as Toor remarks, 'popular and widespread'.[12] Four months later, in February 1989, I attended the carnival in Huejotzingo, Puebla. For two days, thousands of participants staged a raucous street drama ostensibly recalling the defeat of the French at Puebla in 1861. Neither play dealt officially with the conquest of Mexico. Both did so unofficially.

LA FIESTA DE SAN FRANCISCO

Cuetzalán is a picturesque colonial town of red-tiled roofs and winding cobbled streets, terraced into the steep mountainside of a subtropical valley in the Sierra de Puebla. Economically, it 'stagnated in isolation' until a new asphalted road reached the town in 1962; 'since then, development has been very rapid'.[13] The visitor can now reach the town in three or four hours by car from Tlaxcala, passing during the last hour through spectacular forested canyons and over mist-covered peaks. Nowhere is the feast day of St Francis celebrated with greater exuberance. The fiesta is divided, according to the local historian Antonio Santiago, 'into three parts. For the Catholic sector of the community there is a spiritual programme: masses, processions, and a visit from the Archbishop. For the mestizos, there is a social programme: music, dancing, contests, the commercial coffee fair. And for the Nahua Indians, there are the ancient dances and the *feria del huipil*'.[14]

The Indian fiesta is older than the other parts. Sr Santiago cites the report of an official Spanish visitor one October in the early 1550s, shortly after the first Franciscan missionaries arrived in Cuetzalán. Diego Ramírez marvelled at the stream of natives 'issuing, as if by a miracle, from a thousand hamlets' to take part in a celebration full of 'most unusual customs'. Ramírez noted particularly 'a kind of dance on a tall pole, from which they descend in a most dangerous fashion', a reference to the still popular *danza de los voladores*.[15] Sr Santiago suggests that Ramírez saw a feast in honour of Xochiquetzal, the Aztec goddess of flowers. Her name links her to the feathers of the quetzal bird after which Cuetzalán (formerly Quetzalán) is named. And her annual feast day, 6 October, would easily have merged with that of the Christian St Francis two days earlier to form a single Catholic and Nahua festival.[16]

But the ancient heart of the region is not in Cuetzalán itself. Four miles further on, over a road surfaced with jagged rocks that threaten to disembowel a car, is the village of Yohualichán. There, on a series of terraces carved into the mountainside and affording a breathtaking view of the tropical plains sweeping down towards the Gulf of Mexico, lie the ruins of an ancient religious centre.

The pyramids resemble those at the more accessible site of El Tajín; but archaeologists are still uncertain of the origins of Yohualichán. Sr Santiago believes that the complex was built by Totonac Indians in the sixth-century and dedicated to the Sun with the sacrificial blood of defeated Otomís.[17] By the time of the Spanish conquest, Yohualichán was a tributary of the Aztecs, whose Náhuatl-speaking descendants still occupy the region. The Aztecs respected Yohualichán. In the defence of the faith offered to the first Franciscan missionaries by Nahua wise men in the Aztec capital of Tenochtitlán in 1524, Yohualichán was named as one of the six sacred sites where the gods had been 'held in reverence'.[18] The *danza de los santiagos* that I watched at the Feast of St Francis was performed by a troupe from Yohualichán.

For several days before the fiesta the steps of the terraced market-place in Cuetzalán were filled with Nahua Indians in traditional dress buying and selling a cornucopia of local produce. Bananas, peppers, coffee beans, turkeys and embroidered blouses (*huipiles*) were prominent during my visit. An adjacent square was crowded with roundabouts, a ferris wheel and all the trappings of a modern fair. The dances began after dark on 3 October.

The volador pole, a stripped tree trunk 70 feet tall, was in place in the centre of the church square. Excitement mounted as the four *voladores*, accompanied by a fifth playing a flute and hand-held drum, began to dance to each of the cardinal points around the foot of the pole. Suddenly and almost simultaneously, several other troupes of dancers and musicians were pushing their way into the square through the milling crowds, a brass band began to play, fireworks lit up the sky above the church and the *voladores*, who had climbed the pole by means of knotted rope footholds, flung them-selves backwards from the top of the pole. As the ropes that secured them to the 'thimble' on top of the pole slowly unwound, the plat-form revolved, forming a tiny, rotating dance floor for the remaining musician. According to Sr Santiago, the musician ensures his com-panions' safety by offering homage, 'not to the saints that the Span-iards brought, but to Tonacatecutli, his ancestral god'.[19] The *voladores* hit the ground running, the musician slid down one of the ropes, the crowd applauded and the other dancers began to form up in the square.

Gradually we made our way into the church. The brass band played in the porch. The dancers wove their way down the aisles, dancing in groups before the altar, in the side chapels and in the central aisle. The pews were soon packed with spectators, and the parish church was a riot of exuberant noise and colour.

I saw *quetzales* (see Plate 6), whose scarlet costumes connote the sun and the colour of the sacrifices he demands, and whose huge fan-shaped head-dresses recall the rainbow of colours flashing from the play of sunlight on the plumage of the sacred quetzal bird. There were *negritos* dressed in black, sequined costumes to recall the leg-end of a snake-bitten African slave brought back to life by the danc-ing of his peers.[20] *Miguelitos* represented the Archangel Michael in his battle with the devil. And officially the *santiagos* of Yohualichán enacted the victory of Sant' Iago, the patron saint of Spain, over the heathen.

LA DANZA DE LOS SANTIAGOS

There were eight dancers in the group from Yohualichán. Five were *santiagos*, two *pilatos* and one *él señor Santiago caballero*. The *caballero* (see Plates 2 and 3) was the only dancer not masked. Instead, he wore a large straw hat festooned with ribbons and feathers. A miniature, white, wooden horse was strapped to his waist, protruding about eighteen inches before and behind, and he wielded a large metal sword. The five *santiagos* wore lightweight carved wooden masks, painted bright red, with golden eyes, eyebrows, moustache and chin. These masks were pushed back over the forehead, facing upwards. One of the *santiagos* was the *maestro* of the troupe (see Plate 3), and directed the dancers with the short *vara* (wand) that he held.[21] The *pilatos* (see Plate 4) were the clowns and villains of the troupe. They fought the *santiagos*, engaged in comic mimicry and demanded money from photographers in the crowd. The *pilatos* clashed their long wooden swords against pestle-shaped blocks that they carried, and wore pink masks on which were painted a black beard, red cheeks and a red nose tip. Unlike the *santiagos*, they wore their masks over the face. From behind the masks issued a quiet, mocking laugh, sounding as if someone skilled were whistling and gargling at the same time. There were also three musicians. One played a wooden flute; the other two took turns to beat a steady rhythm on a large drum strapped across the shoulder.[22]

For a long time the *danza de los santiagos* consisted only of a series of stylized clashes between the *santiagos* and *pilatos*. All would dance simultaneously, the *pilatos* at one end (away from the altar), the *santiagos* in the middle, and the *caballero* at the other end. Then each of the *santiagos*, designated in turn by the *maestro*, would challenge the *pilatos*, meeting the proffered sword stroke with a raised fist clutching a coloured cloth. The *caballero* did not yet approach the *pilatos*, remaining separated from them by the *santiagos* and brandishing his sword in a series of solitary and self-absorbed dance steps.

I had spoken earlier in the day with Sr Pablo Huerta Ramír, who carves and paints masks for several of the troupes in the area. To my surprise, he had said that the *santiagos* represent the sun. This is why, he explained, the face of the mask is red and there are emblems of the sun on the chin, eyes and eyebrows: golden ovals and circles outlined in black and with black rays extending. It also explains why the *santiagos* wear their masks on their foreheads. 'They are', he told me, 'looking at the sun'. There is also an emblem of the sun on the dancer's shield. Although the Yohualichán dancers did not carry shields, a *santiago* from San Miguel Tzinacapán, whom I had photographed at his home the previous day, did (see Plate 5). The wooden shield, about twelve inches in diameter, is painted sky blue. In its lower half there is a red face, circled by gold and emanating golden rays. Later, this dancer was to confirm to me that the *santiagos*, in his words, 'son el sol [are the sun]'.[23] At the end of the dance, Sr Huerta added, *Santiago caballero*, whom he also called 'el rey sol [King Sun]', would kill 'el rey pilato'.

Who then, I asked, are the *pilatos*? Sr Huerta was unclear. In the dance, he explained, the sun is challenged by 'a less powerful sun', represented by a pink or white mask. The *pilatos* are this less-powerful force. Watching the dancers that evening, it dawned on me that the pale face, rosy cheeks and dark beards of the *pilatos*' masks were intended to represent the features of the Spanish conquistadors.[24] My suspicion was confirmed the next day by a spectator who volunteered the observation that the *pilatos* 'son los españoles'.

The dance I was watching, it became clear to me, was susceptible of two readings, just as much of the missionary drama had been three and a half centuries earlier. The Catholic reading celebrated the defeat of the infidel, represented by twin Pontius Pilates borrowed from the Easter drama. Victory belonged to Santiago, patron saint of Spain and miraculous leader of Spanish forces to victory against the heathen. The masked *santiagos* were, according to this reading, faithful soldiers fighting behind their patron saints. So Toor, an expert on Mexican folklore, had read the dance. But the native reading pitted the Sun and his warriors against the 'weaker' invading force of Spanish conquistadors. According to this reading, it is the conquistadors who are defeated when *el rey pilato* is killed. Indeed, in this reading it is singularly appropriate that the villain should be named after Pontius Pilate. For was not the historical Pilate the representative of a colonial government, subjecting the Jews to foreign laws, gods and institutions, in just the manner of the Spaniards towards the Indians?

Within the terms of this second reading, some of the comic antics of the *pilatos* make more sense. When photographed, the *pilatos* demanded money. At one point, the leader of the two took the money offered, grumbling as always that it was insufficient, retreated some distance inside the church and then knelt facing the donor. With the coin he had been given he made the sign of the cross and then placed it on his tongue as if it were a communion wafer. This is the kind of blasphemy that folk clowns enjoy.[25] But it also served to recall the conquistadors' confusion of religion and gold. On another occasion, when the brass band began to play again in the porch, one of the *pilatos* posed in front of it, blocking the spectators' view. The other, using his pestle-shaped block as an imitation camera, pretended to take his partner's photograph, mimicking the rotation of a zoom lens and the antics of a photographer trying to obtain the best possible vantage point. It was funny, but it also identified him with the most recent foreign invaders: tourists and anthropologists. The *pilatos*, I was told by the dancer from San Miguel, '*representan dinero*'. That they 'represent money' could refer to both tourists and conquistadors.

Wachtel reads the Dances of the Conquest as evidence of an unequivocal resentment still felt by the indigenous peoples of Latin America against the violent disruption of their world by the Spanish conquistadors. But Mercedes Díaz Roig, pointing out that at least in Mexico the performers are often mestizo and Catholic, has suggested that the attitude of the dancers is more complex. The texts of the plays, she writes, 'move between the poles of evangelization and conquest', dramatizing in varying degrees both aspects of the Spanish invasion. This dual focus creates 'grave problems' for the dancer. On the one hand,

> he feels himself to be part of the native world, not so much by blood, since the majority of the performers are not Indians, but on account of a historical consciousness of three centuries of Spanish domination. . . . For the Mexican, the Spaniard is the conquistador, the enemy, the one who subjugated him and from whom liberty had to be won by force of arms.

On the other hand, the dancer is aware that 'the light of the gospel was brought by the oppressor'. His Indian ancestors were 'idolatrous' and 'needed to be conquered by the Spaniard if they were to know the true religion'. The encounter between two worlds dramatized in the Dances of the Conquest is not, therefore, 'external to [the performer], but internal: his *indigenismo* and his *catolicidad*; neither one nor the other can be conquered'.[26] The Nahua *santiagos* in Cuetzalán were ethnically 'part of the native world'. But they were also Catholics, performing, as the dancer from San Miguel explained, '*por el patrón* [for our patron saint]'.

The dancers from Yohualichán were the last to leave the church that night and the first to return the next morning. But the first event of the next day, the feast day of St Francis, was the coronation of the *huipil* queen. This drew the largest crowd of the entire fiesta. A select group of young Nahua girls, each representing an outlying Nahua village, gathered in the church square (see Plate 7). The girls wore native dress, their hair interwoven with wool and piled high on their heads in a traditional style known as *maxtáhuatl*. An old woman perfumed the air with the scent of copal from an Aztec censer or 'smoking bowl' [*popocaxtli*]. Each girl was led past a jury of six Nahua elders, delivered a short, shy speech in Náhuatl, and then mounted a decorated platform to await her companions. The platform, according to Sr Santiago, was meant to recall the pyramids of Yohualichán.[27] Meanwhile, the *santiagos* cleared a space in the crowd to one side of the square and began to dance.

When the verdict of the elders was announced, the crowd burst into applause, and the new queen and her court retired to the *palacio municipal*. Other dance troupes filled the square, their multicoloured costumes seeming to refract the sunlight. From time to time the *voladores* swooped down in widening gyres from the top of their pole, momentarily clearing the square below. Finally, the queen of the *huipil* was carried from the *palacio municipal* through the twisting streets of Cuetzalán on a litter borne by four young Nahua men. A *quetzal* head-dress formed a vast, many-coloured halo behind her throne. She and her companions wore garlands of brightly coloured flowers.[28]

The *feria del huipil* as such began in 1963, the year after the asphalted road first reached the town. 'Although it was created', according to Sr Santiago, 'by private initiative, and with a commercial purpose, it has been accepted with great pleasure by the Indians. They all take an active part in it: men, women, youngsters and old ones . . . with an inexplicable enthusiasm'.[29] Inexplicable, that is, if one forgets the ancient fair of Xochiquetzal. For Xochiquetzal, in the words of one authority on Aztec religion, 'was conceived as a supremely beautiful maiden'. Her name means Flower Feather and on her feast day, in the person of her *ixiptla* [incarnation], she was seated in an arbour of flowers while people danced about her, 'wearing garlands on their heads and heavy collars of flowers around their necks'.[30] Sr Santiago does not find it hard to explain the popularity of the *feria del huipil* among the Nahua Indians of Cuetzalán.

He is convinced that the fair taps into the tribal memory of the ancient festival of Xochiquetzal.

Throughout the latter part of the *huipil* ceremony, the Yohualichán troupe continued its routine of dance steps and stylized clashes between *santiagos* and *pilatos*. Finally, at about three o'clock in the afternoon, the plot of the drama began to unfold. For the first time *el señor Santiago caballero* approached the *pilatos*, ritually threatening them with his sword, and walking behind them, drawing his sword across the nape of their necks. Several times the *pilatos* escaped, running round the square with the *caballero* in pursuit, weaving perilously through spectators, vendors and other dances in progress. Once they ran into the church but soon rejoined the troupe outside. When the *caballero* chased the *pilatos* into the church a second time, however, they did not reappear. On the contrary, I noticed that the five *santiagos* had quietly followed. I hurried after them.

The dancers were gathered at the foot of the steps leading up to the altar. The senior of the two *pilatos*, *el rey pilato*, was lying motionless on his back, his head towards the altar and his feet facing the west door. The second *pilato* knelt beside the corpse, massaging the king's heart with his wooden block, listening through his sword as if it were a stethoscope, and moaning in quiet desperation. The *maestro* stood beside him, reciting barely audible verses. The *caballero*, his white horse still strapped to his waist, stepped slowly back and forth across the corpse, tears streaming down his face. The other *santiagos* stood to one side. The musicians no longer played the cheerful music of the earlier dance. Now, to a single, slowly repeated drumbeat, the flute played a haunting dirge. The church was dimly lit and there were few spectators. One, an elderly man, took flowers from near the altar and placed them on the dead *pilato*'s chest. Then he put a lighted candle at the corpse's head.

Finally, the *santiagos* lifted the corpse of *el rey pilato* and bore him at shoulder height down the central aisle to the last row of pews before the church door. There the play was over. The pall bearers set the *pilato* on his feet and all filed back, no longer in character, to the altar. They climbed the steps, knelt and prayed to the image of Christ high in the *retablo* behind the altar. The actor who had played the *caballero* was still weeping.

It was a denouement of extraordinary poignancy. Toor had led me to expect a Christian victory. The masks had presaged a triumph of the Sun. Instead, the victory of the *santiagos* was, it seemed, an occasion for grief. As heirs to the prehispanic traditions of

Yohualichán, the Nahua dancers mourned the Spanish victory of Santiago. As Catholic Christians, they mourned the triumph of the pagan Sun. If Díaz Roig is correct, the clash of *indigenismo* and *catolicidad* remains an affair of intense ambivalence. The dissonance between names and masks in *la danza de los santiagos* made possible in performance a theatrical dialogue between the indigenous and Catholic worlds of the performers. With an extraordinary economy of means, the Nahua dancers had preserved the colonial narrative, silently grafting on to its official discourse an expression of their own complex emotions as Catholic Christians and heirs of Yohualichán. Only perhaps in the theatre could so unobtrusive a gesture as the naming of a character (in *The Conquest of Jerusalem*) or the design of a mask (in *la danza de los santiagos*) initiate so powerful a dialogue between worlds.

Intensely moved, I knelt with the dancers before the altar. To my surprise, the *maestro* bent to whisper to me as he descended the steps, 'It's over now. We're leaving'. It was an unexpected gesture of friendliness. Until then the troupe's attitude towards spectators had ranged from studied disregard to vexed belligerence. The *santiagos* formed up again briefly and danced out of the church into the square. There they disbanded and headed for the ice-cream vendor, where they were happy to speak to me. The *maestro* told me pointedly that the dancers were from 'Yohualichán de los Pirámides', and was delighted to discover that I had visited the ruins. As for the dance itself, he confirmed the Catholic names of the characters and explained all the actions and words of the drama with a smile, a shrug of the shoulders and a simple, '*Es de costumbre* [It's a matter of custom]'.[31] What had been danced could not now be spoken to an outsider. But it had been danced, and I from my European Protestant world had been afforded a glimpse into the world of the Nahua Catholic. Much as it may have done in Mexico City in 1530 or in Tlaxcala in 1539, native performance of a Christian script had dramatized and partially communicated to a foreigner the Catholic Indian's internal dialogue between *indigenismo* and *catolicidad*.

8

Hidden Aztecs and Absent Spaniards

Situated at the foot of the snow-capped volcanoes of Iztaccíhuatl and Popocatépetl, Huejotzingo was one of the major prehispanic powers of central Mexico. Like Tlaxcala, it took part in the flower wars with Tenochtitlán; and, as an ally of Tlaxcala, it offered Cortés assistance in his march on the Aztec capital.[1] Huejotzingo has dwindled in both size and importance in the meantime, however, and is now only a small, dusty town known for its Franciscan convent, its cider and its carnival. The carnival is an annual explosion of prodigious street theatre. By my count, some 2500 took part in the carnival play in 1989 and 10,000 to 15,000 filled the square to watch.[2] The Huejotzingo play has none of the delicacy of the final moments of the Yohualichán *danza de los santiagos*. In scale, volume and violence it is more akin to the Tlaxcala *Conquest of Jerusalem* or to the annual *fiesta de moros y cristianos* at Alcoy in Spain. The dialogue between official discourse and unofficial signs, however, is just as powerful.

CARNIVAL AND *CINCO DE MAYO*

None of the reports of the Huejotzingo play that I had read suggested a disguised reading. Rafael García Granados and Lius MacGregor, who have written the most detailed account of the history and architecture of Huejotzingo, dismiss the carnival play as 'three days of innocent recreation'.[3] Frances Toor first saw 'this amazing carnival drama' in 1928 and wrote in *Mexican Folkways* that 'it dramatizes the capture and death of Agustín Lorenzo, a famous bandit, who . . . ran off with the beautiful young daughter of a rich *hacendado*'.[4] Victor José Maya Rubio, an authority on Mexican masks, bypasses the narrative of banditry and elopement and suggests that the play 'stages principally the struggle between French

108

and Mexican armies' during the successful defence of Puebla against French imperial troops on 5 May 1862. The 'religious' narrative of 'Moors and Christians', he writes, has been replaced by a 'nationalist' drama 'closer to the feelings' of contemporary Mexicans.[5] What I had been led to expect, therefore, was something of an eclectic amalgam traceable, at least in part, to the tradition of large-scale missionary battle plays that began with *The Conquest of Rhodes* and *The Conquest of Jerusalem*. This tradition had proved remarkably fertile in the intervening years. Civic parades resembling the initial entry of the troops in *The Conquest of Jerusalem* were enormously popular in the sixteenth and seventeenth-centuries.[6] Large-scale battle plays between Moors (or Turks) and Christians, known as *moros y cristianos* or *morismas*, survived at least into the present century. Alfonso Toro, writing in 1928, described a *morisma* in Zacatecas, lasting 'three days or longer' and involving 'not less than a thousand men'.[7]

In parts of Mexico, as Maya Rubio points out, the tradition was adapted to commemorate the historic defence of Puebla. Known as *Cinco de Mayo* plays, these 'nationalist' re-enactments were first performed, according to Angel Salas, in 'some villages in the state of Puebla'. They soon spread elsewhere. In 1933 Salas described an annual performance in El Peñon, a suburb of Mexico City. Lasting from noon till nightfall, *La batalla del Cinco de Mayo* culminated in a pitched battle between several battalions of Mexican and French troops. In the *Cinco de Mayo* plays, for the first time official victory was accorded to Mexican rather than to European troops.[8]

But, if Bakhtin is right, official victory cannot long provide the material for unofficial carnival drama. The latter thrives on challenge to the status quo. The appropriation of *Cinco de Mayo* by the national government as an officially sanctioned day of patriotic celebration drained it of its unofficial carnival vitality. *La batalla del Cinco de Mayo* is no longer performed in El Peñon, nor do I know of any 'villages in the state of Puebla' where it survives. Somewhere along the way in Huejotzingo, however, legends of banditry, attracted by a fortuitous coincidence of names, revitalized the tradition. The French general defeated at Puebla was named Laurencez. Called Lorenzo by Mexican spectators of *Cinco de Mayo* plays, 'because of the similarity with the real name and the difficulty they find in pronouncing foreign words',[9] he seems to have been replaced in Huetjotzingo by the local bandit hero, Agustín Lorenzo. Bandits and memories of *Cinco de Mayo* are thus the two publicly acknowledged elements in the play's narrative.

My first impressions of the Huejotzingo play were consistent with my expectations of a lively but heterogeneous spectacle. I arrived about 6 p.m. on the Saturday before carnival. The opening festivities were in full swing. On the western side of the square, in front of the *presidencia municipal*, soldiers from the battle play filled the street. All carried long, ornately carved muskets, which they loaded with gunpowder and discharged with considerable noise and smoke. All wore painted masks made of leather. There were, however, five distinct groups of combatants, some having their immediate antecedents in the *morismas* and others in the *Cinco de Mayo* plays. The Turks had black beards and wore feathered turbans, blue jackets and baggy white trousers. The Zouaves each sported a brocaded fez, light brown side-whiskers shaped like corn cobs, a blue jacket and red baggy trousers similar to those of the Turks. They were named after a French light-infantry corps whose original recruits, pressed into service after the French colonization of Algeria in 1830, had been members of the warlike Zouaouah tribe.[10] The unit had fought in the unsuccessful attack on Puebla. The Zacapoaxtlas were distinguished by a voluminous, flowing head-dress made of paper streamers in the national colours of orange, white and green and attached to their wide-brimmed sombreros. They recalled the Indians from the region of Zacapoaxtla, a small town in the Sierra de Puebla south of Cuetzalán, who had fought with the Mexican army in the defence of Puebla. The Indios or Inditos (see Plate 9) wore battered straw hats, long grey wigs, colourful tunics or serapes, and white cotton trousers. Their pale beards were made from animal fur and each had fastened to his bandolier a stuffed squirrel or skunk. The Zapadores (see Plate 8) were recognizable by their tall, black, brocaded hats, dark beards and sunglasses.[11]

Soldiers advanced into the space between battalions and fired their rifles at an oblique angle into the air or the pavement in the direction of the neighbouring troupe (see Plate 11), reeling back from the explosion with a rotating dance step and a gurgling laughter akin to that of the *pilatos* at Cuetzalán. Each battalion had its own small band, consisting of brass and wind instruments and a drum, which struck up periodically. Stray dogs, terrified of the gunfire, cowered beneath the horse-drawn carts in which some of the soldiers had arrived. The furore lasted another hour or so and then the actors began to drift away.[12]

CARNIVAL IN HUEJOTZINGO: MONDAY

Sunday was a day of rest. On Monday the carnival play was given the first of two full performances. The morning was spent in preparation. Banks of seats had been erected across the street from the *presidencia municipal* to accommodate civic dignitaries and their guests. Police were clearing parked cars from the perimeter of the square. A water-truck drove back and forth in front of the *presidencia*, discharging water to settle dust and rinse the street. A ladder was placed against the central balcony of the *presidencia* and decorated with branches, ribbons and paper flowers. This would be the scene of the elopement later in the day. More and more battalions of *máscaras* [masked actors] paraded individually and informally through the town towards their assembly point. Actors playing the bandit Agustín Lorenzo and his men galloped into the square to inspect the *presidencia*. A small hut made of dry branches, fronds and stubble, representing the bandits' hide-out, had been built in an open space at the north-west corner of the square. Bands played, vendors displayed their wares, meat and tortillas were being cooked at open air stalls, beer was being drunk in large quantities. Spectators began to line the streets.

At midday, to the roar of musketry and martial music, the procession swept into the square from the north-west corner. First came a group that had not appeared the previous evening. 'Apaches', dressed in multi-coloured feather kilts and high, feathered head-dresses with small mirrors before and behind, led the parade (see Plate 10). They wore masks of various designs, the most striking being dark-skinned with gilt nose-rings. Many carried a full-sized wooden replica of a *macana* or *maquahuitl*, the obsidian-edged club wielded in battle by Indian warriors at the time of the conquest. A few bore what Toor had described as 'a shield of feathers radiating from a mirror',[13] now a disk of cardboard wrapped in aluminium foil and bordered with brightly coloured material. Unlike the later battalions, the Apaches were accompanied by a band playing only primitive shawms and a drum.

These 'Apaches' had a dual referent. Historically the Apaches, who roamed either side of the Río Grande, succeeded the Chichimecas as the source of primitive native resistance to the northern expansion of New Spain. 'For two centuries, marauding Apaches swooped down on the thin line of Spanish settlement in hit-and-run raids, which baffled the defending troops and exacted an almost regular toll in persons and possessions from the terrorized colonists'.[14] In Mexican folk drama, therefore, the Apaches serve as a symbol of opposition to Spanish rule. But the Apaches of Huejotzingo had an additional referent. The *macana*, shield, nose-rings, and feathered costumes recalled the finery worn in battle and in flower wars by the tribes of central Mexico at the time of Aztec dominance. The actors therefore represented two enemies of Spanish empire, both Apaches and Aztec or Huejotzinga warriors from the time of the conquest.

Riding behind the Apaches was the General-in-Chief. Dressed in nineteenth-century military uniform and flanked by aides-de-camp on horseback, he was the titular head of all the armies. He was also the *corregidor* (mayor) and rich *hacendado* (landowner) whose daughter would later be abducted by the bandit Lorenzo. There followed battalions of Zapadores, Indios, Zouaves, Turcos and Zacapoaxtlas. Many of the groups were led by a general on horseback. The Turks were commanded by a richly costumed Sultan. Mounted and brandishing a scimitar, he was crowned by a turban bearing a silver crescent. The Sultan Cortés in the Tlaxcala *Conquest of Jerusalem* may well have looked like this. And, like the Moorish King in the Zacatecas *morisma*,[15] the Huejotzingo Sultan was accompanied by his harem, a contingent of young women dressed as odalisques.

The procession circled the square twice, halting when the General-in-Chief reached the *presidencia* for the third time. By now the noise of thousands of muskets being repeatedly discharged was deafening. Some of the spectators had their ears stuffed with cotton. Those of us on the inside of the square were completely surrounded. There was little of the 'festive folk laughter'[16] that Bakhtin found so readily in the medieval carnival. This was much more akin to the 'ancient popular drama'[17] that Artaud invoked as a precedent for his Theatre of Cruelty. Artaud would have loved the unrelenting assault on the audience's senses: the explosion of the guns; the acrid smell of gunpowder that filled the air, often driving the spectators to cover nose and mouth with handkerchiefs or else be seized by fits of coughing; the mass of brilliant and eccentric costumes dazzling the sight; the tactile senses of taste and touch being seduced by vendors hawking edible wares. It was a Theatre of Cruelty in which the line separating the audience from real physical danger could easily be crossed. Toor remarked in 1928 that the actors played their parts so well 'that some years a few of them never leave the battlefield alive. When that happens the Indians say it has been a *good carnival*'.[18] A man standing next to me assured me that the carnival play left 'many wounded, some dead each year'. Before the day was out I would learn to heed these warnings.

As the troops stationed in front of us continued to fire their muskets, the General-in-Chief dismounted and led his daughter into the *presidencia municipal*. Although in Toor's day the daughter (or *dama*) was played by 'a man disguised as a woman',[19] she is now played by a young woman in a white bridal dress trimmed with pink. Shortly, the bride reappeared on the central balcony, where she danced with her father. A Zapador stood guard on each of the two flanking balconies.

At about two o'clock, a messenger rode up to the *presidencia*. Dressed only in shorts and a brief feathered head-dress, his face and body stained with purple dye, he represented a Chichimeca Indian belonging to Agustín Lorenzo's band.[20] Climbing the ladder, he delivered a written message from Lorenzo to the *corregidor*'s daughter. The girl penned a hasty reply and the messenger rode away.

Her reply was positive. As the noise of musket fire rose to a crescendo, Lorenzo and his men galloped into the square, adding dust to smoke. Lorenzo climbed to the balcony and embraced his bride. He lingered a while, enjoying the moment, and then helped the girl over the iron railing on to the ladder.[21] Once the *dama* was safely received by his companions at street level, Lorenzo fired a pistol twice into the air and clambered down the ladder himself. The bandit chieftain, his men and their willing captive rode swiftly away. This was the signal for the most intense outburst yet of gunfire. The two battalions facing one another across the front of the *presidencia municipal* – Zapadores to the south, Indios to the north – advanced again and again, firing, dancing away, reloading and firing again. All around the square similar engagements were taking place. The air was filled with incessant explosions and clouds of acrid smoke.

After about fifteen more minutes the noise began to die down. It was now over two hours since the procession had entered the square, bombarding our senses, and I was beginning to feel I could stand the noise no longer. Gradually and mercifully, the *máscaras* began to drift away, some to stores and homes, others to the marketplace stalls, to eat and drink and prepare for the next act. It was a relief to see the human faces behind the masks, calmly eating lunch, sucking popsicles, some of the younger ones playing basketball.

During the break, Bakhtin's carnival humour surfaced briefly. A bizarre group wandered from stall to stall and occasionally stopped passing cars, playing a kind of trick-or-treat on merchants and motorists. The troupe consisted of three small boys in masks, each playing a drum or tambourine, a masked man in a sombrero leading on a rope another dressed as an opossum, two 'gorillas' and, most eccentric of all, a man in a skirt and a woman's mask carrying a dead, stuffed baby donkey. The donkey would 'nibble' food from stalls, roll on its back on the hood of stopped cars, or be ridden at the crowd by one of the gorillas. Toor had made no mention of such a group, but it was explained to me with the inevitable '*Es tradición*'. I take it to have developed from what Toor does mention and which I did not see, namely, the 'robbing' of stores by the bandits at this stage in the day.[22]

At about 3.30 p.m. the *máscaras* began to return, surrounding the hut in the open area in the north-west corner of the square that represented Lorenzo's hideaway. Toor reported that the wedding of the bandit and his bride took place here and that sometimes a priest would perform a mock ceremony. The soldiers, she wrote, launched their attack during the ensuing celebrations and dancing.[23] When I saw the play, Lorenzo and his bride were absent and there was no sign of a wedding. None the less, the hut was assaulted with full ferocity. For half an hour the soldiers fired their muskets into the hut, dancing away after they had fired to reload and shoot again. Piece by piece, the hideaway was blown apart until, at last, a tongue of flame from one of the rifles set it on fire (see Plate 12). The actors continued their attack on the burning and finally charred *casa*. When only a blackened frame remained, it was still enveloped in clouds of smoke from the blast of muskets and in sudden gusts of ashes exploding from the wreckage. These last moments of the vacant and devastated hideout still under exuberant fire left me with an indelible impression of senseless violence. 'Like the plague', wrote Artaud,

> the theater restores us all our dormant conflicts and all their powers, and gives these powers names we hail as symbols: and behold! before our eyes is fought a battle of symbols, one charging against another in an impossible mêlée. . . . Like the plague the theater is the time of evil, the triumph of dark powers that are nourished by a power even more profound until extinction. . . . Like the plague, the theater has been created to drain abscesses collectively.[24]

Artaud never managed to stage such a performance. But he longed to 'rejoin the ancient popular drama, sensed and experienced directly by the mind without the deformations of language and the barrier of speech'.[25] Only in Huejotzingo have I seen theatre that came so close to that of which Artaud dreamt.

Eventually, the battalions left the devastated hut and reformed around the perimeter of the square, advancing repeatedly into the intervening spaces to fire on one another. As I approached too close to gain a better vantage point for my camera, I heard my seven-year-old son, running behind, yell in pain. I turned and, horrified, saw that his upper lip seemed to be split open. We ran diagonally across the square, weaving between spectators and behind armed 'soldiers' to reach the hospital. The doctor on duty cleaned my son's lip and, to my intense relief, pronounced that there would be no scar, only a temporary and very painful swelling. It was, he said, as if my son had been struck in the mouth in a boxing match. The blow had been delivered not by a fist but, at close range, by the wadding exploding outward from the striking hammer of a musket. The doctor prescribed a medicine to reduce the swelling. As we left, a Zapador stood in the foyer, his sleeve rolled up to reveal eighteen inches of raw flesh around the elbow from which the skin had been completely burned away. We had been lucky.

Back in the hotel that evening I thought about what we had seen. Most of the battalions in the carnival drama had their immediate roots in the *Cinco de Mayo* plays: Zapadores and Zouaves were French troops, Zacapoaxtlas and Indios fought for the Mexicans. The skirmishes around the circumference of the square, the incessant firing of the muskets and the final siege of the *casa del bandido*, were all that remained of the elaborate battles of the *Cinco de Mayo* play. The Turks had strayed from the *morismas*. Both *morismas* and *Cinco de Mayo* plays in all likelihood had deeper roots in Spanish *moros y cristianos*, Nahua flower wars and the battle plays staged immediately after the conquest. Muskets had replaced the skyrockets used to simulate artillery in *The Conquest of Jerusalem*, and cannons and bows had been abandoned. But the splendour of the costumes, the number of participants and the ferocity of the fighting had not diminished. I could well understand now Motolinía's relief that no one had been wounded during the fighting in the Tlaxcala play. I remembered, too, that the Christians in *The Conquest of Jerusalem* had set fire to 'a house of reeds' in the rear of the city, and that, in *The Play of St Francis* that followed, hell had been ignited and 'burned frightfully'. The burning of Lorenzo's hideout had a long theatrical pedigree.

Lorenzo himself had strayed into the play from local legend.[26] The name of the defeated French General Lorencez seems to have acted as a magnet to the stories of the bandit Lorenzo, whose challenge to the authority of the powerful *corregidor* appealed to the unofficial spirit of carnival. The one faded in dramatic prominence as the historical referent of the *Cinco de Mayo* play became more distant; the other rose to the position of dramatic hero as the play became more and more a carnival challenge to official control.

But I also found myself wondering if there might be a more guarded reading of the performance, as there had been at Tlaxcala and Cuetzalán. Intriguingly, the Mexican army was made up exclusively of Indians (Indios and Zacapoaxtlas). There was a fondness for 'infidel' battalions. There were Turks but no Christians. There were Zouaves, named after the Zouaouah, a Berber tribe whose armed resistance to French colonization in Algeria had finally been quashed in 1857,[27] just five years before the Mexican defence of Puebla. And there was Zapadores, whose headgear recalled both the high turban of a Moorish King and the stone head-dress of Indian warriors in prehispanic sculpture.[28] Moreover, the procession was headed by 'Apaches', whose name recalled a tribe that had successfully resisted Spanish colonization and evangelism, and whose costumes represented Mexican warriors from the time of the conquest. There were no Christians, no Spaniards, no unequivocally French troops.

There was another detail that puzzled me: on almost every costume, irrespective of its wearer's official character, there was stitched a colourful portrait of an Indian warrior and his bride, sometimes accompanied by other warriors. I had been told by one spectator that this was nothing more than decoration ('*Nada más es adorno*'). But a woman selling mantles embroidered with the design had said that the warrior and his bride represented Popocatépetl and Iztaccíhuatl. According to Durán, the Aztecs had worshipped the volcanoes as fertility gods, offering human sacrifice to them in temples and caves on their slopes.[29] But the woman mentioned only popular legend. Iztaccíhuatl, it is said, was the beautiful daughter of an Aztec emperor and Popocatépetl a young warrior in love with her. When Iztaccíhuatl died, Popocatépetl built a great pyramid on which he laid his betrothed and another by its side where he stood holding a

1. William Hogarth: *A scene from 'The Conquest of Mexico'*, 1732

2. *El señor Santiago caballero*

3. The *maestro* and the *caballero*

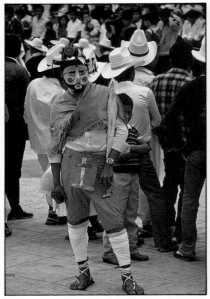

4. A *pilato*

5. A young *santiago*

6. *Quetzales*

7. *Huipil* contestants

8. A *zapador*

9. *Los inditos*

11. Confrontation

flaming torch to guard her corpse. Over the years the snows covered both pyramids and now they appear as snow-capped peaks, the one, it is said, resembling a recumbent woman, the other from time to time shooting flame into the air.[30] Behind the warrior and his bride on the mantles worn by the *máscaras* loomed the twin peaks of Popocatépetl and Iztaccíhuatl. I wondered if the love of Agustín Lorenzo for the *corregidor*'s daughter and the constant association of the warrior bandit and his bride with *'las montañas'* might be a veiled allusion to this legend. I was, however, to be given a third and, to my mind, more cogent explanation of the portrait of the Indian warrior and his bride the next day.

CARNIVAL IN HUEJOTZINGO: TUESDAY

Tuesday is the most important day of the carnival. It brings out the largest number of *máscaras* and spectators and the greatest abundance of food and drink. When we arrived, shortly before noon, the marketplace was packed with improvised stalls, kitchens and outdoor restaurants. Meat was being cut and cooked in vast kettles over wood fires, the simmering stew stirred from time to time with huge paddles. Chickens roasted, strings of sausages hung out of reach of the dogs. Loaves of sweet bread, papayas, coconuts, oranges and bananas, sugared pink and white *dulces*, ice cream, rainbows of bottled soft drinks, peppers and assorted spices were displayed in grand profusion. I was reminded of Bakhtin's insistence that 'feasting is part of every folk merriment', not simply because gathered crowds of necessity consume much food but because 'man's encounter with the world in the act of eating is joyful, triumphant; he triumphs over the world, devours it without being devoured himself. . . . The banquet always celebrates a victory'.[31]

The dramatization of victory, the precise nature of which was still unclear to me, began again at noon. I watched with my son from the safety of a raised balustrade behind several rows of spectators. The play followed the same narrative line as it had the day before: the opening parade, culminating in the abduction of the *dama*; the mid-afternoon respite; the devastation of the bandit's hideout; and the concluding skirmishes around the perimeter of the square. There were, however, a few minor additions.

The battalions in the parade were introduced over a loudspeaker by an announcer who repeatedly invoked the official line that the purpose of the carnival was to generate *'alegría y entusiasmo* [joy and enthusiasm]' and to promote the honour of the city. The parade was led not by the Apaches but, as had often been the case in seventeenth-century *mascaradas*, by 'a disorganized band of wild Chichimeca Indians'.[32] Their skin was dyed black, their feet were bare, and they wore the same shorts and brief feathered head-dress as Lorenzo's Chichimeca messenger. A few wore primitive masks, one held aloft a stuffed bird of prey, and two others carried a kind of totem pole. The Apaches followed. The procession was thus led by the two tribes who had most doggedly resisted Spanish colonization.

Another contingent taking part in the parade for the first time on Tuesday bore a banner announcing themselves as *'Casamiento indígena* [Native Wedding]'. This group included women and children, some men dressed as women and others imitating drunken wedding guests. The wedding party had presumably become detached from the marriage of Agustín Lorenzo. Although the marriage was no longer performed, the guests still took part in the procession.

When Lorenzo and his men concluded their second circuit of the square in front of the *presidencia municipal*, they flung money to the crowd. Children rushed into the street to pick it up from between horses' hooves and firing *máscaras*. The bandits repeated this gesture immediately after the abduction of the *drama*. On this occasion, too, Lorenzo threw money from the balcony into the street. Like Robin Hood, these outlaws robbed the rich to feed the poor.

Finally, when Lorenzo's *casa* was being blown apart and burned, the General-in-Chief and father of the bride was more evident than he had been the day before, directing the attacking troops and enacting consultation with the general of the Zapadores. The play concluded, I was told (for I left shortly before this was to take place) with speeches in which both the General-in-Chief and Agustín Lorenzo gave thanks to all who had taken part.

For me, however, the most enlightening event of the second day was a conversation I had with one of the participants after lunch. My son and I ate in a small restaurant near the entrance to the convent. In the back room of the restaurant a group of Zacapoaxtlas were dining. They had left the outer layers of their costumes piled on a table near ours. When one of the older Zacapoaxtlas caught me admiring these, I enquired about the Indian warrior and his bride portrayed on the mantle. 'Oh,' he said at once, 'We're all Aztecs.' He went on to explain that the carnival play represents a battle between Aztecs and Spaniards from the time of the conquest. I asked if any of the participants represented Spaniards. 'No,' he said. 'We're all Aztecs. The Spaniards have been defeated.' In the carnival drama, he acknowledged, *se mezcla algunas historias distintas* [several distinct stories are mixed]'. There are the *'fuerzas del Cinco de Mayo'*; there is Agustín Lorenzo and all the forces that chased him into the mountains; and, most importantly, there are the Aztecs who conquer the Spaniards.

Only the first two groups were named. The last, it now became clear to me, were identified by the costumes; some more openly with feathered head-dresses and *macanas*, all with the silent stitching into the costume of the portrait of an Aztec warrior. Like the renaming of the Sultan of Babylon and his Captain General in *The Conquest of Jerusalem* and the design of the masks in the Yohualichán *danza de los santiagos*, the portrait of the Aztec warrior and his bride in Huejotzingo is the small key that unlocks the powerful unofficial reading of the play. Turks, Zouaves, Zapadores, Zacapoaxtlas, Indios, Apaches and Chichimecas are official designations, chosen because they can imply without actually naming the unofficial identity of the performers. Within the terms of the unofficial reading, however, all these infidel groups represent Indian warriors who have driven the Spaniards from the field.

Since the French invasion which provides the official narrative bore no evangelistic purpose, the tension between *indigenismo* and *catolicidad* is muted in the Huejotzingo play. Although the defeat of Catholic Spain is implicit in the triumph of native Mexico, the actors represent it only indirectly. It is the victory of *indigenismo* that shines from all three facets of the narrative: the repulse of the French by Mexican troops; the outwitting of the creole *hacendado* by the Indian Lorenzo; and the expulsion of the Spaniards by Aztec warriors.

THE VISION OF THE VANQUISHED

The indigenous readings of the Yohualichán and Huejotzingo dramas do not reside in the text. They are discreetly revealed in performance. Once noticed, however, they shift the entire focus of the play. Frances Toor remarked on a similar distinction between the voice of the text and that of the performance in a version of the *danza de las plumas* that she saw in Cuilapán, Oaxaca, in 1925. The text of this dance, dramatizing the conquest of Mexico, ends properly with the defeat of Montezuma and his warriors by the Spaniards. 'But', wrote Toor, 'the Conquest was a lie'. Montezuma and his captains 'looked and danced like gods'. Dressed in high feathered head-dresses and performing exuberant leaps and twists, they contrasted most favourably with Cortés, 'a little man, accompanied by a lot of small boys stiffly dressed in [plain] blue uniforms'. Although Cortés gained the official textual victory, it was clear that, at the aesthetic or 'symbolic' level, Montezuma had defeated the 'military oppressors'.[33]

Victoria Bricker, too, has noticed a complex 'disjunction between costume and role' in the Mayan carnival plays of highland Chiapas. In language that might well be applied to the Huejotzingo play, she writes that the Mayan 'rituals' are not simple 'historical' dramas; instead, they 'consist of a hodge-podge of elements drawn from different historical periods'. But there is, she discovers, an 'underlying structure' to this 'seeming chaos'. All has to do with

> ethnic conflict – warfare, death, rape, soldiers, weapons, fireworks, and the division of people into two groups: the conquerors and the conquered. The ritual of Carnival *is* historical drama, but drama which treats the history of ethnic conflict in symbolic terms. What is important in ritualized ethnic conflict is not the order of historical events, but the message communicated by their structure.[34]

The 'message', she implies, is one of resistance to conquest.

The theatrical dialogue begun by the Indians of Tlaxcala, when they let it be known in performance that the Sultan of Babylon 'was Hernán Cortés' and his second-in-command 'was Pedro de Alvarado', is still being conducted in dance-dramas and carnival plays throughout Mexico. The evidence of these modern folk performances, however, does more than just support the understanding of the *Conquest of Jerusalem* advanced by Horcasitas and Arroníz. It allows us insight into what both Leon-Portilla and Wachtel have called 'the vision of the vanquished'. The texts assembled by Leon-Portilla in *Visión de los vencidos* represent the Indian point of view as it was transcribed by European minds.[35] The folk plays, no less than the indigenous chronicles, reflect European influences. But the players, whether at Tlaxcala in 1539 or in the neighbouring states of Puebla and Oaxaca today, have encoded their vision in a performance that officially speaks of something else: the triumph of Christianity or the defeat of the French. This allows the vision of Spanish defeat to be played at once discreetly and with great power. And, if Díaz Roig is correct, it is this very overlay of Roman Catholic and indigenous Mexican viewpoints that gives accurate expression to the ambiguous vision of the vanquished in Mexican folk dramas. The people of sixteenth-century Tlaxcala and of twentieth-century Yohualichán, Huejotzingo, Cuilapán and Chiapas have adopted (and no doubt adapted) the Catholicism of their conquerors. And they have repeatedly defeated, in most earnest play, the conquering armies of Spain. Their folk plays, for nearly 500 years, have expressed, as Díaz Roig puts it, this 'existing tension between piety [*religiosidad*] and nationalism',[36] between *indigenismo* and *catolicidad*.

We can, in fact, conceive of the dialogue between worlds in much of the missionary drama and in the folk plays we have considered, in terms of four pairs of interlocutors: text:performance: :official :unofficial: :Old World:New World: :*catolicidad:indigenismo*. In each case, the second partner in the dialogue relativizes the monological pretensions of the first. But in each case, too, the first perspective is partially accepted by the second. The indigenous voice, heard unofficially in performance, rejects its conquest by the Old World but embraces, at least in part, the Catholicism of the Old World, in so far as this is offered rather than imposed. The drama testifies to an ongoing dialogue.

This dialogue, as Díaz Roig pointed out, is internal to the performers. But it is also capable of being communicated to those who attend. Motolinía was sensitive to the indigenous perspective in Tlaxcala. Frances Toor heard the Mexican voice in the *danza de las plumas* in Cuilapán. And what I have learned of the vision of the once-vanquished but still-resilient native peoples of Mexico, I have learned in great part from the drama.

The dialogical character of the dramatic genre has been demonstrated in the first two parts of this book in literary dramatizations of the conquest of Mexico in Europe and in indigenous dramatizations of the same theme in Mexico itself. The drama has shown itself capable of dialogue between differing points of view within a single social world (Dryden's *The Indian Emperour*) as well as in the context of an encounter between two vastly different worlds (*The Conquest of Jerusalem*). We are now ready to apply this theatrical paradigm to the broader moral questions raised by Tzvetan Todorov concerning the justice of cross-cultural relationships. This will form the subject matter of Part Three.

Part Three
The Question of the Other

9

Barbarians and Other Neighbours

To bring any new paradigm to bear on the ancient question of the other is to enter an enduring debate. There is not space here to review the history of that debate in detail. But by attending in this chapter to the models of alterity at work during the Spanish conquest and evangelism of Mexico, we shall be able to focus on a number of its strands. For there were, on the Spanish side, those who invoked Aristotle's classicist view that 'others' are incapable of rational self-determination. And there were those who, without jettisoning the classicist assumptions of their culture, nevertheless opposed Aristotle with the biblical injunction to 'love your neighbour as yourself'. Moreover, as we shall see, the Aztec model of alterity may be said to resemble the classicist pattern. Complicating matters further, it is in this historical context that Todorov believes he can discern, along with much that is to be condemned, 'the first sketches of a future dialogue, the unformed embryos that herald our present'.[1] In Todorov's critique of the sixteenth-century encounter, therefore, we can also hear the voice of one committed to a dialogical model of alterity.

This portfolio of sixteenth-century views of the other, seen at least in part through Todorov's twentieth-century eyes, will also remind us of the moral problems entailed in 'the discovery that the self makes of the other'. We shall then be better prepared, in Chapter 10 and 11, to assess the potential contribution of the language of the dialogical theatre to the ethics of cross-cultural encounter. We begin with Aristotle.

ARISTOTLE AND THE AZTECS

The classical Greek tradition was frankly contemptuous of the external other, grouping all who were not members of the closed Hellenic community under the single-title of alterity and inferiority: bar-barian. Unable to speak Greek, the *barbaroi* were suspected of irra-tionality. Lacking a fully operational faculty of reason, they were considered incapable of controlling bestial passions, of acquiring virtue, or of forming the kind of civilized *polis* in which alone 'it was possible to be truly human'.[2]

The aristocratic Greek adult male was only marginally less con-temptuous of the internal other. Artisans, merchants and farmers were too busy earning their livelihood to cultivate the virtues neces-sary for full citizenship.[3] Within the home, Nature's decree that some should rule and others be ruled yielded, according to Aristotle's *Politics*, 'three pairs – master and slave, husband and wife, father and children'.[4] All possessed reason, but only the first in each pair pos-sessed the capacity for deliberation [βουλεύεσθαι] which was con-sidered essential to wise leadership. 'The deliberative faculty in the soul', Aristotle believed, 'is not present at all in a slave; in a female it is present but ineffective, in a child present but undeveloped'.[5] Slaves were the social and economic base of this internal hierarchy. Aristotle had no doubt that some human beings were 'slaves by nature', constitutionally incapable of deliberative choice or moral action and therefore needing to be under the care and command of a free Greek citizen who was able to do their thinking for them.[6]

Combining internal and external hierarchies of alterity, Aristotle accepted the view that 'non-Greek [βάρβαρος] and slave are by nature identical'.[7] As Anthony Pagden points out, it was 'this iden-tification of the natural slave with the barbarian'[8] that rendered the theory of natural slavery pertinent to the sixteenth-century dis-covery and conquest of America. For if the Indians could be viewed as barbarians, then, in Aristotle's words, it would be 'both just and expedient that they should serve as slaves'.[9]

The most articulate spokesman for this position in sixteenth-century Spain was Juan Ginés de Sepúlveda, a humanist scholar of considerable repute and a recognized authority on Aristotle. His Latin translation of Aristotle's *Politics* was for many years consid-ered the best available.[10] Sepúlveda incorporated Aristotle's theory of natural slavery into his own influential *Democrates secundus*. In-tending to justify the Spanish conquest of the New World, Sepúlveda began with the argument that the Indians were natural salves and must, for their own good, be made to submit to their natural lords (the Spanish).[11] Sepúlveda defended this view against the indignant Las Casas in a debate summoned by Carlos V at Valladolid in 1550.

The outcome of the debate was inconclusive. *Democrates secundus*, which had circulated widely in manuscript form, was denied publication. Those who supported the conquest, however, continued to cite Sepúlveda's views with approval. López de Gómara, for example, justified in this way the events described in his *La conquista de México* (1552). Were his readers to consult Sepúlveda, he assured them, they would 'be completely satisfied on this matter'.[12]

The Spanish were not the only ones to invoke Aristotle's theory of natural slavery. One of the more intriguing moments in the Tlaxcala *Conquest of Jerusalem* occurred when the defeated Sultan Cortés asked that his people be received in mercy as the Emperor's 'natural vassals'. No doubt the Indians had heard the language of natural slavery from their conquerors. They were inclined, however, to apply it differently.

Aristotle's concept would not have seemed odd to the Tlaxcalans. For, although it would be naive to suppose that Greek and Nahua views of social and ethnic difference were identical, the two cultures bore striking similarities in this matter. The Aztec nobility, the *pipiltin*, regarded themselves alone as 'fit to govern', and referred to the *macehualtin* or commoners metaphorically as burdens that must be borne or as helpless eggs that needed the protective cover of a mother bird.[13] Children too 'grew up in a hierarchical environment', in which age was privileged over youth and male was exalted over female. 'Woman' was an insult hurled at cowards.[14]

The Nahua attitude towards the external other may also be said to resemble the classicist model. Tlaxcalteca contempt for the weak and uncivilized Indians of the Caribbean was evident in *The Conquest of Jerusalem*. More broadly, Todorov draws attention to the apparently universal tendency, from which the Indians of central Mexico were not exempt, to regard those whose language one cannot understand as barbaric. 'The Aztecs themselves call the people south of Vera Cruz *nonoualca*, "mutes", and those who do not speak Náhuatl they call *tenime*, "barbarians", or *popoloca*, "savages" '. Todorov also quotes from Durán the argument advanced about 1454 by the powerful Aztec general Tlacaelel that prisoners should not be taken for sacrifice from distant tribes because 'our god does not like the flesh of those barbarous peoples. They are yellowish, hard, tasteless bread in his mouth. They are savages [*bárbaros*] and speak strange tongues'.[15]

Nor was such a judgement reserved only for distant Indians. When Montezuma's lordly ambassadors brought gifts of gold and quetzal feathers to Cortés as he first approached Tenochtitlán, Span-

ish greed prompted Aztec disdain. 'The Spaniards', according to
the native sources, 'picked up the gold and fingered it like monkeys
. . . ; they hungered like pigs for that gold'. Bestial similes proving
inadequate, the account reaches for the greater insult. The Spaniards, it adds, 'were like one who speaks a barbarous tongue
[*tlapopoloca*]: everything they said was in a barbarous tongue'.[16]

THE NEIGHBOUR AND THE SELF

Christianity's entry into Mexico might have been expected to offer a
radical alternative to 'classicist' Nahua society. For Christianity can
be viewed, in part, as a reaction against the racial, economic and
sexual divisions of the classical world. In Christ all such divisions
were declared of no account: 'There is neither Jew nor Greek, there
is neither slave nor free, there is neither male nor female, for you are
all one in Christ Jesus' (Galatians 3: 28). The universal church replaced the local *polis* as the community within which true humanity
was to be found. 'You have put on the new humanity [νέος
ἄνθρωπος]', the Colossians were told; 'here there cannot be Greek
and Jew, circumcised and uncircumcised, barbarian [βάρβαρος],
Scythian, slave, free man, but Christ is all, and in all' (Colossians
3: 9–11). Furthermore, the church, unlike the Greek *polis*, was in
theory an open community: every human being was invited to join.
In practice, however, the structure of Spanish society, like that of so
much of Christendom, owed more to the hierarchical instincts of
Aristotle than it did to the egalitarian impulse of the New Testament.
Aztec and conquistador were, in this respect, kindred spirits. Moreover, there remained outside the church, by choice or ignorance, the
infidel and the pagan. While the biblical narrative may be said to
endorse pluriformity within the Christian community, its attitude
towards the external other is arguably more ambivalent.

On the one hand, the classic texts of the Christian faith claim that
love of the other who is the Christian's neighbour is no less important than love of God (Mark 12: 28–31; Leviticus 19: 17–18). Some
have wanted to restrict this love to neighbours of their own kind.
But the Jesus of the gospels forbids any such limitation, insisting, in
the Gospel of Matthew, that the injunction to love one's neighbour
does not carry with it license to hate one's enemy (Matthew 5: 44–5),

and, in the Parable of the Good Samaritan, that the Jew's neighbour was to be found not only within his own cultural and religious tradition but also in the other whom his tradition regarded as alien (Luke 10: 25–37). The Samaritan, Jesus taught, must be welcomed as a neighbour by the Jew. The Spaniard, insisted the friars, must recognize a neighbour in the Indian.

On this matter the friars were adamant. Firing the first salvo against exploitation in the New World, the Dominican Anton Montesino demanded of his congregation in Hispaniola in 1511, 'Aren't [the Indians] human beings? Have they no rational souls? Aren't you obliged to love them as you love yourselves?'[17] Sahagún began his encyclopedic *Historia general de las cosas de Nueva España* with the certainty that 'these people are our brothers, proceeding from Adam's stock even as we ourselves; they are our neighbours whom we must love as ourselves'.[18] Las Casas reminded his hearers in Valladolid in 1550 that 'we are commanded by divine law to love our neighbour as ourselves. . . . This we owe to all men. Nobody is excepted'. For all that the Indians may appear 'completely barbaric, they are nevertheless created in God's image . . . [and] redeemed by Christ's most precious blood. . . . Good-bye, Aristotle!' he exulted. 'From Christ, the eternal truth, we have the command "You must love your neighbour as yourself" '.[19]

But as Enrique Dussel has pointed out in his *History of the Church in Latin America*, to love another as oneself may mask a denial of the alterity of the one loved. 'Since the time of Aristotle', he writes, 'the pedagogy of domination has insisted that parents "love their children as themselves" ', suppressing alterity in the replication of parental values:

> The cultural conquest of other peoples has likewise been represented as the extension of 'the Self'. The conqueror or the pedagogical dominator controls by force of arms, and then by violence imposes upon another human being (such as the Indian, the African, the Asian, the masses, the worker, or the defenceless) the conqueror's civilization, religion, and deified cultural system in its ideological Totality.

To establish 'dominion over another by controlling his or her analytical horizon'[20] is to love another only in so far as he or she becomes like oneself.

Thus the missionary friars, who insisted on the Christians' obligation to love their Indian neighbours, also insisted that evangelism
was a necessary expression of such love. Las Casas repudiated physical violence not only out of love for his neighbour but also in the
conviction that peaceful persuasion was 'the one way to draw all
peoples to the true religion'. 'Yet is there not already a violence',
Todorov asks, 'in the conviction that one possesses the truth oneself,
whereas this is not the case for others, and that one must furthermore impose that truth on those others?'[21] One could argue that
'impose' is a loaded word, connoting a violence that Las Casas's
more neutral 'draw' does not intend. But evangelism has often been
justified in terms of universal authority and international obedience:
since 'all authority in heaven and on earth has been given' to the
risen Christ, his followers are to 'make disciples of all nations'
(Matthew 28: 18–20). To the friars, obedience to this command was
an expression of love towards their Indian neighbours. This may
have been the view, in retrospect, of many who embraced the gospel.
But evangelism can also appear to preclude love for the neighbour
in her or his otherness and to demand instead that the neighbour
become as oneself in order to be loved.

The sixteenth-century appropriation of Aristotelian and Christian
views of the other strikes Todorov as being deeply egocentric.
Values in general, he observes, were extrapolated from the values of
the self; others were considered to be like and equal to oneself, or
different and lacking. Todorov writes, for example, of Columbus:

> Either he conceives the Indians (though without using these words)
> as human beings altogether, having the same rights as himself;
> but then he sees them not only as equals but also as identical, and
> this behavior leads to assimilationism, the projection of his own
> values on others. Or else he starts from the difference, but the
> latter is immediately translated into terms of superiority and in-
> feriority (in his case, obviously, it is the Indians who are inferior).
> What is denied is the existence of a human substance truly other,
> something capable of being not merely an imperfect state of one-
> self. These two elementary figures of the experience of alterity are
> both grounded in egocentrism, in the identification of our own
> values with values in general, of our *I* with the universe – in the
> conviction that the world is one.[22]

As Todorov sees it, both the assumption of identity and that of superiority preclude true dialogue. What is needed is an acknowledgement of difference and equality, a willingness to grant that one's own world and that of the other may be differentiated by point of view and not by degree of conformity to a single world 'out there'.

Of this kind of modern sophistication Columbus was not capable. Initially he assimilates the Indians as equals into his own world, claiming to have found them already 'predisposed to Christianity' and possessed of 'Christian virtues'. As Todorov remarks, this image depends on 'the suppression of every feature of the Indians that contradicts it'. But when the Indians prove recalcitrant in the matter of supplying gold and other material goods necessary to support spiritual expansion, Columbus switches to the model of superiority. He knows best, and the Indians must be forced to co-operate. 'Thus, by gradual stages', Todorov observes, 'Columbus will shift from assimilationism . . . to an ideology of enslavement'. The other must be incorporated into the world of the colonist either as a replica or a slave.[23] It would not perhaps be simplifying matters too much to suggest that it is his Christianity that inclines him to seek replicas and his Aristotelian heritage that prompts him to settle for slaves.

DE INDIS ET DE JURE BELLI

We could cite others who, like Sepúlveda and Columbus, openly used the language of Aristotle and Christianity to justify the colonization of the New World. But we can take a step closer to Todorov's discovery of 'the first sketches of a future dialogue' if we turn instead to the work of Francisco de Vitoria. For Vitoria's *De Indis et De Jure Belli*[24] is widely admired as a model of humane and judicious reasoning, an example of genuine Spanish sympathy for the plight of the Amerindian other. Nevertheless, it is among the works whose fundamental morality Todorov calls into question. An understanding of Todorov's negative judgement on Vitoria will bring into clearer focus the character of the incipient dialogue he discerns elsewhere.

A second reason for attending to *De Indis et De Jure Belli* in this study stems from a coincidence of dates and themes. Although Vitoria's material may have been prepared as early as 1532, it was first made public in a series of lectures at the University of

Salamanca in June 1539. Coincidentally, *The Conquest of Jerusalem* was performed in Tlaxcala in the same month.[25] The play, at least in its European reading, assumes the justice of a Christian reconquest of Turkish-occupied Jerusalem; and, at least in its Mexican reading, calls into question the justice of the Spanish conquest of Mexico. Vitoria addresses the latter concern, but he does so in an academic rather than a dramatic mode. Different forms generate different effects. For all the sympathy that Vitoria may have for the Indian position, his choice of medium excludes the Indian voice. In the lectures we hear a Spanish voice expressing Spanish thoughts about the plight of the absent Indian other. In the play we hear Indian and Spanish voices speaking alongside one another. The drama is dialogic; the lectures are, quite literally, univocal.

In his published text, Vitoria begins by asking 'whether the aborigines in question were true owners in both private and public law before the arrival of the Spaniards'. He lists four grounds on which the Indians had been supposed to lack any claim to legitimate ownership – namely, 'that they were sinners or were unbelievers or were witless or irrational'.[26] That the Indians were 'in mortal sin' and 'unbelief' he does not dispute but argues, with ample quotation from scripture and church fathers, that they cannot therefore be 'barred from being true owners', and that 'such sin [does not] entitle Christians to seize their goods and lands'. He concedes that lack of reason, as in the case of animals, precludes ownership, and that 'unsoundness of mind', in the case of human beings, may jeopardize ownership without suspending all rights. But these strictures do not apply to the Indians, for 'they are not of unsound mind, but have, according to their kind, the use of reason'. Vitoria concludes, therefore,

> that the aborigines undoubtedly had true dominion in both public and private matters, just like Christians, and that neither their princes nor private persons could be despoiled of their property on the ground of their not being true owners.[27]

The importance of Vitoria's defence of Indian ownership is, of course, that just cause or 'title' must now be demonstrated if the Indians' natural legal ownership is to be overridden. Vitoria rejects all titles based on 'the right of discovery', the refusal of the Indians to 'accept the faith of Christ', 'the sins of these Indians aborigines', the supposed 'voluntary choice' of the Indian populace to submit to

Spanish authority or the claim of 'special grant from God'. All of these, Vitoria asserts, are 'false and inadequate titles'. To speak of the 'discovery' of occupied lands or of the 'choice' of the Indians to submit to coercion is, he insists, to misrepresent the facts. To 'punish' the Indians' rejection of the gospel or their continuing 'sins' is to assume an unwarranted authority over the spiritual life of unbelievers. And to see in God's delivery of Canaan to the Israelites proof that he has delivered the New World to Spain is to misread scriptural precedent.[28]

But the title most cherished by Spaniards was that embodied in the *Requerimiento*, a startlingly monological document to which we have already referred in our discussion of Dryden's *The Indian Emperour*. Drafted in 1513, with the intention that it be read to Indians before hostilities could be legally launched, the *Requerimiento* announced the jurisdiction of the Pope over the whole earth and his 'donation' of the New World to the King and Queen of Spain. The Indians were therefore 'required', after proper deliberation, to yield voluntary submission to the Spanish crown and to listen attentively to the preaching of the 'religious fathers'. Should they do so, they would be left in all other respects 'free without servitude'. Should they refuse, the Spanish forces would press their claim by warfare.[29]

Not only did the *Requerimiento* naively presume ideal conditions, under which Indians who had never before seen Europeans would voluntarily and peacefully assemble to hear an armed landing party read to them, but it also overlooked the obvious problem of translation from Spanish into the unknown tongue of the native. Moreover, it displays, as Todorov is quick to point out, the most blatant form of ethnocentric bias. The Spaniards never question their own innate superiority to the Indians, allowing the Indians to choose 'only between two positions of inferiority: either they submit of their own accord and become serfs; or else they will be subjugated by force and reduced to slavery'.[30]

Vitoria challenges the *Requerimiento* by taking issue with the 'vehemently asserted' dogma of papal donation. Neither Holy Roman Emperor nor Pope, he writes, may be considered 'civil or temporal lord of the whole world'. Papal authority is spiritual alone, and extends neither to civil matters nor, 'as even our opponents admit', to unbelievers. So the refusal of the Indians to recognize papal claims of lordship or grants of Spanish sovereignty 'furnishes no ground for making war on them and seizing their property'.[31]

Having disposed, however, of the false claims, Vitoria turns his attention to 'the lawful and adequate titles whereby the Indians might have come under the sway of the Spaniards'.[32] The word 'might' is important. Vitoria is not justifying the historical conquest. Rather he is claiming that, had the Spaniards approached the Indians in a different fashion, there might have ensued just occasion for war, from which just conquest could have followed. It is possible, therefore, that future conquests could be just, should they arise from lawful title.

Vitoria bases his first such title on the international right to travel and trade. Spaniards, so long as they behave well, must be allowed to travel in other lands and to trade with the inhabitants. Should the Indians of the New World obstruct this right, the Spanish may protect it. Likewise, 'Christians have a right to preach and declare the Gospel in barbarian lands' and may, if necessary, defend that right with force. In either case, 'in favor of those who are oppressed and suffer wrong [Spanish merchants and missionaries impeded in their task], the Spaniards can make war' and 'may enforce against [the Indians] all the rights of war, despoiling them of their goods [and] reducing them to captivity'.[33] Although the rights of trade and evangelism may now seem outmoded, it is worth remembering that as recently as 1900–1 the Boxer rebellion in China was crushed on just such grounds. And the free flow of oil from the Middle East, when it can be linked in the popular mind to 'the gospel of democracy and freedom',[34] is still considered grounds for protective military intervention.

A third and a fourth title follow from the freedom to propagate Christianity. Should any of the native converts to Christianity be forced by their princes to return to idolatry, the Spaniards may, if 'other methods fail', depose those rulers by force of arms. Similarly, if a large part of the Indians were converted to Christianity, the Pope might, 'in the interests of the faith', depose their unbelieving rulers and 'give them a Christian sovereign'.

A more persuasive cause to modern ears is that which depends on the responsibility to protect the innocent. If the Indians cannot be persuaded peacefully to abstain from 'the sacrifice of innocent people for cannibalistic purposes', then they may justly be persuaded by war. A 'true and voluntary choice' on the part of the Indians, 'both rulers and ruled', to submit to 'the prudent administration and humanity of the Spaniards' would also confer lawful title on the Spaniards. So would victory in a war waged in defence of Indian 'allies and friends'. Finally, but with considerable hesitation, Vitoria concedes that lawful title could stem from the need of the aborigines, in their cultural infancy, for such mature administration as could be provided by the Spanish crown.[35]

Certainly, Vitoria's argument represents a considerable advance on the *Requerimiento*. 'But', Todorov points out, 'the more or less weakened traces of [the *Requerimiento*'s] spirit are to be noted even' in Vitoria. Although some of Vitoria's just titles are based on reciprocity and therefore, in theory at least, apply equally to Indian and Spaniard, this is not the case in practice. The Indians can exercise their right of trade with the Spaniards in the New World, but Vitoria does not conceive of them travelling to Spain for that purpose. And, when it comes to 'the circulation of ideas',

> Vitoria thinks only of the Spaniards' freedom to preach the Gospels [*sic*] to the Indians, and never of the Indians' freedom to propagate the *Popul Vuh* in Spain, since Christian 'salvation' is an absolute value for him.[36]

The 'natural right to society and communication',[37] on which Vitoria bases much of his argument, is thus defined in practice as the right of the Spaniard to speak and of the Indian to listen.

Even the defence of the innocent from the tyranny of human sacrifice and cannibalism strikes Todorov as ethnocentric. For only the Spaniards may enforce this rule, and it is they who have decided, for example, 'that human sacrifice is the consequence of tyranny, but massacre is not'. The same charge can be made yet more forcibly against the title based on cultural and administrative 'guardianship': 'even admitting that one is to impose "the good" on others, who, once again, decides what is barbarity or savagery and what is civilization?' Todorov concludes, therefore, that the received view of Vitoria's contribution to just war theory is in need of correction:

> We are accustomed to seeing Vitoria as a defender of the Indians; but if we question, not the subject's intentions, but the impact of his discourse, it is clear that his role is quite different: under cover of an international law based on reciprocity, he in reality supplies a legal basis to the wars of colonization which had hitherto had none (none which, in any case, might withstand serious consideration).[38]

There is a need for care here, especially with the charge that the defence of the innocent against tyranny is necessarily ethnocentric. Humanitarian intervention, however it may in reality be mixed with less-noble motives, is still widely accepted as a just cause for war. One may recognize the innate perils of unilateral moral judgement and, in particular, the mixed motives of the conquistadors in suppressing human sacrifice in Mexico, or of the allied forces in protecting 'democracy' in Kuwait. But it must be remembered that it was such a judgement (that the slaughter of ethnic groups and political dissidents in Nazi gas chambers was wrong and not a legitimate cultural variant) that occasioned the Second World War. It is hard to imagine Todorov's critique of racial bias being freely published in Western Europe had that decision not been made.

With this caveat in place, however, we may grant Todorov's point that Vitoria's plea for justice remains ethnocentric. Prior justifications for the conquest and evangelism of the New World are rejected on the basis of natural and Christian law. But they are replaced with principles designed to protect the Christians' right to profit financially from and to impose ideologically on all whom the Christians consider to be 'barbarians'. The opinion of the Indians is neither asked nor heard.

SAHAGÚN AND DURÁN

The voice of the Indian was, however, transcribed in the latter half of the sixteenth-century in the work of the Franciscan Bernardino de Sahagún and the younger Dominican Diego Durán. Accidental ethnographers, concerned to document Indian beliefs and practices in order to uproot all traces of idolatry, they 'heralded, without fully achieving', Todorov believes, 'the dialogue of cultures that characterizes our own age'.[39]

The declared motive of both Sahagún and Durán was unashamedly Christian and evangelistic. What Todorov writes of the one could, with little modification, be said of the other. 'Durán', he comments, 'links the two following inferences: to impose the Christian religion, all trace of the pagan one must be uprooted; to eliminate paganism successfully, it must first of all be known thoroughly'.[40] The ultimate goal may have been the eradication of the other's religion. But the intermediate goal, that of first knowing the other thoroughly, led necessarily, in Todorov's view, to a form of dialogue.

For Sahagún, this dialogue began on his arrival in Mexico in 1529, as it had for many of his Franciscan predecessors, with learning the Náhuatl language. 'This fact', Todorov comments, 'is in itself already significant: usually it is the conquered who learns the conqueror's language'. The Spanish conquistadors, for example, had made no effort to learn the native tongues, but had depended on Indian interpreters who mastered Spanish. To learn the language of the conquered was at once to relativize the categories of 'civilized' and 'barbarian' (based since the Greeks as much on linguistic as on ethnic difference), and to step, however tentatively, into the world constructed by the other's language. Even if their purpose was 'only to identify the other with [themselves]' by bringing the Indian into the Christian fold, the missionaries began, Todorov remarks, 'by identifying [themselves], at least in part, with the other'.[41]

Sahagún is best known for his *Historia general de las cosas de Nueva España*, 'a priceless work',[42] providing, in Todorov's words, 'an inestimable encyclopedia of the spiritual and material life of the Aztecs before the conquest'.[43] The value of Sahagún's work derives not only from the wealth of material he recorded but also from the variety of independent voices present in his text. Munro Edmonson explains:

> Perhaps the most startling innovation in Sahagún's mode of procedure was his rigorous and systematic use of informants. The result is the inclusion in the work of a wide range of materials corresponding to different interests and purposes, collected in different ways, and expressed in different styles. Parts of the text are made up of preconquest Náhuatl rhetoric – formal orations directly recorded from the still extant oral tradition. Other parts are clearly shaped by more or less explicit questionnaires designed to elicit specific information. Some passages are just as clearly spontaneous elaborations by informants, clarifying particular points. Yet others reflect an explicit concern with collecting and preserving Náhuatl vocabulary. And finally there are passages of commentary and interpretation added by Sahagún himself.[44]

What is striking, however, is the care taken by Sahagún to separate his own voice from that of his informants. Rather than incorporate the words of the Nahua elders into a discourse of his own, in the manner of most historians, Sahagún preserves them in a separate Náhuatl text, to which he then adds his own loose translation, commentary and glosses in Spanish. Sahagún, as Todorov puts it, 'chooses the path of total fidelity' to the other's discourse.

But, Todorov adds, 'total fidelity does not . . . signify total authenticity'.[45] It is Sahagún who conceives the design of the whole according to 'a scholastic and medieval hierarchy'[46] of topics, thereby suppressing any difference that might have surfaced had his informants been free to organize their material according to an Aztec conceptual framework. Likewise, it is Sahagún who frames the specific questions, inadvertently curtailing discussion in areas where 'the gap of understanding between questionnaire and informants' was too great. López Austin suggests, for example, that Sahagún 'asked about the nature of the sky with totally Occidental expectations', thereby reducing the Nahua elders to bewilderment in the face of 'questions they considered ingenuous in their lack of knowledge'.[47] Finally, it is Sahagún who chooses the European medium of linear writing for his book, thereby introducing a form of translation even into the Náhuatl text. For the Nahua elders provided their information initially in the form of painted codices, that being, Sahagún notes, 'the writing they employed in ancient times'.[48] Their oral commentary on these codices was then transcribed, using the Latin alphabet, by Indians trained in this skill in mission schools.

If the purity of the Indian voice is compromised even in the Náhuatl text, it is of course further modified in the Spanish translation. But neither is the voice of the translator his own. It is the other's words which he translates. At times, too, he faces a choice between fidelity to the Indian voice and loyalty to his own Christian convictions. Should he, for example, translate the Aztec term for deity as 'gods' or 'devils', and should he call those who officiate at Aztec sacrifices 'priests' or 'necromancers'? The first term legitimates, the second disputes the Indian point of view. Language does not offer him a neutral word. Sahagún alternates terms, effectively allowing both points of view to be heard.[49]

It may have been Sahagún's intention to juxtapose voices, contrasting the 'idolatry' of the Aztec view with the 'truth' of the Christian faith, the latter represented by his own commentary and by his lengthy quotation from the Bible.[50] But Todorov finds instead in the *Historia* an 'interpenetration of the two voices', and it is this that prompts him to pronounce Sahagún's book not merely 'the addition of two monologues' but 'the first sketches of a future dialogue'.

De Indis et De Jure Belli is the product of one voice, albeit one that contemplates the other with a measure of sympathy. Sahagún's work was intended to introduce a second voice but to maintain a strict delineation between the voice of the self and that of the other. In Todorov's view, however, Sahagún was unable to keep the two voices apart. Like the *Conquest of Jerusalem* or the *danza de los santiagos*, Sahagún's work is, he believes, 'the product of the interaction of two voices, two cultures, two points of view'.[51]

This interpretation is even more evident in the case of Durán. Arriving in Mexico as a young child with his parents, he soon spoke Náhuatl as fluently as he did Spanish, and in time acquired 'an understanding of Indian culture from within unequaled in the sixteenth-century'.[52] His studies of Aztec religion and history are preserved in his *Historia de las indias de Nueva España y islas de la tierra firme*. No less determined than Sahagún to eradicate all traces of paganism by a thorough understanding of all its forms, he is also committed, like Sahagún, to a textual preservation of the Indian voice. Although he writes in Spanish, Durán intends to separate his own point of view from that of the Náhuatl codices that provide much of his source material. 'I must tell the truth according to the stories and traditions of the Indians', he writes. Todorov comments, 'This is obviously something different from telling the mere truth. . . . [Durán's] goal is not truth, for which he himself would be responsible, but fidelity to a different voice'.[53]

But Durán's own voice is not single. He is at once an evangelist and an advocate for the Indians in the face of Spanish cruelty. He opposes pagan religion, and he admires prehispanic social organization. He speaks of preserving the memory of Aztec heroes. 'Durán's point of view', Todorov observes, is 'both Indian and Christian'. This internal dialogue between points of view is evident in Durán's evaluation of the conquest itself. 'Although, for the care of their souls', he writes, '[the year of the conquest] was a happy and fortunate one, on account of the benefit that flowed and continues to flow from their receiving our Faith, when have the Indians ever experienced more suffering than they did that year?' Durán, comments Todorov, is 'a divided being: a Christian converted to "Indianism" who converts the Indians to Christianity'.[54]

We are reminded of the tension between *indigenismo* and *catolicidad* in the sixteenth-century missionary theatre and in the modern folk plays that we discussed in Part Two. This tension is characteristically Mexican: it is not present in the uniformly Spanish voice of Vitoria, nor is it present in prehispanic codices and architecture. Todorov's conclusion, therefore, is that, 'rather than being either Aztec or Spanish, Durán's history is one of the first *Mexican* texts, in the new sense of the word, that is "hybrid" '.[55] It is 'a voice whose multiplicity is internal to it'.[56]

In this respect, the work of Durán and the performances of the Franciscan missionary theatre serve to illuminate one another. Both, at first sight, seem to be enlisting Indian help (actors or informants) in the propagation of an exclusively Christian point of view. Both, on closer examination, reveal an Indian voice that speaks independently of its Spanish interlocutor. Both, finally, emerge as prototypically Mexican works, in which the internal dialogue is not between distinct voices from the Old World and the New but between voices formed in the New World: on the one hand, that of the Indian who has embraced Christianity without renouncing his *indigenismo*, and, on the other hand, that of the Christian missionary who has embraced the Indian without renouncing his own *catolicidad*.

The missionary theatre may even surpass the work of Durán and Sahagún in one respect. The latter remained a matter of private conversation and lost manuscripts until they were finally published in the nineteenth-century.[57] The Franciscan theatre, by contrast, was a matter of contemporary public spectacle. When the question of just conquest was raised in public discourse or debate of the time, as it was by Vitoria and by Las Casas and Sepúlveda, the Indian was absent. When the Indian voice was transcribed, as it was by Durán and Sahagún, it remained unpublished. But in *The Conquest of Rhodes* and *The Conquest of Jerusalem*, behind the dual mask of theatrical performance and disguised reconciliations, Indian – and African – voices found a means of expressing themselves publicly and immediately on a matter of vital moral concern.

Nevertheless, it is probably fair to say that whatever dialogue between cultures took place in Mexico in the second quarter of the sixteenth-century was, as Todorov puts it, a matter of 'uncontrolled slippage'. The plurality of simultaneous voices discernible at times in the work of Sahagún and Durán, and in the indigenous performances of missionary drama, did not stem from a commitment on the part of the friars to intercultural dialogue. Rather, it was, in Todorov's phrase, 'fortuitous and unconscious',[58] a happy consequence of formal choices that offset the classicist assumptions of the Spanish invaders.

Todorov, however, writes within a tradition that consciously aspires to a dialogical mode of encounter and communication. In the present century, too, the church has begun to think of its relationships with multiple cultures and with 'neighbours of other faiths' in dialogical terms.[59] It is to this way of thinking, enriched by the language of the theatre, that we now turn.

10
Performing the Scriptures

This book began with literary theory. Drama, I suggested, is a dialogical genre and theatre is a dialogical medium. An examination of plays by Dryden and 'Zárate' and of a scenario by Artaud advanced my argument. I chose these works not because they stand out from other dramatic literature as paragons of dialogism but because they share a common historical referent: the conquest of Mexico. For the discovery and conquest of America was, in Todorov's words, 'the most astonishing encounter of our history', a unique opportunity for dialogue between worlds largely squandered through the Spanish failure to conceptualize an otherness both equal and different. But even in this difficult historical context theatre proved to be a dialogical medium. Indigenous dramatizations of the theme of conquest in Mexico, whether under the auspices of the early Franciscan missionaries or as part of a still-vital folk tradition, have proved to be fruitful vehicles for what Bakhtin would call 'communication between simultaneous differences'. The task now before me is to apply what I have learned of the dialogical theatre to the questions raised by Todorov concerning the ethics of cross-cultural encounter.

One of those questions has to do with what Todorov calls 'the Christianization of the Mexicans'.[1] The church's conviction that it is called of God to convert others to the Christian faith has both prompted and complicated cross-cultural encounters for nearly two millennia. The outworking of this conviction in sixteenth-century Mexico provided Todorov with an exemplary instance of the moral problems raised by 'the export of any ideology or technology'.[2] The recent inclination of the church to define its mission in dialogical terms provides me with a similar opportunity. Unable to 'speak of everything all at once', I shall focus the last part of my book on the exemplary question of Christian foreign missions.

As Todorov is well aware, however, political questions also lurk beneath the surface of any discussion of cross-cultural encounter. The cross-cultural mission of the church does not take place in a political vacuum, and one of the difficulties facing the missionary church then as now is that of confusing the gospel with the particular political and social structures in which it has historically been embedded.

The reverse is also true: secular expansion is often accompanied by religious rhetoric. The Aztecs and the conquistadors are not the only ones to have bolstered the quest for empire with the discourse of religion. A recent exhibition at the National Museum of American Art in Washington, D.C. documented the way in which nineteenth-century American artists evoked missionary ideals to justify western expansion. The director of the museum, Elizabeth Broun, commented:

> The artists who portrayed westward expansion would have us believe that homesteaders went west not only for 160 acres to farm but for the larger purposes of taming the wilderness, Christianizing the savages, or spreading the gospel of democracy and freedom. . . . Artists skated over the low points of the historical record . . . with a consoling rhetoric of grand purpose.[3]

One of the most striking paintings in the exhibition was Emmanuel Leutze's *The Storming of the Teocalli by Cortez and his Troops* (1848), a detailed 'historical' depiction of Spanish forces driving the Aztecs from their temple in Tenochtitlán. According to William Truettner, this painting was hailed by contemporary critics as a celebration of 'the decisive death-grapple of the savage and civilized man' not only in sixteenth-century Mexico but also on the nineteenth-century western frontier. 'Contemporary viewers', Truettner writes, 'must have had little trouble shifting the scene from the Aztecs to the Comanche, Sioux, Blackfoot, and other western tribes considered especially fierce adversaries of white encroachment'. Setting the scene of the painting on a pagan temple where, to the left of the clash of warriors, a child is being ritually disembowelled by an Aztec priest and, to the right, a Christian priest is offering the gospel to a dying Indian, provides the religious justification for such encroachment.[4]

Secular foreign policy is still arguably conducted with missionary zeal. Albert Blaustein, for example, has recently written with admiration of 'the American penchant for constitutional proselytizing'.[5] 'The framers of the American Constitution', he explains, 'believed that they were creating a new Eden for all of humanity and spent much of their efforts in sending this message. Americans of succeeding generations have continued this role as constitutional missionaries'.[6] More broadly, and more critically, John Howard Yoder notes the survival, in different guise, of the rhetoric of holy war. 'When appeal is made', he writes, 'to transcendent ideological causes not subject to political measurement, like the defense of "the free world" or the liberation of "the working class", it is in fact the holy-war concept that is still at work'.[7] Recent events in the Middle East have only served to confirm the religious dimension of modern warfare. My focus, therefore, on the form of cross-cultural encounter generated by Christian evangelism should not inhibit the application of the theatrical paradigm to other aspects of human community and conflict.

In the present chapter I shall begin to bring the language of the dialogical theatre to bear on the ethics of cross-cultural evangelism by looking at Nicholas Lash's essay 'Performing the Scriptures'.[8] I shall glance, too, at what I take to be the dialogical impulse of the biblical narrative itself and at the church's historical struggle to come to terms with this impulse. Finally, I shall draw attention to a New Testament parable which may challenge traditional notions of the role of the 'chosen people' in cross-cultural encounter.

PLAYING BEETHOVEN AND THE BIBLE

Lash begins his essay with the suggestion that 'different kinds of text call for different kinds of reading'. Although the same text may properly be used in various ways, there are limitations ('It would be silly to sing railway timetables, rather than to use them to catch trains') and there are priorities. Those 'black marks on white paper', for example, 'which are recognizable as the score of one of Beethoven's late string quartets', may be interpreted by scholars intent on establishing a definitive score or on offering new insight into the 'meaning' of the piece; or they may be performed by 'four people playing the quartet'. Lash argues for the primacy of the latter 'strategy of use'. He readily acknowledges the value of the part played by 'the academics . . . in contributing to the quality and appreciation of the performance'. Their role is 'indispensable'. But it is also 'subordinate': 'The fundamental form of the interpretation of Beethoven consists in the performance of his texts'.

So it is, Lash continues, with a dramatic text. *King Lear*, for example, was written to be performed by a 'company of actors and an audience'. The 'readings' of *King Lear* generated by 'textual critics, historians of Elizabethan drama, literary critics and philosophers' are 'indispensable but subordinate' to the 'fundamental form of [its] interpretation' in performance. Lash concludes, therefore, 'that there are at least some texts that only begin to deliver their meaning in so far as they are "brought into play" through interpretative performance'.

The texts that together constitute the New Testament are, Lash believes, of this kind:

> Not all the texts of the New Testament are stories but, taken together, they 'tell the story' of Jesus and the first Christian communities. I want to suggest, first, that, although the texts of the New Testament may be read, and read with profit, by anyone interested in Western cultures and concerned for the human predicament, the fundamental form of the *Christian* interpretation of scripture is the life, activity and organization of the believing community. Secondly, that Christian practice, as interpretative action, consists in the *performance* of texts which are construed as 'rendering', bearing witness to, one whose words and deeds, discourse and suffering, 'rendered' the truth of God in human history.

The 'performative interpretation' of the biblical text by the Christian community 'needs (just as much as does the interpretation of Beethoven and Shakespeare) the services of scholarship and critical reflection'. But, Lash suggests, the New Testament is first and foremost an account of past performance and a score for the future life of the church. The 'fundamental form' of its Christian interpretation is its performance.

From this analogy with musical score and dramatic script, Lash draws two further conclusions. First, performing the scriptures is a full-time, communal affair. 'It takes two to tango and rather more to perform *King Lear*', but the participants properly resume their everyday identities and activities once the performance is over. It is not so with the scriptures. Some texts, among which, Lash suggests, the scriptures are to be included, call for interpretative performance in the ongoing 'social existence of an entire human community'. An 'isolated individual' can no more perform such texts than he or she can perform a Beethoven quartet or a Shakespearean tragedy. Moreover, the Christian's part in the 'collaborative enterprise' of enacting the scriptures is not an intermittent exercise. Although the Christian life properly includes both relaxation and solitude, one does not cease to be a Christian at such moments in the way that an actress sloughs off the role of Cordelia or Goneril on leaving the theatre.

Lash offers another analogy, from the political arena, to illustrate the kind of ongoing, communal performance he has in mind:

> The fundamental form of the political interpretation of the American Constitution is the life, activity and organization of American society. That society exists (not without change, conflict and confusion) as the *enactment* of its Constitution. Similarly, we might say that the scriptures are the 'constitution' of the church.

This leads Lash to a second conclusion. The analogy of performance, whether it be of an artistic or a political document, suggests the legitimacy of wide variation in the performative interpretation of scripture by different companies of Christians. We have remarked already on the multiplicity of performances engendered by the single text of *The Tempest*. Lash is well aware of this phenomenon of performance. 'Each new performance of Beethoven or Shakespeare', he writes, 'is a new event in the history of the meaning of the text. There is no such thing as an interpretation that is "final" and "definitive" in the sense of bringing that history to an end'. So it is, he suggests, with the performance of a political document:

> Even in the case of societies that have a written constitution, the interpretation of that constitution is an unending enterprise. Times change, circumstances change. The 'meaning' of the constitution is never definitively 'captured'; it is, ever and again, sought and constructed.

And so it is, Lash concludes, with the performance of the biblical text.

I want now to draw three further conclusions from Lash's analogy. The first has to do with the presence of an audience. The performance of the scriptures by the Christian community, if it is to be more than a rehearsal or 'workshop' closed to outsiders, will be before an audience made up, at least in part, of others not professing the Christian faith. For most Christians, those others are members of the Christians's own national or ethnic community and of the same social class. In some situations, however, members of the Christian community will find themselves performing the biblical text before an audience made up almost entirely of what Todorov calls 'the exterior and remote other'.

Moreover, if we are to take seriously the classic texts and historic practices of the church, the Christian community is not simply engaged in 'putting on a show'. The church invites its audience to join in the performance. Or, to put it another way, the Christian company offers the biblical text for performance by others. There is, however, an important difference between these two ways of phrasing the analogy. To invite an audience to join in a performance, even in the most experimental theatrical milieu, is to require the audience to conform to the pattern of the performance in progress. An audience that insisted on taking control of the performance, jettisoning cast, costume and set, and acting the script in its own way would be considered disruptive, not participatory. To offer a text for performance, on the other hand, is to allow for the possibility of significant difference in interpretation and mode of performance.

To 'perform the scriptures', therefore, necessarily involves a decision, conscious or otherwise, as to the intended effect of that performance on its audience. Is the goal of the performance to swell the ranks of the cast by incorporating as many members of the audience as possible into a single, ongoing performance? Or is it, by interpreting text in performance, to offer that same text for interpretative performance by others? The two goals may be partially reconciled by conceiving all performances of the same text to constitute a single community of diverse performances bound together not by uniformity of interpretation but by allegiance to a common text and to the story told by that text. But at the moment of encounter the question remains as to whether the text is being offered for performance by the other or whether the attempt is being made to impose both text and, as far as possible, definitive performance of that text on the other. The former strategy risks challenge to one's own mode of seeing and doing the text or, from a positive point of view, invites fresh insight into the text and into one's own performance of it. The latter strategy is a mode of colonization, risking violent resistance but making possible the suppression and even in certain circumstances, the eradication of an alien and arguably dangerous point of view. I shall argue, in the pages that follow, that the nature of the biblical script, like its dramatic counterpart, is to resist the imposition of uniform performance.

A second conclusion that I want to draw from Lash's analogy of performative interpretation has to do with reciprocity. Even the model of offering text for performance by the other entails only limited reciprocity. It is still a matter of performing and offering for performance 'our' text alone. But the other also has a text that he or she may offer for my performance. Reciprocity would require that 'we' who constitute the missionary community also be open to attending the performance of the other's text and to performing a version of that text ourselves. This is something that the Christian community, in its fear of contamination by 'paganism' or 'syncretism' or of participation in 'idolatrous worship', has often been reluctant to attempt. It is worth remembering, therefore, that the biblical narrative bears witness to the performance of one who, 'being in very nature God' (Philippians 2: 6), entered fully into the human world, being made like us 'in every way' (Hebrews 2: 17), and who yet, it is claimed, 'was without sin' (Hebrews 4: 15). To put this in theatrical terms, God began by playing the other's part. Rather than approach humanity as a divine outsider wielding a prescriptive text, or even as an understanding dramatist offering the human race a script for its communal performance, he became human, offering his own performance within the human community as a model for subsequent human mimesis (Ephesians 5: 1). And he did so, we are assured, without in any way compromising his integrity as God. I shall propose in Chapter 11, that the Christian doctrine of the incarnation has a significant contribution to make to a reciprocal ethics of cross-cultural encounter.

A final, brief conclusion has to do with the nature of the 'texts' that govern social performances. Often these do not appear in written form. Most societies, religious or otherwise, base their communal life more or less on oral tradition as well as (or rather than) on written documents. 'Text', as I use the term in this final third of the book, should therefore be understood to include, wherever appropriate, other forms of narrative or communal tradition that call, as Lash puts it, for 'enactment as the social existence of an entire human community'.

POLYPHONIC SCRIPTURES AND MULTICULTURAL CHURCHES

Having accepted and amplified Lash's argument that the scriptures call for performance as their primary mode of interpretation, we can now turn our attention to the biblical text itself. For this, in Lash's scheme of things, is the 'script' which the Christian community is called to enact. In Chapter 4 we noted Derrida's description of the biblical word as the inscribed voice of an absent other seeking, like a playwright and a tyrant, to colonize and to govern human performance from a distance. But the theatrical analogy, as Lash develops it, envisages a much looser relationship between scripture and performance, one that corresponds more closely, if I have understood the dialogical nature of the theatre correctly, to the actual and necessary relationship between dramatic script and theatrical performance. It is, of course, true that the church has acquired something of a reputation through the centuries for wanting, like many a misguided playwright and director, to control the details of performance. But the biblical text, it seems to me, is more wisely read not as a mandate for uniformity but as a celebration of diversity quite in keeping with the multiplicity of 'faithful' performances that it generates.

The very form in which the biblical narrative is inscribed can be read as an affirmation of diversity. For the Bible is the meeting place of many voices. The Old Testament was written in Hebrew (and Aramaic) and the New Testament in Greek, languages that embody very different cultural perspectives. Within each national language there are further languages or genres (lyric, apocalyptic, legal, prophetic, didactic, parabolic, narrative and so on), each giving voice, as Bakhtin would insist, to different points of view. Each genre is then used by a plurality of authors, whose distinct voices enhance the diversity. Furthermore, the Bible has lent itself to translation in a way that the Quran, for example, has not. Unlike Muslims, who believe that Arabic is the very 'language of God',[9] Christians regard the languages of the Bible as contingent. Finally, the central narrative of the Christian scriptures – the life, death and resurrection of Jesus of Nazareth – is given in four different versions. The Bible is, in Bakhtin's sense, a heteroglot text.

Perhaps the Bible is also polyphonic. 'A polyphonic work', as Morson and Emerson put it, citing Bakhtin, 'embodies dialogic truth by allowing the consciousness of a character to be truly "*someone else's* consciousness". . . . The direct power to mean, which in a monological work belongs to the author alone, belongs to several voices in a polyphonic work'. Christians view the Bible, in some sense, as both the word of a single author (God), and as the work of many human voices who are, as Bakhtin would put it, 'subjects of

150 *The Question of the Other*

their own directly signifying discourse'.[10] Even in the most conservative circles, the biblical authors are rarely thought of as
mere channels for another's voice. Thus B. B. Warfield, one of the
nineteenth-century's most vehement defenders of the inspiration of
the scriptures, wrote:

> The whole of Scripture is the product of divine activities which
> enter it, however, not by superseding the activities of the human
> authors, but confluently with them; so that the Scriptures are
> the joint product of divine and human activities, both of which
> penetrate them at every point, working harmoniously together
> to the production of a writing which is not divine here and human
> there, but at once divine and human in every part.[11]

Morson and Emerson have even suggested that 'the ethical agenda'
of Bakhtin's Dostoevsky book, in which he develops most fully the
theory of the polyphonic novel, 'is related to a theological one'. 'We
may imagine', they write, 'that God created the world . . .
polyphonically. He created unfinalizable beings, who are truly free
and capable of surprising Him, as Dostoevsky's characters surprised
their creator'.[12]

Nor is this simply a matter of form. For some of the stories told by
this heteroglot and arguably polyphonic text may be read as celebrations of diversity, congruent with the variety of performances the
text engenders. One strand of the creation narrative, for example,
may be taken as an affirmation of simultaneous difference within
both the divine and the human community. 'Let us', God says in the
first chapter of Genesis, 'make humanity in our image, in our likeness' (Genesis 1: 26). The divine use of the first-person plural is no
accident of grammar. For it is immediately followed by an announcement of plurality and difference within the human race: 'Male and
female he created them' (Genesis 1: 27). The two may later 'become
one flesh' (Genesis 2: 24), but there is nothing in the narrative to
suggest that this will involve the erasure (rather than the celebration) of difference. Something in the nature of God, the account
implies, is reflected in the community and diversity (and genders) of
the human race.

The legal system under which the Old Testament Jews subsequently laboured seems to have reversed the creation account's
affirmation of difference and to have placed instead a premium on
conformity even in the least details of ceremonial and civil life. But

many of the Jewish prophets anticipated a time when difference would once again be embraced and preserved in a community of justice and peace, and the New Testament writers believed they were witnessing the beginning of that era. The story of the 'new creation' of the church, as it is told, for example, in the opening chapters of the Book of Acts, celebrates the variety of languages and language groups to be found in the 'new humanity'. Although diversity in gender, age and class is not overlooked – the apostle Peter interprets the events of Pentecost in the light of the prophetic word that God would pour out his Spirit on 'sons and daughters', 'young men' and 'old men', and on his 'servants, both men and women' (Acts 2: 17–18; Joel 2: 28–9) – it is the spectacular gift of 'tongues' that propels the narrative. Pilgrims 'from every nation under heaven' listen to the apostles' sudden linguistic versatility with astonishment. 'How is it', they ask,

> that each of us hears them in his own native language? Parthians, Medes and Elamites; residents of Mesopotamia, Judea and Cappodocia, Pontus and Asia, Phrygia and Pamphilia, Egypt and the parts of Libya near Cyrene; visitors from Rome (both Jews and converts to Judaism); Cretans and Arabs – we hear them declaring the wonders of God in our own tongues.   (Acts 2: 8–11)

For those familiar with Bakhtin's thought, the divine endorsement of 'heteroglossia' at Pentecost may be read as a declaration that the God to whom the New Testament bears witness envisages a 'new humanity' that is unabashedly multilingual and multicultural and which finds its unity in the presence of the Spirit of Christ rather than in the tyranny of monological discourse.

But even those sharing the experience of Pentecost did not at once grasp its multicultural implications. Later in the Book of Acts, we are told that Peter three times needed to hear the voice of God declare every variety of animal clean before he could bring himself to visit the Gentile household of Cornelius in Joppa. Only there was Peter persuaded, by what he took to be the evident descent of the Holy Spirit on the Gentile audience, that the church was truly open to those who were not part of his own Jewish culture (Acts 10). The Jerusalem Council, called to mediate in a dispute over the degree to which Gentile Christians should observe the religious laws of Israel, believed itself led by the Holy Spirit to require tact and minimal conformity. The 'Gentiles who are turning to God' were to be subject only to moderate and, as it turned out, temporary Jewish direction of their performance of the scriptures (Acts 15). 'From the very beginning', Lash remarks, 'from Peter's vision at Joppa and the Council at Jerusalem, Christianity has acknowledged *in principle* its vocation to catholicity'.[13]

Principled commitment, however, has often struggled with monocultural impulse. Aylward Shorter, writing from a Roman Catholic perspective, describes rather bluntly the history of his church: 'For nearly sixteen centuries, from late Roman times until our own, a monocultural view of the world held sway among bishops, theologians and thinkers of the Catholic church.' The church, he says, simply 'adopted the imperial, Roman view of culture':

> The Roman understanding of culture was of a universal system of values and laws that could be elicited through philosophical reflection and imposed through education. Thus the entire human race could be divided into two camps: the civilized and the barbarian, the cultured and the uncultured. When Church and Empire united to become the politico-religious system known to history as 'Christendom', Roman monoculturalism received a powerful reinforcement. The superior world culture was identified with Christianity. In other words, it was assumed that the Gospel must be proclaimed everywhere in a single, 'perfect' cultural form.[14]

Both Lash and Shorter, following Bernard Lonergan, name this monocultural impulse 'classicist'.[15] But it may be misleading to suggest that such universal aspirations were peculiar to the classical European cultures of Greece and Rome. The apostle Peter's initial assumption that the blessings of Pentecost were aimed exclusively at those who embraced Jewish laws and values was not borrowed from the Roman world. It was part and parcel of his own Jewish heritage. Moreover, as we saw in the previous chapter, Aztec views of the other made a similar distinction between the cultured Aztec and the incomprehensible barbarian. The 'classicist' view of culture was (and is) more widespread than the name suggests.

The movement of the New Testament church towards catholicity may be seen as a break with the classicist assumptions of the surrounding Jewish and Roman worlds. And the subsequent history of the church may be read as a struggle between the monocultural aspirations of its 'bishops, theologians and thinkers', on the one hand, and the overwhelming weight of human diversity and, if you like, the impulse of the Holy Spirit, on the other hand. For the fact remains that, despite the efforts of generations of classicists, the church displays an astonishing diversity.

The fragmentation of the visible church into a plurality of churches may also be viewed, not as a consequence of human sinfulness or, from the Protestant point of view, as a triumph of biblical truth, but simply and positively, in the words of Abraham Kuyper, as an 'unfolding of multiformity'.[16] 'The truth of God', Kuyper wrote at the end of the nineteenth-century, 'was too rich and the great salvation in Christ too aboundingly precious, by reason of the Divine character exhibited in both, for them to be able to reach their full expression in one human form'.[17] Anticipating twentieth-century theories of inculturation, Kuyper insisted that confessional expressions of faith in Christ should properly vary not only between Roman Catholicism and Protestantism but, with the expansion of the church into other cultures, from one ethnic group to another. For revelation, he believed, is not an 'objective truth' suspended above human life; rather, as G. C. Berkouwer puts it, 'revelation has entered into human life'. 'Consequently', Berkouwer continues, 'Kuyper characterize[d] opposition to pluriformity as a form of dualism that does not allow the gospel to penetrate the fabric of life'.[18]

We may conclude that the community that believes itself called to perform the scriptures before an audience of 'others' is also called, by voices embedded in those same scriptures, to be a community of mutually 'upbuilding' (Ephesians 4: 29) communication between simultaneous differences. The dialogical pluriformity of the church (or churches) may be seen, once classicist assumptions are laid aside, to be part of the performance proposed by the biblical script.

THE MERCY OF THE OTHER

This being the case, cross-cultural missions may be viewed not as a means of increasing the numbers of participants in a definitive performance but as a way of extending the range of performances that, in their very differences, bear witness to the riches of their common script. Lonergan, accordingly, distinguishes between 'preaching the gospel and . . . preaching the gospel as it has been developed within one's own culture'. Setting aside the question of whether it is possible to speak of a gospel that is not already inculturated, even in its biblical expression, we can grant the main point of Lonergan's argument: to preach the gospel 'as it has been developed within one's own culture' is to ask 'others not only to accept the gospel but also [to] renounce their own culture and accept one's own'. This, of course, poses no problem for the classicist. But a 'pluralist', Lonergan observes, 'acknowledges a multiplicity of cultural traditions' and will 'proceed from within' the other's culture, seeking 'ways and means for making it into a vehicle for communicating the Christian message'.[19]

The biblical injunction to 'love your neighbour as yourself' is pertinent here. The reader will remember that Montesino, Las Casas and Sahagún, among others, invoked this rule when insisting on the equal humanity of European and Indian and the obligation of the one to love the other. But Enrique Dussel found the command deeply troubling, sensing in it a licence to suppress difference and to love the other only in so far as he or she becomes like oneself. Dussel's concern has strong historical warrant. But the command may also be interpreted as an affirmation of equality and difference.

For it is the clear witness of the New Testament commentary on this law that 'neighbour' is an inclusive rather than an exclusive term. He who loves his neighbour as himself is synonymous with 'he who loves the other [ὁ ἕτερος]' (Romans 13: 8–9). The follower of Christ is to aim at a 'perfect' or 'all-embracing [τέλειος]' love, as unrestricted as the Father's gracious provision of sun and rain to 'the righteous and the unrighteous' alike, and extending even to those for whom difference has become an occasion for enmity (Matthew 5: 43–8).[20] And, in the Parable of the Good Samaritan, Jesus identifies the Jew's neighbour by telling the story of a Samaritan's cross-cultural mercy (Luke 10: 25–37).

But, the critic might respond, this very parable nicely illustrates the problem of affirming both the equality and the difference of the neighbour. For while the story depends for its force on the difference between the Jew and the Samaritan, it also implies, it might be said, the inferiority of the one to be loved, offering for our admiration and imitation the love of the healthy Samaritan for the injured Jew. The love of one's neighbour is thus reckoned to be that of the privileged for the disadvantaged, of the civilized European for the barbaric Indian, of the Christian for the one who is not yet a Christian.

There is, however, an alternative reading of the parable. Karl Barth has suggested that, in its narrative context in the Gospel of

Luke, the parable teaches that love is first given to the other not from a posture of strength but from a position of weakness. At the end of his story Jesus asks the lawyer, whose question about the identity of his neighbour had prompted the tale, which of the three – priest, Levite or Samaritan – proved to be neighbour to the man who fell among thieves. The lawyer properly replies, 'The one who showed mercy on him'. It is not, therefore, Barth writes, 'the poor wounded man with his claim for help' who is the Jewish lawyer's neighbour. Rather it is 'the anything but poor Samaritan who makes no claim at all but is simply helpful'. The love of neighbour in question is that of the Jew who, in his need, allows the Samaritan to help him. This is, Barth comments, 'all very unexpected':

> For the lawyer had first to see that he himself is the man fallen among thieves and lying helpless by the wayside; . . . and above all, he has to see that he must be found and treated with compassion by the Samaritan, the foreigner, whom he believes he should hate, as one who hates and is hated by God.

The love of one's neighbour begins, according to this account, not with 'charity', offered from a position of power, but with humility, receiving mercy from the culturally despised. The parable thus undermines rather than endorses classicist assumptions about the other's spiritual poverty, drawing attention instead to the need of the self for the help of the other. To love another as myself is not, if we accept the commentary of this parable, to love her in so far as she is like myself, but to love her precisely as a different self who, from her place outside me, is able to grant me a mercy that I cannot grant myself.

This principle also extends, according to Barth, beyond love of neighbour to love of God. For the lawyer in Luke's parable had initiated his conversation with Jesus by summarizing the Law in terms of love for God and of love for neighbour. Taking the righteousness of his own love of God for granted, the lawyer chose to focus the discussion on the identity of his human neighbour. But Jesus's parable draws him back to the deficiency of his love for God. For the lawyer lacks, according to Barth, a readiness to receive mercy from the Other who 'stands before him incarnate, although hidden under the form of one whom the lawyer believed he should hate, as the Jews hated the Samaritans'. The 'eternal life' to which the lawyer aspires does not come by 'doing' the law but by yielding to the mercy of the one whose law he breaks and who stands before him unexpectedly in the person of Jesus of Nazareth, even as the Samaritan stood unexpectedly ready to help the beaten Jew. Only when the lawyer sees himself as one who receives mercy from both God and neighbour will he be ready to follow Christ and the Samaritan in also being, as Barth puts it, 'the neighbour who must bring comfort, help, the Gospel to someone else'.[21]

The Christian community's performance of the scriptures, therefore, if it is to bear witness to the mercy of the incarnate Other, will also embody a readiness to receive mercy from the more immediate other who is the Christian's neighbour. To conceive the other's culture as a convenient vehicle for 'our' message, as Lonergan does, may move the church beyond classicism, but it still arguably falls short of true reciprocity. For the other may also, mercifully, offer the Christian insight he does not yet have and of which he is, like the battered Jew, in need.

The Christian, in short, reads a text which invites performance in a multitude of cultural tongues and which encourages openness to the insights embedded in the other's performance. There is, however, one further step to be taken. For the most radical commentary on the Old Testament command to 'love your neighbour as yourself' is Jesus's announcement of 'a new command', refining and even replacing the old. 'Love each other', he is reported to have told his disciples, 'as I have loved you' (John 13: 34, 15: 12). In the final chapter, I shall return to the doctrine of the incarnation, reading this central event in the Christian narrative as a paradigmatic instance of dialogical and performative ethics.

I shall open the chapter, however, by looking at Bakhtin's version of the dialogical principle. For Bakhtin, too, wrote that the nature of Christian faith is to 'turn to the outside of myself and surrender myself to the mercy of the *other*'.[22] And I shall pay heed, in particular, to his advocacy of 'live entering' (*vzhivanie*) as a dialogical mode of interpersonal and intercultural relationships. For Bakhtin viewed the incarnation as 'the great symbol' of *vzhivanie*.

11

Incarnation and Other Dialogues

What Martin Buber has called 'the dialogical principle'[1] requires that the other be recognized not only as an object of which we may speak or whom I may address as a Thou but also as a subject, an I who speaks about me within his or her own circle and who in turn addresses me as a Thou. Buber quotes, as a precursor of his own celebration of reciprocity, Feuerbach's observation that the real I is 'only the I that stands over against a Thou and that is itself a Thou over against another I'.[2] This realization that the other is not merely an object of my discourse and my gaze, but that he or she is also a subject observing me, leads to the startling insight that the other has a point of view that is not my own and which is no more a defective version of mine than mine is a defective version of his or hers.

Not all who recognize the other's subjectivity share Buber's delight in it. Sartre, for example, finds that 'the existence of others' generates the disconcerting emotions of 'shame, . . . anger and fear':[3] it is when I am discovered peeking through a keyhole or when I hear branches crackling in the darkness that I suddenly perceive myself as the object of another's gaze. In the first instance, 'I am ashamed of myself as I appear to the other'; in the second instance, I realize 'that I am vulnerable, that I have a body which can be hurt'.[4] In either case, although I am given by the presence of the other a new perception of myself, it is an unwelcome and alienating gift.

But for Bakhtin the other was a source of joy. Bakhtin's 'dialogism', according to Clark and Holquist, 'celebrates alterity: it is a merry science, a *fröhliche Wissenschaft* of the other'.[5] His 'other' signals the diversity of human experience, joyously challenging the totalitarian assumption that there can ever be a single human point of view.

LIVE ENTERING

Bakhtin begins one of his early essays with the simple observation that no two bodies can occupy the same space at the same time, and therefore that no two viewpoints can be identical:

> When I contemplate a whole human being who is situated outside and over against me, our concrete, actually experienced horizons do not coincide. For at each given moment, regardless of the position and proximity to me of this other human being whom I am contemplating, I shall always see and know something that he, from his place outside and over against me, cannot see himself: parts of his body that are inaccessible to his own gaze (his head, his face and its expression), the world behind his back, and a whole series of objects and relations, which in any of our mutual relations are accessible to me but not to him. As we gaze at each other, two different worlds are reflected in the pupils of our eyes.[6]

You may, for example, see things behind my back, such as a painting or passing clouds, that are hidden from my view, while I may see things that your position denies to your vision, such as a different painting on the other wall or other clouds moving behind your head. This difference determines that, although we may both be in the same event, that event is different for us both.[7] If we stand alongside one another, facing in the same direction, the difference will be minimal. But to the degree that we stand far apart or face in opposite directions, the difference will be great, and for that very reason, the 'surplus' or 'excess of seeing' that each of us can offer the other will be all the more interesting. It may be, therefore, that 'the exterior and remote other', with whom dialogue is admittedly most difficult, offers me the greatest enlargement of vision.

Bakhtin explores the implications of this 'surplus of seeing' in terms of both interpersonal and intercultural relationships.[8] His early essays focus on the former. If my relationship with another individual is to be 'rendered meaningful ethically, cognitively, or aesthetically', Bakhtin writes, it requires 'live entering [*vzhivanie*]', a simultaneous exercise of empathy and 'outsidedness [*vnena-khodimost*]'. If I am to help, to understand or to paint, for example, a particular man who is suffering, I must first 'empathize or project myself into this other human being, see his world axiologically from within him as *he* sees this world.' As I do so, 'a whole series of features accessible to me from my own place will turn out to be absent from within this other's horizon'. Empathy alone, however, merely exchanges my limited horizon for another's. There must also, Bakhtin asserts, be 'a *return* to my own place outside the suffering person', for it is only from this place that I will be able to 'render' the other 'ethically, cognitively, or aesthetically'. 'The excess of my seeing', in short,

> must 'fill in' the horizon of the other human being who is being contemplated, must render his horizon complete, without at the same time forfeiting his distinctiveness. . . . I must put myself in his place and then, after returning to my own place, 'fill in' his horizon through that excess of seeing which opens out from this, my own, place outside him.[9]

In the same way, Bakhtin writes, a creative actor 'in imagination, experiences the hero's life as his *own* life'. But he also 'shapes *from outside* the image of the hero' whom he plays, seeing the hero, as the hero could not see himself, 'as a constituent in the whole' drama. Bakhtin makes a similar case, 'after discounting certain mechanical factors', for the playwright and the director. And, like Brecht, he welcomes the 'active spectator', who retains 'his place *outside* and *over against* the imaged life of the dramatic personae'. 'Creative activity' in the theatre, he insists, involves a willingness both to enter the other's world and to retain one's own perspective.[10]

Bakhtin's use of the imagery of projection and return might be taken to imply that empathy and outsideness occur in sequence. But as we have noted before, Bakhtin's dialogism is a matter of 'communication between simultaneous differences' rather than one of alternating points of view. What distinguishes Bakhtin from other modern thinkers about difference, Clark and Holquist aver, is 'his concentration on the possibility of encompassing differences in simultaneity'.[11] Bakhtin is careful, therefore, to specify that in 'live entering' empathy and outsideness 'do not follow one another choronologically' but occur simultaneously.[12] As Morson and Emerson put it, first paraphrasing and then citing Bakhtin directly:

> In *vzhivanie*, one enters another's place *while still maintaining one's own place*, one's own 'outsidedness,' with respect to the other. 'I

actively live into (*vzhivain*) an individuality, and consequently do
not, for a single moment, lose myself completely or lose my singular place outside that other individuality.'[13]

Just as I can understand the other better in this way, so I can be
understood by the other. But, Bakhtin adds, it is also the other who
enables me to understand myself. For he or she is able to see me as
I cannot see myself. By way of simple physical illustration, Bakhtin
notes that only another can see me from behind, or view the expression of joy or sorrow on my face without the distorting self-
consciousness of a mirror. What is true of my outward appearance is
also true, Bakhtin suggests, of my inner being. The other's place
outside me both limits what she can know of my inner world and
affords her a perspective that I do not have. As I learn to see myself
'through the eyes of the other', as well as through my own, I am
granted a more complete perception of myself than I could gain
alone. In significant measure, 'the self', as Clark and Holquist put it,
'is an act of grace, a gift of the other'.[14]
    In a later essay Bakhtin applied the same dialogical principle of
'live entering' or, as he was calling it by then, 'creative understanding', to cross-cultural relationships. His immediate concern was that
literary scholars should try to understand the total cultural context
in which works from past epochs were written. But the closing
paragraphs of the essay admit a broader application. He writes:

> These exists a very strong, but one-sided and thus untrustworthy,
> idea that in order better to understand a foreign culture, one must
> enter into it, forgetting one's own, and view the world through
> the eyes of this foreign culture. . . . Of course, a certain entry as a
> living being into a foreign culture, the possibility of seeing the
> world through its eyes, is a necessary part of the process of under-
> standing it; but if this were the only aspect of this understanding,
> it would merely be duplication and would not entail anything
> new or enriching. *Creative understanding* does not renounce itself,
> its own place in time, its own culture; and it forgets nothing. In
> order to understand, it is immensely important for the person
> who understands to be *located outside* the object of his or her
> creative understanding – in time, in space, in culture. For one
> cannot even really see one's own exterior and comprehend it as a
> whole, and no mirrors or photographs can help; our real exterior

can be seen and understood only by other people, because they are located outside us in space and because they are *others*.[15]

It is not, then, simply a matter of furthering my understanding of the other culture by this simultaneous empathy and outsidedness. It is also the case, Bakhtin claims, that a culture, like an individual or a work of art, can yield its 'meaning' to an outsider in a way that it cannot to itself or, in the case of a work of art, to its author. Earlier in the essay, he had applied this principle to the works of Shakespeare and of the Greeks, arguing that subsequent epochs have genuinely found 'new significance' embedded in ancient texts, which neither the authors themselves nor their contemporaries 'could consciously perceive and evaluate in the context of the culture of their epoch'.[16] A twentieth-century production of *Oedipus Rex*, for example, may choose to incorporate or to ignore Freud's reading of the Oedipal myth. But a post-Freudian audience will certainly bring questions to the play that its original audience did not. And these questions will cause the text to resonate in ways that it could not have done for Sophocles. One could make a similar case for a late twentieth-century scholar who reads *The Indian Emperour*, *La conquista de México*, and *La Conquête du Mexique* in the light of moral and aesthetic questions raised by Bakhtin and Todorov. One could also cite the Tlaxcalans responsible for *The Conquest of Jerusalem*. Living into the Christian world of the Franciscans, while retaining the perspective of outsiders, they were able to understand and apply the Spanish theories of just reconquest in a way that the Spaniards, from their own perspective, could not.

At the close of his essay, Bakhtin asserts once more the importance of outsidedness in creative understanding and, therefore, in fostering mutually enriching cross-cultural dialogue:

> It is only in the eyes of *another* culture that foreign culture reveals itself fully and profoundly (but not maximally fully, because there will be cultures that see and understand even more). A meaning only reveals its depths once it has encountered and come into contact with another, foreign meaning: they engage in a kind of dialogue, which surmounts the closedness and one-sidedness of these particular meanings, these cultures. We raise new questions for a foreign culture, ones that it did not raise itself; we seek answers to our own questions in it; and the foreign culture re-

sponds to us by revealing to us new aspects and new semantic
depths. Without *one's own* questions one cannot creatively understand anything other or foreign. . . . Such a dialogic encounter of
two cultures does not result in merging or mixing. Each retains its
own unity and *open* totality, but they are mutually enriched.[17]

THE INCARNATION

The most startling illustration that Bakhtin offers, albeit in passing,
for his concept of 'live entering' or 'creative understanding' is the
Christian doctrine of the incarnation. 'One way to imagine Christ',
Bakhtin suggests, according to Morson and Emerson's paraphrase of
his early essay 'Towards a Philosophy of the Act', 'is to see the
incarnation as an act of *vzhivanie*. According to this analogy, Christ
did not empathize with people; rather he became one of them while
still maintaining his divine outsidedness'.[18] 'Christ's descent', Bakhtin
wrote, is 'the great symbol of activity' that conforms to the pattern of
vzhivanie.[19] 'The world from which Christ departed' had been enriched by his living into it, and 'could no longer be that world in
which he had never been'.[20]

Unfortunately these last two tantalizing sentences were separated, according to the editors of the Russian manuscript, by 32
'indecipherable' words, and are followed by a change of topic. Although Bakhtin planned to write a section of the essay that would
deal with theological topics, this is the sole mention of the incarnation in the text as it has come down to us.[21] It is not hard, however,
to imagine his probable train of thought.

For the Christian doctrine of the incarnation bears witness to an
encounter between God and humanity, in the single person of Jesus
of Nazareth, in which both empathy and outsidedness are fully and
simultaneously in play. God, we are taught, entered wholly into the
human world, choosing to see things from the perspective of a
particular human being at a particular place and time in human
history. At the same time, in the words of the Athanasian Creed,
Jesus remained 'perfect God, . . . equal to the Father, as touching his
Godhead'.[22] The empathic identity of God with humanity did not, in
other words, entail the surrender of his outsidedness. The classic
Christian creeds proclaim that Christ's divinity was not diminished

by his adoption of a human nature and that his humanity was not curtailed by his retention of deity. Had either been the case, Barth insists, God would have 'at once ceased to be God' without ever becoming 'a man like us'.[23]

The fourth gospel, in particular, portrays the simultaneous operation of two natures in a single person. We are told, for example, that 'Jesus, tired as he was from the journey', and genuinely in need of the drink of water he requests from the Samaritan woman, also knows, as she puts it, 'everything I ever did' (John 4: 4–29). On the other hand, he 'learns' that an invalid has been paralysed for 38 years, but then heals him and declares himself to be 'equal with God' (5: 1–23). And he weeps at the tomb of Lazarus, knowing he will shortly raise him from the dead (11: 1–44). To suppose either that the Jesus of this gospel is feigning human fatigue, thirst, ignorance or grief, or that his miracles and other claims to deity are to be understood as fraudulent, would be to read against the evangelist, who unashamedly asserts both that 'the Word was God' and that 'the Word became *flesh*' (1: 1, 14). The author of the fourth gospel is testifying, as Barth puts it, to God's 'dialogue with man' in the person of Jesus of Nazareth.[24]

This dialogue, according to one strand of the New Testament witness, may be understood to continue and even to expand after the resurrection. For the Pauline literature proposes a startling intimacy and even identification between the ascended Christ and the church, by virtue of which the incarnate God may be said, in Bakhtin's phrase, to 'live into' an increasing number and variety of human cultures.

When, for instance, in the latter part of the Book of Acts Paul recalls his vision on the road to Damascus, he does not ascribe to Christ the words of rebuke one might expect: 'Saul, Saul, why do you persecute my church?' Rather, he remembers the glorified Christ saying, 'Why do you persecute *me*?' (Acts 26: 14). On another occasion, addressing the Corinthians, Paul compares the church to a body made up of many members. 'The body', he writes, 'is a unit, though it is made up of many parts; and though all its parts are many, they form one body. So it is', he adds – and we expect him to say 'with the church'. But he does not. 'So it is', he concludes, 'with Christ' (1 Corinthians 12: 12). Such is Paul's sense of the solidarity between the risen Christ and the church on earth that he is willing to call both by one name.

Again, writing to the Galatians, he assures them, 'All of you who were baptized into Christ have clothed yourselves with Christ. There is neither Jew nor Greek, slave nor free, male nor female, for you are all one in Christ Jesus. If you belong to Christ, then you are Abraham's seed' (Galatians 3: 29). Earlier, Paul had taken pains to insist that, in the Old Testament promises made 'to Abraham and to his seed', the singular 'seed' referred not to 'many people' but to 'one person, who is Christ' (Galatians 3: 16). By telling a diverse multitude of Christians that they are 'Abraham's seed' he is not revoking his earlier argument, but identifying them all with Christ. 'If you belong to Christ', he is in effect assuring them, 'you are Christ'.

This idea of the union of Christ and the church was also developed by Paul in terms of the Spirit of Christ. Both individual Christians (1 Corinthians 6: 19) and a pointedly multicultural church (Ephesians 2: 19–22) are described in the Pauline epistles as 'the temple of the Holy Spirit'. The same Spirit may thus be said to animate both the head of the church, the risen Christ, and all the manifold members of the body who together comprise the Christ on earth. In this way, as Aylward Shorter puts it, 'Christ in his members, can become African, Indian, American and so on'.[25] We might also add that, in this way, he can become she. Even more startling, perhaps, is the idea that if, in Christian thought, Christ and the church are one, then the Christ who, according to Paul, is at the right hand of God must also somehow be of both genders and of many classes and cultures. 'God raised us up with Christ', the Ephesians – men and women, slave and free, Jew and Greek – are told, 'and seated us with him in the heavenly realms in Christ Jesus' (Ephesians 2: 6). The 'living entry' of the Son of God into the human community in the person of Jesus of Nazareth is thus sustained and extended, according to the Pauline gospel, by the continual expansion of the members of Christ's body into new cultural forms.

Moreover, this dialogue can be thought of as genuinely reciprocal. For there lies at the heart of the New Testament witness the startling (but good) news not only that humanity is being redeemed in Christ but that God, too, is being transformed by the acquisition of a human nature. 'Is it not true', Barth asks, 'that in Jesus Christ, as he is attested in the Holy Scripture, genuine deity includes in itself genuine humanity?'[26] Elsewhere, he answers his own question affirmatively. 'Without ceasing to be God', he writes, 'the Word of God is among us in such a way that he takes over human being, which is his creature, into his own being and to that extent makes it his own being'.[27] We can add, in the light of the Pauline identity of Christ and the church, that God includes in himself (and now we can also say herself) not only the particular humanity of a first-century Jewish working-class male but also, since Pentecost, the particular humanities of a multitude of men and women, who are members both of the church and of an almost uncountable number and variety of languages, worlds and cultures.

CROSS-CULTURAL MISSIONS AND DIALOGICAL THEATRE

To read the incarnation as an act of *vzhivanie* modifies our initial inclination to speak of cross-cultural encounter in terms of the offer of our cherished text for independent performance by the other. This modification is called for even though we imagined such an offer being followed by a reciprocal willingness to attend a performance of the other's text and to perform a version of that text ourselves. For the God of the New Testament, as we have seen, began, not with an offer of text, but by playing the other's part. If the incarnation is to be the model for the Christian's encounter with others, then the church's cross-cultural mission will start with the Christian's 'living entry' into the other's world.

Shorter cites three examples of Jesuit missions in the late sixteenth and early seventeenth centuries which experimented with such an approach.[28] Matteo Ricci in China, Roberto de Nobili in India and Pedro Paez in Ethiopia each sought to live as Christians (retaining thereby their perspective as outsiders) wholly within the terms of the culture to which they had been sent. Ricci, for example, became an accomplished Confucian scholar, writing in Chinese more than twenty scientific treatises much appreciated by the imperial court and by the literate community of Peking. He approved the application of the traditional Chinese title 'Lord of Heaven' to the Christian God, and authorized Chinese converts to Christianity to continue to honour both Confucius and their own ancestors through periodic rituals. Visitors thronged the mission house in Peking, and enquiries about the doctrines Ricci taught came to him from all over the empire. It is, perhaps, a measure of Ricci's success that some 3000 people had been baptized by the time of his death in 1610. Shorter remarks, with approval:

Ricci and his fellow Jesuit missionaries were embarked on a profound dialogue with the religious culture of the Chinese. . . . They were aiming at nothing more nor less than inculturation in the true sense of the word. The goal was to achieve a Christian reinterpretation of Chinese culture which would, in turn, provoke a Chinese reinterpretation of Christianity presented in this sympathetic Chinese form.

De Nobili, adopting the costume and mode of life of a Hindu holy man, lived among the Brahmins of Madras. Under his influence, Brahmin converts to Christianity were allowed to retain much of their former way of life. Paez was captured by pirates on his first voyage to Ethiopia, and spent seven years in captivity as the slave of a Yemeni pasha. When he finally reached Ethiopia, he did not insist on Latin rites but permitted the indigenous church to retain its ancient culture and distinctive liturgy. Each left a legacy of thousands of converts.

The work of Ricci, de Nobili and Paez was subsequently suppressed by church authorities in Rome or abandoned by more-conventional successors. Each missionary was suspected of tolerating superstition. But to adopt the forms of another culture is not to surrender one's own values. The Son of God, it will be remembered, according to the writer to the Hebrews, became fully human without yielding to sin. He learned obedience or, if you will, learned to perform God's script faithfully (with all the interpretative freedom which that implies) in human terms and, more specifically, in terms of a particular human culture.

Christians, whether or not they venture across cultural boundaries, are faced with a similar challenge. Since from all points of view but the classicist no culture is uniquely Christian, even the believer who remains in the cultural world of her birth is engaged in a dialogical performance. She is called to perform, at one and the same time, the text of her faith and that of her culture. If she then decides to engage in cross-cultural evangelism, she is faced with the choice of exporting the gospel as it is performed in her own culture or of living into another culture as a Christian. In either case, the gospel will be embedded in cultural forms. The incarnation models the latter move. For according to the biblical narrative, God chose to enter the other's world and there to perform, dialogically (and therefore simultaneously), his own holy text and a fully human script.

The struggle for Christians, as it was for Christ, is to play the human part without sin. Christians recognize that they fail. But to read the other's cultural forms as sinful (because not our own) confuses rather than clarifies this struggle.

The moral challenge of such an encounter is not only felt by the Christian. For the Christian's outsidedness also raises moral questions for the culture being entered. Shorter reminds us that Jesus, while open to the mercy of the other, also 'challenged the culture of his adoption'. He stood within it as a human being and outside it as a 'stranger', proposing 'a radical revision of the way his contemporaries understood' human life. In a similar fashion, Shorter believes, the faithful performance of the Christian narrative in any cultural setting 'invites people to reappraise their cultures in the light of radically new values – values that turn human thinking upside down'.[29]

It may be, therefore, that Christians living into another culture will be asked to give an account of the way in which their own performance of the prevailing cultural script differs from that of the indigenous performers. Much will depend on the quality of their performance. The writer of the First Epistle of Peter imagined his Christian readers, scattered throughout Asia Minor, being asked by their pagan neighbours, 'Why do you not fear what we fear?' To recount, at this point, 'with gentleness and respect' for the other, the narrative that undergirds their own 'hope' (1 Peter 3: 14–15), would be a dialogical gambit to which Todorov, at least, would not object.

For Todorov is well aware of the tension that exists between the right of 'self-determination and noninterference', on the one hand, and the value of 'cross-pollination' on the other.[30] He is no advocate for the kind of cultural 'apartheid' which, in its concern to avoid the presumptions of 'ethnocentric universalism', swings to the opposite extreme, renouncing what he calls 'the very idea of shared humanity' and thus abandoning the possibility of dialogue between different points of view.[31] 'The essential thing', he suggests, 'is to know whether [cultural influences are being] *imposed* or *proposed*. Christianization, like the export of any ideology or technology, can be condemned as soon as it is imposed, by arms or otherwise'. But to *propose* a change in the other's way of seeing and doing both protects the liberty and makes possible the enrichment of the interlocutors. 'We need not be confined', Todorov concludes, 'within a sterile alternative. . . . To justify colonial wars (in the name of the superiority of Western civilization), or to reject all interaction with a foreign power in the name of one's own identity', are not the only options open to us. In politics, as in religious, racial and sexual encounter, 'nonviolent communication exists, and we can defend it as a value'.[32]

Christians who offer the biblical text (or the story told by the text) as an explanation of their own distinctive performance of the other's cultural script are simply bringing into the open the dialogical relationship between the two worlds and their underlying texts already implicit in the performance. A dialogical gesture of this kind involves no imposition. Having told their story, the Christians can then offer the biblical text for independent performance by the others into whose culture they are living. Such an offer may be refused. A playwright cannot, under ordinary circumstances, insist on his or her text being performed. Nor, if the theatrical analogy is to be observed, can one community insist on its text being performed by another, however strongly it may believe that the other's world would thereby be enriched.

On the other hand, such an offer does not require those making it to relinquish their sense of the high or even superior value of their own text. The theatrical metaphor does not invite the kind of 'generalized relativism' which both Bakhtin and Todorov despise. 'Heterology, which makes the difference of voices heard', is very different, in Todorov's mind, from an 'insipid . . . polylogy', characterized by a 'renunciation of all values' or a flaccid, non-committal sympathy with every option.[33] Commitment to the text one offers is not a liability but a necessary condition of 'heterological' dialogue.

What the theatrical model does require, however, is a willingness to relinquish control over the other's performance of one's own legitimately cherished text. Theatrical performance adapts dramatic text, embedding it in a multi-media presentation that cannot be scored precisely on the page, and a multitude of different performances can claim fidelity to a single text. The sending church or missionary community that follows the theatrical model will resist the temptation to impose on its neighbour either the text or the details, ritual or social, of performance. The limits of interpretation, in the theatre as in missions, will in the end be determined not by a central authority but by the local performers and their audiences.

Experiments of this kind may also result in an enrichment of the missionary community's own understanding of the scriptures. If, as Bakhtin insists, a text, like an individual or a culture, can yield its meaning 'fully and profoundly' only to outsiders, then one would expect the Christian community to benefit from the surplus of seeing generated by fresh cultural performances of its texts. Even a playwright, after all, may learn more about his or her text on seeing it performed by others. The church, too, Shorter suggests, can be 'transformed' by other cultures, 'not in a way that falsifies its message, but in the way in which the message is formulated and interpreted anew'.[34]

This can be true not only when Christians live into another culture, performing the scriptures in dialogue with the other's cultural forms and then watching (and learning) should the other community embark on its own performance of the outsider's text. It can also be true when members of another culture bring their own texts into dialogue with the scriptures in predominantly Christian communities. This involuntary but none the less powerful live entering of African slaves into American culture, for example, has both transformed and enriched Christian worship and theology in the United States.

But the Christian must remember, too, that the theatrical model grants to others equal freedom to act as missionaries on behalf of their own religion. Muslims, for example, may live into European or American culture (as Jews have done for centuries),[35] simultaneously performing their own scriptures and the local cultural text. They may tell the story on which their own distinctive performance is based, and they may offer the Quran for independent performance by Christians. Christians may decline the offer. They may, remembering the Parable of the Good Samaritan, be willing to receive a measure of mercy from an unexpected source, or, remembering Bakhtin, be eager to fill out their own horizon by seeing themselves from another's point of view. They may respond with evangelism of their own, living the gospel into the Muslim community in the hope that the Muslims will become Christians. Either may live into the other's community. Neither may impose their religion on the other.

Nor, one hopes, would Christians ordinarily want to prevent such an outreach on the part of the other. Tolerance under these circumstances would not be just a matter of reciprocity. Can Christians object if their neighbours of another faith model their own cross-cultural outreach on the Christian doctrine of the incarnation? Even a Christian of a classicist frame of mind might find here a dialogical openness to the Christian gospel.

CONCLUSION

It is partly because, as Lash puts it, 'classicist assumptions survive like beached whales on the shores of contemporary culture', and 'even beached whales . . . are a force to be reckoned with',[36] that I have grounded my argument not on the nature of 'truth', about which classicists and pluralists disagree, but on the nature of performing texts. The latter seems to me to be marginally more straightforward. For dramatic, religious and political texts may be observed, as a matter of fact, to generate a diversity of performances. Most of these are intended, in one way or another, to bear witness to the 'truth' of the text. Guardians of a text, or of a particular way of performing the text, may regret that cultural change and cross-cultural encounter engender new performances, but this, I suggest, is inherent in the nature of the text they guard. Texts whose 'fundamental form of interpretation', as Lash puts it, is their communal performance, generate diverse performances in diverse communities. To resist this variety is, I believe, to fight the very nature of performance.

It is the nature, too, of texts that anticipate performance to be evocative rather than prescriptive. I think of the latter part of my own book in this way, as a modest script for the mutually fruitful enactment of cross-cultural encounter. It is certainly not the final word. I would be naive if I thought that playing one's own text in dialogue with the other's cultural forms, and then offering that text for independent performance by the other (while granting to the other the same dialogical freedom), resolved all the problems of cross-cultural encounter. Human interaction is too complex to admit a single solution.

A text, for example, may be performed by others in a way that seems to those who offered it to be so at odds with their own understanding of the text as to be completely unacceptable. Thus the practice of democracy in South Africa has seemed to many to be so restricted as to be no democracy at all. Or the refusal of the other to perform the text offered may mean the continuation of practices whose very suppression the text appears to demand. Human sacrifice presented the European conquistadors of the New World with this dilemma. Or the other may use force to impose performance of his text. Early Christians in Rome, Jews in Hitler's Germany, Arabs in Israel and Indians in the New World have faced such oppression.

A consistent application of the theatrical model might suggest a pacifist response to such situations. Arguing that it is not only wrong but in the end impossible to impose definitive performance of a text on another, the pacifist community would choose to influence others only by the ongoing performance (and free offer) of its own text, in dialogue, wherever possible, with the other's cultural script. Such a performance might well include non-violent and even at times carnivalesque resistance. (One thinks, for example, of the festive atmosphere of Gandhi's salt march in 1930.[37]) Or it may end in martyrdom. A Christian pacifist would well argue that this was the role chosen by Christ, and point to Paul's argument that the 'weakness' of 'Christ crucified' has proven, contrary to what one might expect, to be 'the power of God', effecting radical change in the lives of all 'those who are called, both Jews and Greeks' (1 Corinthians 1: 23–5).

Others, Christians among them, might argue that the text they are called to perform requires a commitment to fight, violently if necessary, against the oppression of others within or without one's own community. This, it will be remembered, was one of the conditions under which Vitoria argued that just war could be waged. It is not an argument to be taken lightly. Had the allies neglected it, it is unlikely that western Europe would now provide a forum for discussion of 'heterology' and the advantages of ethnic diversity.

To extend the theatrical metaphor, the pacifist would argue against all forms of censorship. The advocate of just war would maintain that some texts and some performances are so offensive that they require suppression not just by moral example but, if necessary, by force. The theatrical model cannot settle this argument. It can only point to a mode of cross-cultural exchange which, to the degree that it were practised, would work against the oppression that in many minds is a just cause of war. For the theatre is not an oppressive but a dialogical genre.

Notes

Notes to Chapter 1: Dialogical Genres and Cultural Encounters

1. K. Clark and M. Holquist, *Mikhail Bakhtin* (Cambridge, Mass.: Harvard University Press, 1984) p. 9.
2. Y. Argudín, *Historia del teatro en México* (Mexico: Panorama, 1986) p. 23.
3. T. Todorov, *Mikhail Bakhtine: le principe dialogique, suivi de Écrits du cercle de Bakhtine* (Paris: Seuil, 1981), and *La Conquête de l'Amérique* (Paris: Seuil, 1982).
4. J. H. Elliott, 'Mastering the Signs', *New York Review of Books*, 19 July 1984, p. 31.
5. N. A. Scott, Jr, 'The House of Intellect in an Age of Carnival: Some Hermeneutical Reflections', *Journal of the American Academy of Religion*, vol. 55 (1987) p. 7.
6. S. J. Samartha, *Courage for Dialogue* (Maryknoll, N.Y.: Orbis Books, 1982) p. viii.
7. For a more complete account, see G. S. Morson and C. Emerson, *Mikhail Bakhtin: Creation of a Prosaics* (Stanford, Cal.: Stanford University Press, 1990) pp. 271–470.
8. M. M. Bakhtin, *The Dialogic Imagination*, trans. C. Emerson and M. Holquist (Austin, Tx.: University of Texas Press, 1981). For a convenient bibliography of Bakhtin's work, see Clark and Holquist, *Mikhail Bakhtin*, pp. 353–6.
9. Bakhtin, *Dialogic Imagination*, pp. 262–3, 295–6.
10. M. Edwards, *Towards a Christian Poetics* (London: Macmillan, 1984) p. 55. Edwards is capable (pp. 165–6) of viewing the multiplicity of tongues in a positive light, but still yearns (p. 176) for a single 'pure language' transcending its manifold forms. He is, in this respect, avowedly 'Neoplatonic' (p. 147).
11. Bakhtin, *Dialogic Imagination*, p. 278, compares 'the Tower-of-Babel mixing of languages' to 'the unfolding of social heteroglossia'.
12. A. White, 'Bakhtin, Sociolinguistics and Deconstruction', in *The Theory of Reading*, ed. F. Gloversmith (Brighton, Sussex: Harvester, 1984) p. 145.
13. *Webster's Seventh New Collegiate Dictionary* (Springfield, Mass.: Merriam, 1965) p. 279.
14. Bakhtin, *Dialogic Imagination*, pp. 16–17.
15. Ibid., pp. 297–8.
16. Ibid., p. 66. T. Todorov, *Mikhail Bakhtin: The Dialogical Principle*, trans. W. Godzich (Minneapolis, Minn.: University of Minnesota Press, 1984) p. 90, remarks, concerning Bakhtin's assessment of the various genres, 'We never find (unless it is in the unpublished materials) the confrontation we await, between the novel and the drama'.
17. Bakhtin, *Dialogic Imagination*, pp. 11, 38.
18. Morson and Emerson, *Bakhtin*, pp. 66, 441–3, draw a distinction be-

tween 'Epic and the Novel', in which the ideas summarized in this paragraph appear, and the other (earlier) essays in *The Dialogic Imagination*. 'Epic and the Novel', they suggest, is a 'carnival text', inclined to hyperbole, and therefore closer in spirit to M. Bakhtin, *Rabelais and his World*, trans. H. Iswolsky (Bloomington, Ind.: Indiana University Press, 1984). The distinction may be valid, but it also reflects Morson and Emerson's distaste for and attempt to isolate the carnivalesque elements in Bakhtin's work.

19. Bakhtin, *Dialogic Imagination*, p. 299.
20. Ibid., p. 301.
21. Ibid., p. 306; C. Dickens, *Little Dorrit*, bk 2, ch. 24.
22. Bakhtin, *Dialogic Imagination*, p. 324.
23. Morson and Emerson, *Bakhtin*, p. 314; Bakhtin, *Dialogic Imagination*, p. 366.
24. Bakhtin, *Dialogic Imagination*, p. 271.
25. M. M. Bakhtin, *Problems of Dostoevsky's Poetics*, trans. C. Emerson (Minneapolis, Minn.: University of Minnesota Press, 1984). This is a translation of Bakhtin's revised and expanded 1963 version.
26. Morson and Emerson, *Bakhtin*, p. 232.
27. Bakhtin, *Problems*, p. 6.
28. M. M. Bakhtin, 'Towards a Reworking of the Dostoevsky Book', in *Problems*, p. 285; Morson and Emerson, *Bakhtin*, pp. 240, 267.
29. Morson and Emerson, *Bakhtin*, p. 240. My italics.
30. Bakhtin, *Dialogic Imagination*, p. 266. This paragraph, in Emerson and Holquist's published translation, concludes: 'outside that of the (nondramatic) plot'. This phrase, however, does not appear in the Russian original. See M. Baxtin, *Voprosy literaturi i estetiki* (Moscow: Xudozestvennaja literatura, 1975) p. 79. In a telephone conversation (7 November 1989), Caryl Emerson graciously confirmed my suspicion that the phrase was added in translation 'for clarification', and that an error in transcription wrought confusion by rendering the intended 'dramatic' as 'nondramatic'. In a subsequent letter (9 November 1989), she suggested the following literal translation of the concluding sentence: 'There is no all-embracing language, which has been oriented dialogically to separate languages, there is no second all-encompassing extra-plot (not dramatic) dialogue'. My thanks are due not only to Caryl Emerson but also to Mark Elson, of the Department of Slavic Languages and Literatures at the University of Virginia, for helping me to grapple with this passage.
31. Bakhtin, *Dialogic Imagination*, p. 287.
32. Ibid., p. 327.
33. Bakhtin, *Problems*, p. 17. H. Keyssar, 'Drama and the Dialogic Imagination: *The Heidi Chronicles* and *Fefu and Her Friends*', *Modern Drama*, vol. 34 (1991) pp. 89–90, notes the similarity between Aristotle's and Bakhtin's views of drama.
34. Bakhtin, *Dialogic Imagination*, pp. 49, 287, 405.
35. Ibid., pp. 5, 405.
36. Ibid., pp. 68–82.
37. Ibid., p. 132.

38. Ibid., pp. 36, 53–6, 79–80, and, for the medieval carnival, Bakhtin, *Rabelais*.
39. Bakhtin, *Problems*, pp. 32–4. Elsewhere Bakhtin is more generous to Shakespeare, writing in *Rabelais*, p. 275, of 'the essential carnival element in the organization of Shakespeare's drama', and recognizing that the 'logic of crownings and uncrownings . . . organizes the serious elements' as well as the comedy.
40. M. Pfister, 'Comic Subversion: A Bakhtinian View of the Comic in Shakespeare', *Deutsche Shakespeare-Gesellschaft West: Jahrbuch 1987*, ed. W. Habicht *et al.* (Bochum: Kamp, 1987) pp. 27–43.
41. G. Pechey, 'On the Borders of Bakhtin: Dialogization, Decolonization', *Oxford Literary Review*, vol. 9 (1987) pp. 76–7.
42. Keyssar, 'Drama and the Dialogic Imagination', pp. 95–104.
43. J. Docker, 'In Defence of Melodrama: Towards a Libertarian Aesthetic', *Australasian Drama Studies*, vol. 9 (1986) pp. 63–81.
44. M. D. Bristol, *Carnival Theater: Plebeian Culture and the Structure of Authority in Renaissance England* (New York: Methuen, 1985).
45. D. Pollock, 'The Play as Novel: Reappropriating Brecht's *Drums in the Night*', *Quarterly Journal of Speech*, vol. 74 (1988) pp. 296–309.
46. V. Popovici, 'Is the Stage–Audience Relationship a Form of Dialogue?', *Poetics*, vol. 13 (1984) pp. 111–18. Cf. Pechey, 'On the Borders of Bakhtin', p. 78: 'Drama is perhaps not so much monological in essence as *monologized* by being read as literature rather than theatre'. In 'Author and Hero in Aesthetic Activity' (*c.* 1924), Bakhtin encouraged actor, spectator and director to retain perspectives '*outside* and *over against* the imaged life event of the dramatis personae'. But he did not develop this observation into a dialogical theory of theatrical performance. See M. M. Bakhtin, *Art and Answerability*, ed. M. Holquist and V. Liapunov, trans. V. Liapunov (Austin, Tx.: University of Texas Press, 1990) pp. 73–8.
47. Todorov, *Bakhtin*, p. 94.
48. T. Todorov, *The Conquest of America: The Question of the Other*, trans. R. Howard (New York: Harper & Row, 1984) p. 3.
49. Todorov, *Bakhtin*, p. 13. Cf. M. M. Bakhtin, *Speech Genres and Other Late Essays*, ed. C. Emerson and M. Holquist, trans. V. M. McGee (Austin, Tx.: University of Texas Press, 1986) p. 19.
50. Todorov, *Conquest*, pp. 3–5.
51. Bakhtin, *Dialogic Imagination*, p. 370.
52. Todorov, *Conquest*, p. 42.
53. Ibid., p. 4.
54. R. González-Echevarría, 'America Conquered', *Yale Review*, vol. 74 (1985) pp. 281–90
55. D. Root, 'The Imperial Signifier: Todorov and the Conquest of Mexico', *Cultural Critique*, vol. 9 (1988) pp. 197–219.
56. R. Adorno, 'Arms, Letters and the Native Historian in Early Colonial Mexico', in *1492–1992: Re/discovering Colonial Writing*, ed. R. Jara and N. Spadaccini (Minneapolis, Minn.: Prisma, 1989) pp. 201–24.
57. Elliott, 'Mastering the Signs', pp. 29–30; Root, 'Imperial Signifer', pp. 211–15.

58. Adorno, 'Arms, Letters', pp. 205–6.
59. Bakhtin, *Speech Genres*, p. 7.
60. Todorov, *Conquest*, pp. 250–1.
61. Ibid.
62. M. de Certeau, *Heterologies: Discourse on the Other*, trans. B. Massumi (Manchester: Manchester University Press, 1986) p. 78; Adorno, 'Arms, Letters', p. 207.
63. J. Culler, 'A Clash of Symbols', *New York Times Book Review*, 5 August 1984, p. 22.
64. R. Potter, 'Abraham and Human Sacrifice: the Exfoliation of Medieval Drama in Aztec Mexico', *New Theatre Quarterly*, vol. 2 (1986) p. 306.

Notes to Chapter 2: Aztec Maidens in Satin Gowns

1. John Dryden, *The Indian Emperor, or The Conquest of Mexico by the Spaniards*, in *The Works of John Dryden*, vol. 9, ed. J. Loftis and V. A. Dearing, (Berkeley, Cal.: University of California Press, 1966) pp. 1–112.
2. The play has its 'amusing' moments, as is noted by both M. M. Alssid, *Dryden's Rhymed Heroic Tragedies* (Salzburg: Institut für Englische Sprache und Literatur, 1974) p. 144, and J. A. Winn, *John Dryden and His World* (New Haven, Conn.: Yale University Press 1987) p. 154. But its occasional humour is genteel rather than carnivalesque.
3. A. T. Barbeau, *The Intellectual Design of John Dryden's Heroic Plays* (New Haven, Conn.: Yale University Press, 1970) pp. 24–54.
4. A full-colour reproduction of Hogarth's painting, together with a detailed commentary, can be found in M. Webster, *Hogarth* (London: Studio Vista, 1978) pp. 79–80, 84–5. Cf. J. Powell, *Restoration Theatre Production* (London: Routledge & Kegan Paul, 1984) pl. 35.
5. F. Antal, *Hogarth and his Place in European Art* (New York: Basic Books, 1962) p. 66.
6. In 1663 Aphra Behn supplied a set of 'glorious Wreaths' of feathers from Surinam to be worn by the heroine in Dryden and Howard's *The Indian Queen. See The Works of Aphra Behn*, ed. M. Summers (1915; New York: Blom, 1967) vol. 5, p. 130. These feathers doubtless reappeared in Dryden's sequel, *The Indian Emperour*. In the prologue to the latter play, Dryden notes, 'The Habits are the same / We wore last year'. See *Works*, vol. 9, p. 29.
7. J. Dryden, 'Epilogue to the King and Queen, at the Opening of their Theatre', lines 5–8, in *Works*, vol. 2, ed. H. T. Swedenberg Jr and V. A. Dearing (1972) p. 198. Cf. Powell, *Restoration Theatre Production*, pp. 13–15.
8. Webster, *Hogarth*, p. 79.
9. J. Derrida, *Writing and Difference*, trans. A. Bass (Chicago, Ill.: University of Chicago Press, 1978) p. 176.
10. A. Artaud, *The Theater and its Double*, trans. M. C. Richards (New York: Grove, 1958) pp. 126–32.
11. A. Pagden, 'The Savage Critic: Some European Images of the Primitive', *Yearbook of English Studies*, vol. 13 (1983) p. 35.

12. T. Todorov, *The Conquest of America: The Question of the Other*, trans. R. Howard (New York: Harper & Row, 1984) p. 249.
13. Dryden, *Indian Emperour*, I, i, 1–20. Cf. Lucretius, *De rerum natura*, bk 5, 772–836, trans. W. H. D. Rouse, rev. M. F. Smith (Cambridge, Mass.: Harvard University Press, 1975) pp. 438–45. Lucretius compares the fruitfulness of 'the world's infancy' with the old earth's inability to bear, 'like a woman worn out by old age'. But he adds that, while 'one thing crumbles and grows faint and weak with age, another grows up and comes forth. . . . What [the earth] bore she cannot, but can bear what she did not bear before'. *De rerum natura* was read widely in England in the seventeenth-century. See G. D. Hadzsits, *Lucretius and his Influence* (New York: Longmans, Green, 1935) pp. 284–317. Dryden knew *De rerum natura* well and was to publish a translation of parts of the poem in 1685. See *Works*, vol. 3, ed. E. Miner and V. A. Dearing (1969) pp. 44–66.
14. Dryden, *Indian Emperour*, I, i, 21–6. Cf. Lucretius, bk 5, 818–19, in Rouse's translation, pp. 442–3: 'The infancy of the world produced neither hard cold nor excessive heat nor winds of great force'.
15. Dryden, *Indian Emperour*, I, i, 11–14. Cf. Montaigne, 'Of Cannibals', *Essais*, liv. 1, cap. 31, in *The Essays of Montaigne*, trans. E. J. Trechmann (New York: Random House, 1945) p. 176: 'We call barbarism that which does not fit in with our usages. And indeed we have no other level of truth and reason but the example and model of the usages of the country we live in. . . . Those people are wild in the sense in which we call wild the fruits that Nature has produced by herself and in her ordinary progress; whereas in truth it is those we have altered artificially and diverted from the common order, that we should rather call wild'.
16. D. Hughes, *Dryden's Heroic Plays* (Lincoln, Neb.: University of Nebraska Press, 1981) p. 40. Cf. Alssid, *Dryden's Rhymed Heroic Tragedies*, p. 144.
17. Winn, *John Dryden*, p. 152, points to another way in which the second scene discredits the Spanish assumptions of the first scene. Cortez (I, i, 1–4) describes the New World as the child of the Old, implying that future relations between the two cultures should resemble those between parents and children. But, as Winn notes, the 'struggle between the generations in the Indian camp' in scene 2 quickly serves notice that such relations 'are not always warm and nurturing'.
18. Todorov, *Conquest*, p. 42. Todorov defines egocentrism as 'the identification of our own values with values in general'. For Todorov's critique of Spanish theories of just conquest, see ibid., pp. 146–82.
19. Hughes, *Dryden's Heroic Plays*, p. 48.
20. For an English translation of the *Requerimiento*, see L. Hanke (ed.), *History of Latin American Civilization*, 2nd edn (Boston, Mass.: Little, Brown, 1973) vol. 1, pp. 94–5. For a brief history of the *Requerimiento*, see L. Hanke, *The Spanish Struggle for Justice in the Conquest of America* (Philadelphia, Pa: University of Pennsylvania Press, 1949) pp. 31–6. For Todorov's critique of the document, see Todorov, *Conquest*, pp. 146–9.

21. Montaigne, 'Of Coaches', liv. 3, cap. 6, in *Essays of Montaigne*, pp. 795–801. For a discussion of Dryden's debt to Montaigne and of his possible use of Montaigne's own sources, see Dryden, *Works*, vol. 9, pp. 310–15.
22. Dryden, *Indian Emperour*, I, ii, 282–8, 293–4. Cf. Montaigne, *Essays of Montaigne*, p. 798: 'The man who parcelled out things in that way must be fond of broils, to go and give to another person what did not belong to him'.
23. Alssid, *Dryden's Rhymed Heroic Tragedies*, p. 143. Cf. Barbeau, *Intellectual Design*, pp. 83, 89; and J. M. Armistead, 'The Occultism of Dryden's American Plays in Context', *Seventeenth Century*, vol. 1 (1986) p. 139.
24. Todorov, *Conquest*, pp. 189, 250.
25. M. M. Bakhtin, *The Dialogic Imagination*, trans. C. Emerson and M. Holquist (Austin, Tx.: University of Texas Press, 1981) pp. 311–12.
26. J. Loftis in Dryden, *Works*, vol. 9, p. 306.
27. D. Hughes, 'Dryden's *The Indian Emperour* and Georges de Scudéry's *Alaric*', *Review of English Studies*, vol. 31 (1982) pp. 47–51. Cf. Hughes, *Dryden's Plays*, pp. 160–2, for Dryden's debt to La Calprenède.
28. Hughes, *Dryden's Heroic Plays*, pp. 168–9, provides a lengthy bibliography of this debate, in which he serves as the most articulate spokesman for the view that Dryden finds fault with his heroes.
29. Armistead, 'Occultism', p. 151; Barbeau, *Intellectual Design*, pp. 84–5.
30. Pagden, 'Savage Critic', pp. 34–6.
31. Montaigne, 'Of Coaches', p. 799.
32. Loftis, in Dryden, *Works*, vol. 9, p. 316, n. 96.
33. Hughes, *Dryden's Heroic Plays*, p. 57; Dryden, *Indian Emperour*, V, ii, 111.
34. J. A. Winterbottom, 'The Place of Hobbesian Ideas in Dryden's Tragedies', *Journal of English and Germanic Philosophy*, vol. 57 (1958) p. 668.
35. Dryden, *Indian Emperour*, I, i, 169; Barbeau, *Intellectual Design*, pp. 86–7.
36. Cf. Winterbottom, 'Place of Hobbesian Ideas', p. 669, and Alssid, *Dryden's Rhymed Heroic Tragedies*, pp. 159–61.
37. Bakhtin, *Dialogic Imagination*, pp. 375–6. Cf. G. S. Morson and C. Emerson, *Mikhail Bakhtin: Creation of a Prosaics* (Stanford, Cal.: Stanford University Press, 1990) pp. 344–8.
38. Dryden, *Indian Emperour*, II, i, 88–104; Virgil, *Aeneid*, bk 6, 440–74; Armistead, 'Occultism', p. 143.
39. Armistead, 'Occultism', p. 141.
40. Dryden, *Indian Emperour*, V, ii, 356–7; Barbeau, *Intellectual Design*, pp. 33–8.
41. Powell, *Restoration Theatre Production*, p. 76.
42. Ibid., p. 108: 'The stance of the actors is reminiscent of soloists in an oratorio. . . . Their words begin addressed to their companions on the stage, but as the speeches develop, a turn of the head directs the description straight to the audience in the theatre'. Cf. Powell's discussion of the performers in Hogarth's painting (ibid., pp. 101–2).
43. Ibid., p. 105.
44. Ibid., p. 60.

45. B. Brecht, *Brecht on Theatre*, ed. and trans. J. Willett (New York: Hill & Wang, 1964) p. 39.
46. Derrida, *Writing and Difference*, p. 190.
47. Artaud, *Theater*, p. 39.
48. Brecht, *Brecht on Theatre*, p. 39.
49. For a complete record of known performances of *The Indian Emperour* on the London stage, see Ben Ross Schneider, Jr, *Index to the London Stage, 1660–1800* (Carbondale, Ill.: Southern Illinois University Press, 1979) pp. 254–5, and the appropriate references in *The London Stage: 1660–1800*, ed. W. Van Lennep *et al.*, 11 vols (Carbondale, Ill.: Southern Illinois University Press, 1960–8).
50. J. Lindsay, *Hogarth: His Art and His World* (London: Hart-Davis, MacGibbon, 1977) p. 76.
51. The last performance of *The Indian Emperour* on the London stage was on 7 May 1737. I know of no subsequent revival of the play. *The Indian Queen*, however, with music by Henry Purcell, was revived in Oxford in February 1984. For a review of the production, see C. Rawson, 'Beyond the Mexique Bay', *The Times Literary Supplement*, 24 February 1984, p. 192.
52. For the stage history of *The Tempest*, see W. Shakespeare, *The Tempest*, ed. S. Orgel (Oxford: Clarendon Press, 1987) pp. 64–87; and, with particular attention to the theme of colonialism, T. R. Griffiths, ' "This Island's mine": Caliban and Colonialism', *Yearbook of English Studies*, vol. 13 (1983) pp. 159–80; or M. Harris, 'Theater, Colonization, and the Conquest of Mexico', dissertation, University of Virginia, 1989, pp. 194–207.
53. Todorov, *Conquest*, p. 4.

Notes to Chapter 3: A Marrano in Montezuma's Court

1. C. Swietlicki, 'Lope's Dialogic Imagination: Writing Other Voices of Monolithic Spain', *Bulletin of the Comediantes*, vol. 40 (1988) pp. 220–1. For an account of the Inquisition, see H. C. Lea, *A History of the Inquisition in Spain*, 4 vols (1906; New York: American Scholar, 1966), or H. Kamen, *The Spanish Inquisition* (New York: New American Library, 1965).
2. F. M. M[ontero] de E[spinosa], *Relación histórica de la judería en Sevilla* (Seville: J. J. Franco, 1849) pp. 85–99. For a generic description of *autos de fe*, see Lea, *History of the Inquisition*, vol. 3, pp. 209–29.
3. For a history of the Marranos, see C. Roth, *A History of the Marranos* (1932; New York: Jewish Publication Society of America, 1966); Y. Baer, *A History of the Jews in Christian Spain*, 2 vols (Philadelphia, Pa: Jewish Publication Society of America, 1961); or J. Caro Baroja, *Los judíos en la España moderna y contemporánea*, 3 vols (Madrid: Arion, 1961–2). For a history of the laws requiring purity of blood, see A. A. Sicroff, *Les Controverses des statuts de 'pureté de sang' en Espagne du XVe au XVIIe siècle* (Paris: Didier, 1960).
4. T. Oelman (ed.), *Marrano Poets of the Seventeenth-Century* (London:

Associated University Presses, 1982) pp. 137–218, translates a number of Enríquez Gómez's poems, including *Romance al divín mártir*, a ballad celebrating a convert to Judaism executed by the Inquisition in 1644. For a full critical edition of this poem, see A. Enríquez Gómez, *Romance al divín mártir, Judá Creyente [don Lope de Vera y Alarcón] martirizado en Valladolid por la Inquisición*, ed. T. Oelman (London: Associated University Presses, 1986). I. S. Révah, 'Un Pamphlet Contre l'Inquisition d'Antonio Enríquez Gómez: La Seconde Partie de la "Política Angélica" (Rouen, 1647)', *Revue des études juives*, vol. 121 (1962) pp. 81–168, includes and comments at length on Enríquez Gómez's *Política angélica*, a pamphlet containing scathing criticism of the Inquisition. J. G. García Valdecasas, *Las 'Academias morales' de Antonio Enríquez Gómez* (Seville: Publicaciones de la Universidad de Sevilla, 1971) pp. 102–11, draws attention to those passages in the *Academias morales* that would have angered the Inquisitors.

5. M[ontero] de E[spinosa], *Relación histórica*, p. 97; García Valdecasas, *Las 'Academias Morales'*, pp. 31–5.
6. G. F. Dille, *Antonio Enríquez Gómez* (Boston, Mass.: Twayne, 1988) p. 143; C. H. Rose, 'Las comedias políticas de Enríquez Gómez', *La torre*, vol. 118 (1982) p. 196.
7. *Parte treinta, Comedias nuevas, y escogidas de los mejores ingenios de Espana* (Madrid: Domingo Garcia Morrás, 1668) pp. 228–59, reproduced in *Spanish Drama of the Golden Age: The Comedia Collection in the University of Pennyslvania Libraries* (New Haven, Conn.: Research Publications, 1971) microfilm, reel 7, #317. Subsequent parenthetical references are to the page numbers of this edition. There are no modern editions of *La conquista de México*. Since the text of the play is not readily available, I shall often quote both the Spanish text and my own translation.
8. A. de Castro (ed.), *Poetas líricos de los siglos XVI y XVII*, Biblioteca de Autores Españoles 42 (1857; Madrid: Rivadaneyra, 1875) pp. xx–xxiii, lxxxix–xci. For a brief account of the argument surrounding the rediscovery of the identity of Enríquez Gómez and Zárate, see G. Dille, 'Antonio Enríquez Gómez: Alias Fernando de Zárate', *Papers on Language and Literature*, vol. 14 (1978) pp. 11–21.
9. R. de Mesonero y Romanos (ed.), *Dramaticos posteriores a Lope de Vega*, Biblioteca de Autores Españoles 47 (Madrid: Rivaneyra, 1858) p. xxxiii.
10. Dille, 'Antonio Enríquez Gómez', p. 15.
11. Révah, 'Pamphlet'. Additional biographical material on Enríquez Gómez can be found in A. Enríquez Gómez, *El siglo pitagórico y vida de don Gregorio Guadaña*, ed. C. Amiel (Paris: Hispanoamericanas, 1977) pp. xv–xxi; J. A. Cid, 'Judaizantes y carreteros para un hombre de letras: A. Enríquez Gómez (1600–1663)', in *Homenaje a Julio Caro Baroja*, ed. A. Carreira *et al.* (Madrid: Centro de Investigaciones Sociologicas, 1978) pp. 271–300; Dille, *Antonio Enríquez Gómez*, pp. 9–20; and Oelman, (ed.), *Romance*, pp. 19–28.
12. Dille, *Antonio Enríquez Gómez*, p. 142. García Valdecasas, *Las 'Academias morales'*, p. 12; D. Gitlitz, 'La angustia vital de ser negro, tema de un drama de Fernando de Zárate', *Segismundo*, vol. 11 (1975) pp. 2–4; and

Oelman (ed.), *Marrano Poets*, p. 139, and *Romance*, pp. 24–5, expressed initial doubts as to Révah's conclusions. The identity of Enríquez Gómez and Zárate was, however, accepted by C. H. Rose, 'Antonio Enríquez Gómez and the Literature of Exile', *Romanische Forschungen*, vol. 85 (1973) p. 75; J. Caro Baroja, *Inquisición, brujería y criptojudaísmo* (Barcelona: Ariel, 1974) pp. 153–5; Amiel (ed.), *El siglo pitagórico*, pp. xix–xxi; Cid, 'Judaizantes', p. 280; and Dille, Antonio Enríquez Gómez, pp. 11–21. W. A. Reynolds, *Hernán Cortés en la literatura del siglo de oro* (Madrid: Nacional, 1978) pp. 60–2, seems to have been unaware of Révah's work.

13. Dille, *Antonio Enríquez Gómez*, p. 149.

14. Cid, 'Judaizantes', p. 291. Cid's views are shared, in varying degree, by Révah, 'Pamphlet', p. 83; Amiel (ed.), *El siglo pitagórico*, pp. xx–xxi; and Oelman (ed.), *Romance*, pp. 29–57. García Valdecasas, *Las 'Academias morales'*, p. 75, adopts the unusual stance of denying Enríquez Gómez's identity with Zárate and yet affirming the former's genuine Christianity.

15. Dille, *Antonio Enríquez Gómez*, p. 151.

16. Reynolds, *Hernan Cortés*, p. 61.

17. Despite the recent revival of interest in Enríquez Gómez, alias Zárate, the play has received little critical attention. S. J. Ruffner, 'The American Theme in Selected Dramas of the Golden Age', dissertation, University of Southern California, 1953, pp. 49–64, summarizes extensively and comments briefly on the play. N. D. Shergold, *A History of the Spanish Stage from Medieval Times until the End of the Seventeenth-Century* (Oxford: Clarendon Press, 1967) p. 374, makes brief mention of the spectacular staging implied by 'Zárate's' text. Reynolds, *Hernán Cortés*, pp. 60–2; Cid, 'Judaizantes', p. 296; and Dille, *Antonio Enríquez Gómez*, pp. 51, 143–51, make passing reference. The two articles by C. Romero Muñoz, cited below, contain the only detailed analysis of the text published to date. These, however, focus on style and provenance rather than on meaning.

18. C. Romero Muñoz, *'La conquista de Cortés*, comedia perdida (¿y hallada?) de Lope de Vega', *Studi di letteratura ibero-americano offerti a Giuseppe Bellini* (Rome: Bulzoni, 1984) pp. 105–24. W. L. Fichter, 'Lope de Vega's *La conquista de Cortés* and *El Marqués del Valle*', *Hispanic Review*, vol. 3 (1935) p. 165, had speculated in a footnote on the possible relationship of the two plays.

19. Romero Muñoz, *'La conquista'*, p. 110.

20. C. Romero Muñoz, 'Lope de Vega y "Fernando de Zárate": *El Nuevo Mundo* (y *Arauco domado*) en *La conquista de México'*, *Studi di letteratura ispano-americana*, vols 15–16 (1983) pp. 243–64.

21. Ibid., p. 252.

22. C. Stern, 'Lope de Vega, Propagandist?', *Bulletin of the Comediantes*, vol. 34 (1982) pp. 1–36, nicely summarizes and then challenges the prevailing views of Lope as an uncritical propagandist for conservative Spanish values.

23. Ibid.; A. Zuckerman-Ingber, *El bien más alto: A Reconsideration of Lope de Vega's Honor Plays* (Gainesville, Fla: University Press of Florida,

1984); J. B. Norden, 'Lope de Vega's Use of Discretion: An Indication of a Change in Spanish Thought', *Bulletin of the Comediantes*, vol. 39 (1987) pp. 99–114.

24. D. Gitlitz, 'The New Christian Dilemma in Two Plays by Lope de Vega', *Bulletin of the Comediantes*, vol. 34 (1982) pp. 63–81; Zuckerman-Ingber, *El bien más alto*, pp. 145–74; Swietlicki, 'Lope's Dialogic Imagination', pp. 205–26.

25. Swietlicki, 'Lope's Dialogic Imagination', p. 205. Cf. R. Z. Lavine, 'The Jew and the *converso* in the Dramatic Works of Lope de Vega', dissertation, Catholic University of America, 1983, who concludes that Lope's 'occasional "sympathetic" portrayals of the Jew and the *converso* . . . stem from the aesthetic demands of individual dramas, and do not signify Lope's advocacy of the Jewish or *converso* cause.'

26. G. F. Dille, 'The Tragedy of Don Pedro: Old and New Christian Conflict in *El valiente Campuzano*', *Bulletin of the Comediantes*, vol. 35 (1983) p. 106. Cf. Gitlitz, 'La angustia', p. 84.

27. Oelman (ed.), *Romance*, pp. 24–5.

28. Gitlitz, 'La angustia,' pp. 65–9, 77. Cf. G. F. Dille, 'A Black Man's Dilemma in *Las misas de S. Vicente Ferrer*', *Romance Notes*, vol. 20 (1979) pp. 87–93.

29. Romero Muñoz, '*La conquista*', p. 106.

30. Gitlitz, 'La angustia', p. 83, and 'La actitud cristiano-nueva en *Las cortes de muerte*', *Segismundo*, vol. 9 (1973) pp. 141–64. Carvajal's play may be found in J. de Sancha (ed.), *Romancero y cancionero sagrados*, Biblioteca de Autores Españoles, vol. 35 (Madrid: Rivaneyra, 1872) pp. 1–41. The Indians appear in scene 19.

31. A. Enríquez Gómez, *Loa sacramental de los siete planetas*, ed. C. H. Rose and T. Oelman (Exeter: University of Exeter Press, 1987) p. xxxiv.

32. Dille, *Antonio Enríquez Gómez*, p. 151, adduces this passage as evidence of the playwright's own Christianity, a conclusion that shows too little sensitivity to dramatic context.

33. F. López de Gómara, *La conquista de México*, ed. J. L. de Rojas (Madrid: Historia 16, 1987).

34. Kamen, *Spanish Inquisition*, p. 150. Cf. Lea, *History of the Inquisition*, vol. 2, pp. 315–87.

35. Révah, 'Pamphlet', p. 82.

36. My translation of Enríquez Gómez's Spanish citation.

37. Révah, 'Pamphlet', p. 135.

38. Romero Muñoz, 'Lope', pp. 248, 257–8; Lope de Vega, *El Nuevo Mundo descubierto por Cristóbal Colón*, ed. J. Lemartinel and C. Minguet (Lille: Presses Universitaires de Lille, 1980) pp. 24–8.

39. Gómara, *La conquista*, p. 117.

40. For a discussion of Enríquez Gómez's private use of Jewish symbols in a 'Catholic religious work of impeccable public orthodoxy', written and performed anonymously in Seville in 1659, see Rose and Oelman, in Enríquez Goméz, *Loa sacramental*, pp. vii–liv. Montezuma's emblematic use of the sun and moon is mentioned by Gómara, *La conquista*, p. 86.

41. Cf. John 6–8, where Jesus, in the context of the Passover Feast (6: 4)

and Feast of Tabernacles (7: 2), declares himself to be 'the bread of life' (6: 35), the source of 'living water' (7: 37–8), and 'the light of the world' (8: 12).

42. Roth, *History of the Marranos*, pp. 69–71; Kamen, *Spanish Inquisition*, p. 217.

Notes to Chapter 4: Aspiring Tyrants and Theatrical Defiance

1. Paraphrasing Bakhtin's remarks in 'Toward a Philosophy of the Act' (*c*. 1924), G. S. Morson and C. Emerson, *Mikhail Bakhtin: Creation of a Prosaics* (Stanford, Cal.: Stanford University Press, 1990), p. 34, write, 'That "something new" which an actor imparts to his actions or which interlocutors impart to an utterance must always include an evaluative stance, which is carried by the "emotional-volitional tone" of the act or utterance. . . . Often, gestures serve a similar function, carrying a silent intonation'. Cf. G. S. Morson and C. Emerson, 'Introduction', in *Rethinking Bakhtin*, ed. Morson and Emerson (Evanston, Ill.: Northwestern University Press, 1989) pp. 15–16. Despite these observations about human utterances and actions in general, Bakhtin does not appear to have recognized the dialogical implications of tone and gesture on stage.

2. J. Derrida, *Writing and Difference*, trans. A. Bass (Chicago, Ill.: University of Chicago Press, 1978) p. 190.

3. A. Artaud, *The Theater and its Double*, trans. M. C. Richards (New York: Grove, 1958) pp. 89, 126. To avoid confusion between 'Zárate's' *La conquista de México* and Artaud's *La Conquête du Mexique*, whose titles would be identical if translated into English, I have referred to both by their original titles. I have also, when quoting from an English version of Artaud's work, replaced the translated title of his scenario with the original *La Conquête du Mexique*.

4. P. Deharme, quoted in M.-C. Dumas, *Robert Desnos ou L'Exploration des limites* (Paris: Klinksieck, 1980) p. 196.

5. A. Artaud, *The Peyote Dance*, trans. H. Weaver (New York: Farrar, Straus & Giroux, 1976) p. 61.

6. The invitation is printed in A. Artaud, *Oeuvres complètes*, 12 vols (Paris: Gallimard, 1956–74) vol. 5, p. 369.

7. Dumas, *Robert Desnos*, pp. 83–103.

8. Y. Desnos, *Les Confidences de Youki* (Paris: Fayard, 1957) p. 177.

9. J. Hort, *Antonin Artaud, le suicidé de la société* (Geneva: Connaître, 1960) p. 58, quoted in translation in N. Greene, *Antonin Artaud: Poet Without Words* (New York: Simon & Schuster, 1970) p. 20.

10. Quoted in translation in C. Innes, *Holy Theatre* (Cambridge: Cambridge University Press, 1981) p. 91.

11. Artaud, *Theater*, pp. 65, 46.

12. J. Flanner, 'Introduction', in Greene, *Antonin Artaud*, p. 11.

13. Desnos, *Confidences*, p. 178.

14. Artaud, *Oeuvres*, vol. 5, p. 369. An abbreviated version of *La Conquête du Mexique* had been published the previous year as part of a 16-page

brochure, *Le Théâtre de la cruauté (second manifeste)* (Fontenay-aux-Roses: Denoel, 1933). It is this abbreviated version that was included in the French edition of *Le Théâtre et son double* (Paris: Gallimard, 1938). See Artaud, *Oeuvres*, vol. 4, pp. 151–3, 378. The complete text read by Artaud at the Deharmes' soirée was first published in *La Nef* (March–April 1950) and is reprinted in *Oeuvres*, vol. 5, pp. 20–9; cf. p. 323. M. C. Richards's English translation of *The Theater and its Double* includes the full text of the scenario (pp. 128–32), but the abbreviated version of its preface (pp. 126–8). In what follows I have quoted, wherever possible, from Richards's translation; where necessary, I have translated directly from the full version of the preface.

15. Artaud, *Theater*, pp. 15–32.
16. Ibid., p. 125.
17. For an account of events leading up to and including the Night of Sorrows, see W. H. Prescott, *The Conquest of Mexico* (1843; New York: Random House, n.d.) pp. 413–53, or R. C. Padden, *The Hummingbird and the Hawk* (Columbus, Ohio: Ohio State University Press, 1967) pp. 192–202.
18. P. L. Podol, 'Contradictions and Dualities in Artaud and Artaudian Theater: *The Conquest of Mexico* and the Conquest of Peru', *Modern Drama*, vol. 26 (1983) p. 522.
19. Greene, *Antonin Artaud*, p. 220, concludes that 'Artaud's ideal theater was essentially unrealizable'. Derrida, *Writing and Difference*, pp. 247–8, agrees: 'Fidelity is impossible. There is no theater in the world today which fulfills Artaud's desire.' Works influenced by Artaud's scenario, such as Peter Shaffer's *The Royal Hunt of the Sun* (1964) and Claude Demarigny's *Cajamarca* (1978), depart from Artaud not only in historical referent (the Conquest of Peru) but also in significant aspects of theatrical style. For a discussion of their similarities and differences, see Podol, 'Contradictions', pp. 518–27.
20. Artaud, *Theater*, pp. 40, 69, 106.
21. Artaud, *Oeuvres*, vol. 5, p. 369.
22. Derrida, *Writing and Difference*, pp. 176, 189, 236, 185, 191, 235, 190, 175, 240.
23. Ibid., p. 180.
24. Ibid., pp. 235, 239.
25. Artaud, *Theater*, pp. 68, 39.
26. Ibid., p. 111.
27. Ibid., p. 128.
28. Ibid., pp. 109–10.
29. Ibid., p. 60.
30. Derrida, *Writing and Difference*, p. 192.
31. Artaud, *Theater*, pp. 115, 85, 28, 31.
32. Artaud, *Oeuvres*, vol. 2, p. 14.
33. Artaud, *Theater*, pp. 81, 121.
34. Ibid., p. 32.
35. Ibid., pp. 53, 57–8. For a comparison of Artaud's 'impressions' with 'Balinese theatre as it was and is', see P. A. Clancy, 'Artaud and the Balinese Theatre', *Modern Drama*, vol. 27 (1985) pp. 397–412. Although

Clancy finds Artaud to have been generally sensitive to the 'spirit' of the Balinese theatre, she asserts (p. 409) that he 'was definitely mistaken' in his assumption that the director played a dominant role.

36. Artaud, *Theater*, p. 79. For the role of the Soviet censor, see *Literature and Revolution in Soviet Russia*, ed. M. Hayward and L. Labedz (London: Oxford University Press, 1963).

37. Artaud, *Theater*, p. 94.

38. B. L. Fontana, *Tarahumara* (Flagstaff, Ariz.: Northland, 1979) p. 46.

39. Charles Marowitz, a modern director influenced by Artaud, is unabashed by the colonial aspirations of his trade: 'The director is a self-obsessed colonizer who wishes to materialize power through harnessing and shaping the powers of others'. See C. Marowitz, *Prospero's Staff* (Bloomington, Ind.: Indiana University Press, 1986) p. xvi.

40. A. Wesker, 'Interpretation: To Impose or Explain', *Performing Arts Journal*, vol. 32 (1988) p. 75.

41. K. E. Maus, 'Arcadia Lost: Politics and Revision in the Restoration *Tempest*', *Renaissance Drama*, n.s. vol. 13 (1982) pp. 189–209.

42. Frank Benson's performance of Caliban at Stratford-upon-Avon in 1891 was based on D. Wilson, *Caliban: The Missing Link* (London: Macmillan, 1873). See J. C. Trewin, *Benson and the Bensonians* (London: Barrie & Rockliff, 1960) pp. 71–4; and M. M. Nilan, ' "The Tempest" at the Turn of the Century: Cross-Currents in Production', *Shakespeare Survey*, vol. 25 (1972) pp. 114–15.

43. T. R. Griffiths, ' "This Island's mine": Caliban and Colonialism', *Yearbook of English Studies*, vol. 13 (1983) pp. 169–70, notes a 'pro-Imperial' flavour in Beerbohm Tree's 1904 production.

44. Jonathan Miller directed the play in 1970 as a parable of colonialism. See J. Miller, *Subsequent Performances* (London: Faber & Faber, 1986) pp. 159–62; and R. Berry, *On Directing Shakespeare* (London: Croom Helm, 1977) p. 35.

45. P. Brook, *The Empty Space* (New York: Avon, 1968) p. 86. Brook is describing conventional productions of *The Tempest*.

46. Peter Brook directed *The Tempest* in 1968 under the influence of Artaud. See ibid., p. 86; and M. Croyden, *Lunatics, Lovers and Poets: The Contemporary Experimental Theatre* (New York: McGraw-Hill, 1974) pp. 246–50.

Notes to Chapter 5: Flower Wars and Battle Plays

1. The account of the play is found in Toribio de Motolinía, *Historia de los indios de la Nueva España*, trat. 1, cap. 15, ed. G. Baudot (Madrid: Clásicos Castalia, 1985) pp. 202–13. The translation from which I quote is Motolinía, *History of the Indians of New Spain*, trans. F. B. Steck (Washington, D. C.: Academy of American Franciscan History, 1951) pp. 159–167.

2. The number of actors is calculated by F. Horcasitas, *El teatro náhuatl* (Mexico: Universidad Nacional Autónoma de México, 1974) p. 507. I use the name Nahua after the manner of M. Leon-Portilla, *Aztec Thought*

and Culture, trans. J. E. Davis (Norman, Okla: University of Oklahoma Press, 1963) pp. xvii–xviii: 'At the beginning of the sixteenth-century, the ancient Mexicans – Aztecs, Texcocans, Cholulans, Chalcans, and Tlaxcaltecs – were people of diverse cultural interests and activities. . . . Despite their differences, these ancient Mexicans shared the same cultural heritage, bequeathed them by the founders of Teotihuacán and Tula. Because of their cultural similarities and their common linguistic bond, Náhuatl – the lingua franca of Middle America – these groups will hereafter be referred to generically as the Nahuas.'

3.   O. Arroníz, *Teatro de evangelización en Nueva España* (Mexico: Universidad Nacional Autónoma de México, 1979) pp. 17–18, 53. B. de Las Casas, *Apologética historia sumaria*, lib. 3, cap. 64 (Mexico: Universidad Nacional Autónoma de México, 1967) vol. 1, pp. 333–4, recalls seeing in Tlaxcala in 1538 'Our Lady' raised from one stage to another 'in a cloud'.

4.   Motolinía, *Historia*, pp. 21–7; C. Gibson, *Tlaxcala in the Sixteenth Century*, 2nd edn (Stanford, Cal.: Stanford University Press, 1967) p. 210.

5.   The identity of the author of *The Conquest of Jerusalem* is uncertain. Many, including Baudot, in Motolinía, *Historia*, pp. 24, 42–3, believe Motolinía himself to be the author of the play. Arroníz, *Teatro*, p. 83, suggests an Indian playwright.

6.   Motolinía, *History*, p. 160. Cf. J. L. Phelan, *The Millennial Kingdom of the Franciscans in the New World*, 2nd edn (Berkeley, Cal.: University of California Press, 1970) pp. 17–28; D. C. West, 'Medieval Ideas of Apocalyptic Mission and the Early Franciscans in Mexico', *The Americas*, vol. 45 (1989) pp. 293–313; and T. Todorov, *The Conquest of America: The Question of the Other*, trans. R. Howard (New York: Harper & Row, 1984) p. 11.

7.   Motolinía, *History*, pp. 161, 165.

8.   A. Recinos, *Pedro de Alvarado* (Mexico: Fondo de Cultura Economica, 1952) pp. 176–83; S. de Madariaga, *Hernán Cortés* (New York: Macmillan, 1941) p. 472.

9.   Some, lacking explanation, simply omit the data from their account of the play. See Gibson, *Tlaxcala*, p. 38; and R. Ricard, *The Spiritual Conquest of Mexico*, trans. L. B. Simpson (Berkeley, Cal.: University of California Press, 1966) pp. 196–8.

10. J. García Icazbalceta, *Colección de documentos para la historia de México* (Mexico: Porrua, 1971) p. 89, n. 21.

11. Baudot, in Motolinía, *Historia*, p. 43.

12. R. Baumann, 'Tlaxcalan Expression of Autonomy and Religious Drama in the Sixteenth-Century', *Journal of Latin American Lore*, vol. 13 (1987) p. 143. Cf. A. S. Aiton, *Antonio de Mendoza* (New York: Russell, 1927) pp. 121–3.

13. Horcasitas, *El teatro náhuatl*, p. 508.

14. Arroníz, *Teatro*, p. 83.

15. I. Clendinnen, *Ambivalent Conquests* (Cambridge: Cambridge University Press, 1987) p. xi.

16. *The Play of Antichrist*, trans. J. Wright (Toronto: Pontifical Institute of Mediaeval Studies, 1967). For the date of the play, see ibid., p. 24. For

the Latin text, see K. Young, *The Drama of the Medieval Church* (Oxford: Clarendon Press, 1933) vol. 2, pp. 371–87.

17. E. K. Chambers, *The Mediaeval Stage* (London: Oxford University Press, 1903) vol. 2, pp. 62–4, describes the play in a chapter devoted to 'liturgical plays', and imagines it taking up 'the whole nave of some great church'. But Young, *Drama*, vol. 2, p. 394, concludes, 'There is nothing to show that it was acted in association with the liturgy, or even within a church.'

18. L. H. Loomis, 'Secular Dramatics in the Royal Palace, Paris, 1378, 1389, and Chaucer's "Tregetoures" ', *Speculum*, vol. 33 (1958) pp. 242–55.

19. N. D. Shergold, *A History of the Spanish Stage from Medieval Times until the End of the Seventeenth Century* (Oxford: Clarendon Press, 1967) pp. 116–17. The historical Siege of Balaguer, at which Fernando enforced his claim to the throne of Aragon against the recalcitrant Jaime el Desdichado, lasted from 5 August to 31 October 1413.

20. *Le Mistère du siège d'Orleans*, ed. F. Guessard and E. de Certain (Paris: Imprimerie imperiale, 1862).

21. Ibid., p. 362: '*Lors tous les dessus dits partiront d'Orleans et leurs gens, bien deux mille.*' Cf. below, ch. 8, the 2500 participants in the Huejotzingo carnival play, or, on an even larger scale, the more than 8000 participants in Nikolai Evreinov's commemorative re-enactment *in situ* of *The Storming of the Winter Palace* in Petrograd in 1920. For the latter, see F. Deák, 'Russian Mass Spectacles', *The Drama Review*, vol. 19, no. 2 (1975) pp. 15–21.

22. G. Wickham, *Early English Stages, 1300–1660*, 3 vols (London: Routledge, 1959–81) vol. 2, pt 1, pp. 287–9.

23. T. Gage, *Travels in the New World*, ed. J. E. S. Thompson (Norman, Okla: University of Oklahoma Press, 1958) p. 146. On 21 January 1971 I saw the *combate naval* which is still held annually in Chiapa de Corzo. It consisted then of a flotilla of bamboo boats shooting firecrackers at each other and at *castillos* on the shore. There were no actors, though I was told that within living memory men had fought with lances from dug-out canoes as part of the spectacle. At the same fiesta, some 300 *parachicos*, describing themselves as 'Indians disguised as Spaniards', danced aggressively before the church door, their way barred by church officials. They were in effect besieging the church and, like the boats and fireworks, may have had their origin in the battle plays that Gage witnessed.

24. R. Ricard, 'Les Fêtes de *Moros y cristianos* au Mexique', *Journal de la Société des americanistes*, n.s. vol. 24 (1932) pp. 51–84, 287–91; M. S. Carrasco Urgoiti, 'Aspectos folklóricos y literarios de la fiesta de moros y cristianos en España', *PMLA*, vol. 78 (1963) pp. 476–91.

25. J. L. Mansanet Ribes, *La fiesta de moros y cristianos de Alcoy, y sus instituciones*, 2nd edn (Alcoy, Alicante: Mansanet Ribes, 1981).

26. Horcasitas, *El teatro náhuatl* p. 19.

27. Young, *Drama of the Medieval Church*, vol. 2, p. 542. The translation is from R. Axton, *European Drama of the Early Middle Ages* (London: Hutchinson, 1974) p. 44.

28. K. S. Latourette, *A History of the Expansion of Christianity* (London: Eyre, 1939) vol. 3, pp. 198–200.
29. Ricard, *Spiritual Conquest*, p. 200. Although Ricard is generally correct, it was not unusual for Latin hymns to be incorporated in Náhuatl drama. See Horcasitas, *El teatro náhuatl* pp. 145–6.
30. Las Casas, *Apologética*, lib. 3, cap. 64.
31. M. Leon-Portilla, *Pre-Columbian Literatures of Mexico*, trans. G. Lobanov and M. Leon-Portilla (Norman, Okla: University of Oklahoma Press, 1969) pp. 96–115. An earlier account of prehispanic drama in Mexico can be found in J. J. Rojas Garcidueñas, *El teatro de Nueva España en el siglo XVI* (Mexico: Alvarez, 1935) pp. 21–39.
32. Leon-Portilla, *Pre-Columbian Literatures*, p. 97.
33. M. E. Ravicz, *Early Colonial Religious Drama in Mexico* (Washington, D. C.: Catholic University of America Press, 1970) p. 9.
34. J. de Acosta, *Historia natural y moral de las Indias*, lib. 5, cap. 30 (Seville: Hispano-Americana de Publicaciones, 1987) vol. 2, pp. 88–9. I am quoting from the English translation of this passage in R. Usigli, *Mexico in the Theater*, trans. W. P. Scott (1932; Oxford, Miss.: University of Mississippi: Romance Monographs, 1976) p. 24.
35. Leon-Portilla, *Pre-Columbian Literatures*, pp. 109–15.
36. R. C. Padden, *The Hummingbird and the Hawk* (Columbus, Ohio: Ohio University Press, 1967) pp. 26–43, argues that both the flower wars and the system of human sacrifices they supported were 'political instruments', designed to sustain Aztec domestic and imperial power.
37. B. C. Brundage, *The Fifth Sun: Aztec Gods, Aztec World* (Austin, Tx.: University of Texas Press, 1979) p. 206.
38. For an artist's impression of the visual effect of a flower war, see F. Dávalos's painting reproduced in B. McDowell, 'The Aztecs', *National Geographic*, vol. 158 (1980) pp. 740–1.
39. D. Durán, *Historia de las indias de Nueva España*, tom. 2, cap. 57, ed. A. M. Garibay K. (Mexico: Porrua, 1967–71) vol. 2, pp. 433–7.
40. Ricard, *Spiritual Conquest*, pp. 205–6.
41. Horcasitas, *El teatro náhuatl*, p. 77. The sculptures he compares are on the façade of the Augustinian church of Acolman de Netzahualcóyotl, Mexico, and in the processional chapels of the Franciscan friary at San Andres de Calpan, Puebla.
42. Ricard, *Spiritual Conquest*, pp. 308–9.
43. B. Díaz del Castillo, *Historia verdadera de la conquista de la Nueva España*, cap. 174, ed. J. Ramírez Cabañas (Mexico: Espasa-Calpe Mexicana, 1950) vol. 3, p. 29.
44. Shergold, *History of the Spanish Stage*, pp. 268, 295, 605; Horcasitas, *El teatro náhuatl*, p. 515.
45. G. de Mendieta, *Historia eclesiástica indiana*, lib. 3, cap. 18, ed. J. García Icazbalceta (Mexico: Porrua, 1971) pp. 222–3.
46. J. H. Cornyn and B. McAfee, 'Tlacahuapahualiztli', *Tlalocan*, vol. 1 (1944) p. 316. For the probable text of this play, together with a Spanish translation, see Horcasitas, *El teatro náhuatl*, pp. 448–59.
47. Horcasitas, *El teatro náhuatl*, p. 450; I am citing the English translation of this line from Ravicz, *Early Colonial Religious Drama*, p. 48.

188 *Notes*

48. Ravicz, *Early Colonial Religious Drama*, p. 48.
49. B. de Sahagún, *Historia general de las cosas de Nueva España*, lib. 1, cap. 5 (Mexico: Pedro Robredo, 1938) vol. 1, pp. 17–18.
50. V. R. Bricker, *The Indian Christ, the Indian King* (Austin, Tx: University of Texas Press, 1981) pp. 143–8.
51. F. de Florencia, *La estrella del norte de México* [1675], ed. D. Agustín de la Rosa (Guadalajara: Cabrera, 1895) pp. 29, 115.
52. P. Harrington, 'Mother of Death, Mother of Rebirth: The Mexican Virgin of Guadalupe,' *Journal of the American Academy of Religion*, vol. 56 (1988) p. 32.
53. *Relación breve y verdadera de algunas cosas de las muchas que sucedieron al padre fray Alonso Ponce en las provincias de Nueva España . . .*, 2 vols, *Colección de documentos inéditos para la historia de España*, vols 57–8 (Madrid: Calero, 1872) vol. 2, p. 8; P. W. Powell, *Mexico's Miguel Caldera* (Tucson, Ariz.: University of Arizona Press, 1977) p. 110, provides a translation of this passage.
54. Horcasitas, *El teatro náhuatl*, pp. 561–93.
55. Ibid., pp. 79, 335–6.
56. For confirmation of Motolinía's dating, see Gibson, *Tlaxcala*, p. 38, n. 33.
57. Las Casas, *Apologética*, lib. 3, cap. 64. Gibson, *Tlaxcala*, p. 139, writes of such numerical estimates, 'It should be added that this and other observations for conquest times express only a gross impression and were made by persons to whom statistical accuracy was not a major concern'. None the less, it should also be remembered that the population of Tlaxcala in 1538 may have been as high as 300,000 (ibid., p. 141), and that Las Casas's estimate is not therefore impossible.
58. Motolinía, *History*, pp. 154–9.
59. Motolinía, *Historia*, p. 196. Steck (ibid., p. 155) translates this as 'an excellent motet with organ accompaniment'. Horcasitas, *El teatro náhuatl*, p. 142, points out that '*canto de órgano* does not refer in any way to the instrument of that name' but to polyphonic song, as distinct from the older plain song, or *canto llano*. In *canto de órgano*, the several human voices, singing in counterpoint, recall the multiple 'voices of the organ'.
60. The Tlaxcaltecas may have been adapting a standard Nahua comic routine. Durán, *Historia*, tom. 1, cap. 21 (vol. 1, p. 195), records a song-and-dance routine involving jugglers and a fool who pretended to misunderstand his master's instructions.
61. Horcasitas, *El teatro náhuatl*, p. 84.
62. W. and A. Durant, *The Story of Civilization* (New York: Simon & Schuster, 1935–75) vol. 6, p. 515.
63. Motolinía, *History*, p. 160. Díaz, *Historia*, cap. 201 (vol. 3, p. 182), says the news arrived in 1538. Las Casas, *Apologética*, lib. 3, cap. 64, confirms at least that the festivities celebrating the peace took place in 1539.
64. F. del Paso y Troncoso, *Epistolario de Nueva España* (Mexico: Porrua, 1939) vol. 3, p. 244.
65. Horcasitas, *El teatro náhuatl*, p. 499.

Notes   189

66. Ibid., p. 500; Phelan, *Millenial Kingdom*, pp. 11–12.
67. Las Casas, *Apologética*, lib. 3, cap. 64.
68. Shergold, *History of the Spanish Stage*, pp. 98, 140–1.
69. Díaz, *Historia*, cap. 201 (vol. 3, p. 184). In the following account, I have quoted from both Díaz and Las Casas.
70. *Historia de la nación mexicana Códice de 1576 (Códice Aubin)*, ed. and trans. C. E. Dibble (Madrid: Porrua, Turanzas, 1963) p. 90, contains what Horcasitas, *El teatro náhuatl*, p. 501, believes to be a stylized illustration of the entry of one of the ships in *The Conquest of Rhodes*.
71. Madariaga, *Hernán Cortés*, p. 471; C. Pereyra, *Hernán Cortés* (Madrid: Aguilar, 1931) p. 406; and A. Dotor, *Hernán Cortés* (Madrid: Gran Capitán, 1948) p. 407, all assume, in their account of the festivities, that Cortés himself took part in *The Conquest of Rhodes*.
72. Díaz, *Historia*, cap. 201 (vol. 3, p. 188).
73. Ibid., cap 201 (vol. 3, p. 183): '*garrotes añudados y retuertos*'. A. P. Maudslay, in B. Díaz, *The True History of the Conquest of New Spain* (London: Hakluyt Society, 1908–16), vol. 5, p. 190, translates this as 'knotted and twisted cudgels'. Clubs or cudgels made of knotted and twisted rope are still used by the combatants in the annual 'jaguar fights' in the state of Guerrero. See McDowell, 'Aztecs', p. 743.
74. Horcasitas, *El teatro náhuatl*, p. 503.
75. Durán, *Historia*, tom. 1, caps. 8 and 21 (vol. 1, pp. 86 and 193); Horcasitas, *El teatro náhuatl*, p. 105.
76. Durán, *Historia*, tom. 1, cap. 21.
77. Shergold, *History of the Spanish Stage*, p. 617. Cf. H. V. Livermore, 'El caballero salvaje. Ensayo de identificación de un juglar', *Revista de filología española*, vol. 34 (1950) pp. 166–83.
78. Shergold, *History of the Spanish Stage*, pp. 115–16.
79. I am indebted to Sarah Shaver Hughes, Associate Professor of History at Shippensburg University and a colleague at the Virginia Center for the Humanities in the Fall of 1991, for helping me understand the references to *negros y negras* in this play.
80. C. A. Palmer, *Slaves of the White God: Blacks in Mexico, 1570–1650* (Cambridge, Mass.: Harvard University Press, 1976) pp. 27, 133; D. M. Davidson, 'Negro Slave Control and Resistance in Colonial Mexico, 1519–1650', *Hispanic American Historical Review*, vol. 46 (1966) p. 237.
81. M. Karasch, 'Commentary One', in M. Schuler *et al.*, 'Afro-American Slave Culture', *Historical Reflections/Réflexions historiques*, vol. 6 (1979) p. 139.
82. Palmer, *Slaves of the White God*, pp. 54–5.
83. *Colección de documentos inéditos relativos al descubrimiento, conquista y organización de las antiguas posesiones españolas de America y Oceania* ..., 42 vols (Madrid: n.p., 1864–84) vol. 2, pp. 198–9; Davidson, 'Negro Slave Control', p. 243.
84. Palmer, *Slaves of the White God*, pp. 136–9.
85. J. Williams, 'El teatro de evangelización en México durante el siglo XVI: reseña historico-literaria', dissertation, Yale University, 1980, p. 139.

Notes to Chapter 6: Hernán Cortés: Sultan of Babylon

1. O. Arroníz, *Teatro de evangelización en Nueva España* (Mexico: Universidad Nacional Autónoma de México, 1979) p. 63.

2. Toribio de Motolinía, *History of the Indians in New Spain*, trans. F. B. Steck (Washington, D. C.: Academy of American Franciscan History, 1951), p. 160, and, for the following account of the play, pp. 160–7.

3. C. Gibson, *Tlaxcala in the Sixteenth Century*, 2nd edn (Stanford, Cal.: Stanford University Press, 1967) pp. 164–5.

4. Ibid., pp. 44–5, 124–7. Steck mistakenly translates '*la ciudad que de nuevo* [recently] *han comenzado a edificar*' as 'the city which they have begun to rebuild': cf. T. de Motolinía, *Historia de los indios de la Nueva Espana*, ed. G. Baudot (Madrid: Clásicos Castalia, 1985) p. 203, and *History*, p. 160. For the role of the *cabildo* in Tlaxcala, see Gibson, *Tlaxcala*, pp. 103–15.

5. The square, although now surrounded by colonial buildings of a later date, still serves as the main plaza of Tlaxcala. Tall ash-trees reduce the appearance of horizontal space. Pacing out the square's dimensions, as I did in September 1988, therefore yields something of a surprise. Each side of the square measures approximately 200 yards, encompassing an area about the size of four soccer pitches.

6. The play was not, as Gibson, *Tlaxcala*, p. 38, implies, performed on a single 'stage' but, in the manner of *The Conquest of Rhodes*, used the entire plaza as an elaborate playing area. Figure 6.1 may profitably be compared with the Plan of Central Tlaxcala provided by Gibson (p. 127), so long as it is remembered that the '*cabildo* dwellings' on Gibson's plan are those built around 1550 (ibid., p. 128). The earlier buildings, to which Motolinía refers, were, as Gibson (p. 126) makes clear, on the north-west side of the square. I have followed Gibson's more precise account of the relationship of the square to the points of the compass. Thus what Motolinía calls the western side of the square is, in fact, the north-western side.

7. Steck (in Motolinía, *History*, p. 160) translates '*en la parte oriental fuera de la plaza*' as 'out on the eastern part of the plaza', rather than, as I prefer, 'on the eastern side outside the square'.

8. W. and A. Durant, *The Story of Civilization* (New York: Simon & Schuster, 1935–75) vol. 6, p. 203. The Siege of Granada culminated in the final defeat of the Moors in Spain.

9. F. Toor, 'A Glimpse of Oaxaca', *Mexican Folkways*, vol. 2, no. 1 (1926) pp. 5–6.

10. B. Díaz, *The True History of the Conquest of New Spain*, trans. A. P. Maudslay (London: Hakluyt Society, 1908–16), cap. 149 (vol. 4, p. 98).

11. F. López de Gómara, *La conquista de México*, ed. J. de Rojas (Madrid: Historia 16, 1987) p. 248. My italics.

12. R. Baumann, 'Tlaxcalan Expression of Autonomy and Religious Drama in the Sixteenth Century', *Journal of Latin American Lore*, vol. 13 (1987) pp. 145–6.

13. M. Bakhtin, *Rabelais and his World*, trans. H. Iswolsky (Bloomington, Ind.: Indiana University Press, 1984) pp. 7–12, 155.

14. J. L. Phelan, *The Millenial Kingdom of the Franciscans in the New World*, 2nd edn (Berkeley, Cal.: University of California Press, 1970) p. 33.
15. Gibson, *Tlaxcala*, p. 191.
16. Ibid., p. ix.
17. Motolinía, *History*, pp. 14–15.
18. Ibid., p. 18.
19. J. Williams, 'El teatro de evangelización en México durante el siglo XVI: reseña historico-literaria', dissertation, Yale University, 1980, p. 143.
20. F. Horcasitas, *El teatro náhuatl* (Mexico: Universidad Nacional Autónoma de México, 1974) p. 508.
21. D. Durán, *Book of the Gods and Rites and the Ancient Calendar*, trans. F. Horcasitas and D. Heyden (Norman, Okla: University of Oklahoma Press, 1971) pp. 295–6.
22. Sant' Iago (James) reputedly descended from heaven on a white horse during the (probably legendary) Battle of Clavijo (AD 844) and single-handedly killed 60,000 Moors, ensuring victory for the Spanish. See *Enciclopedia universal ilustrada europeo americana*, 21 vols (Barcelona: Espasa, 1925) vol. 13, pp. 748–9. He was also sighted in a number of later battles, including Cortés's victory at Otumba in 1520 (W. H. Prescott, *The Conquest of Mexico* (1843; New York: Random House, n.d.) p. 464, n. 31). For these and other reputed sightings of Santiago, see W. Starkie, *The Road to Santiago* (New York: Dutton, 1957) pp. 23–4, 29–30, 44.
23. R. Ricard, *The Spiritual Conquest of Mexico*, trans. L. B. Simpson (Berkeley, Cal.: University of California Press, 1966) p. 87.
24. My emphasis. It was on the feast day of St Hippolytus, 22 August 1520, that the Aztecs surrendered to Cortés.
25. See below, ch. 9.
26. Motolinía, *History*, p. 182; Ricard, *Spiritual Conquest*, p. 91.
27. Motolinía, *History*, p. 186.
28. Ricard, *Spiritual Conquest*, p. 93.
29. Easter Sunday fell on 6 April in 1539. See *The Book of Calendars*, ed. F. Parise (New York: Facts on File, 1982) p. 327.
30. Motolinía, *History*, p. 190.
31. The movable feast of Corpus Christi falls on the Thursday after Trinity Sunday. In 1539 this would have been 5 June.
32. Arroníz, *Teatro*, p. 82.
33. Motolinía, *History*, pp. 166–7.
34. Horcasitas, *El teatro náhuatl*, p. 191, suggests that a Náhuatl *Sacrifice of Isaac*, extant in eighteenth-century manuscript form, may be the text of the play performed in Tlaxcala in 1539. He prints (pp. 208–29) both the Náhuatl text and a Spanish translation. M. E. Ravicz, *Early Colonial Religious Drama in Mexico* (Washington, D. C.: Catholic University of America Press, 1970) pp. 83–98 has translated the play into English. A recent discussion of this text can be found in R. Potter, 'Abraham and Human Sacrifice: the Exfoliation of Medieval Drama in Aztec Mexico', *New Theatre Quarterly*, vol. 2 (1986) pp. 306–12. Potter believes that this text 'is almost certainly derived from the 1539 Tlaxcala performance'.

Stylistic evidence for an early date of *The Sacrifice of Isaac* is substantial. Beyond that, however, only the coincidence of subject matter links the text and Motolinía's account of *The Sacrifice of Abraham*.

Notes to Chapter 7: Santiago, the Sun King

1. *Relación breve y verdadera de algunas cosas de las muchas que sucedieron al padre fray Alonso Ponce en las provincias de Nueva España* . . . , vol. 1, pp. 141, 162–3.
2. P. W. Powell, *Soldiers, Indians and Silver* (Berkeley, Cal.: University of California Press, 1969). For 'the Tlaxcalan trek', see P. W. Powell, *Mexico's Miguel Caldera*, (Tucson, Ariz.: University of Arizona Press, 1977) pp. 147–59; and Gibson, pp. 183–9.
3. *Relación breve*, pp. 164–5.
4. Gibson, *Tlaxcala in the Sixteenth-Century*, 2nd edn (Stanford, Cal.: Stanford University Press, 1967) pp. 147–8.
5. *Relación breve*, vol. 2, pp. 8–11.
6. M. M. Bakhtin, *Rabelais and his World*, trans. H. Islowsky (Bloomington, Ind.: Indiana University Press, 1984) p. 9.
7. References to subsequent battle plays in Tlaxcala, in 1640, 1729, 1733 and 1738, may be found in C. Gutiérrez de Medina, *Viaje del virrey Marqués de Villena* (Mexico: Imprenta Universitaria, 1947) pp. 57–9; and *Gacetas de México*, ed. F. Gonzalez de Cossio (Mexico: Secretaria de Educación Publica, 1949–50) vol. 1, p. 176; vol. 2, p. 87; and vol. 3, p. 131. These very brief accounts suggest that the 'unofficial' voice may once again have found expression in the performance of indigenous dances and *moriscos*.
8. Bakhtin, *Rabelais*, p. 9.
9. Ibid., p. 245.
10. K. Clark and M. Holquist, *Mikhail Bakhtin* (Cambridge, Mass.: Harvard University Press, 1984) pp. 310–11.
11. N. Wachtel, *The Vision of the Vanquished*, trans. B. and S. Reynolds (New York: Barnes & Noble, 1977) pp. 7 and 33.
12. F. Toor, *A Treasury of Mexican Folkways* (Mexico: Mexico Press, 1947) p. 349. For an earlier account of the *santiagos* in Cuetzalán, see D. B. and D. M. Cordry, *Costumes and Textiles of the Aztec Indians of the Cuetzalán Region, Puebla, Mexico*, Southwest Museum Papers no. 14 (Los Angeles, Cal.: Southwest Museum, 1940) pp. 12–15.
13. R. J. Bromley, 'Sierra of Puebla: By-passed Zone of Mexico', *Geographical Magazine*, vol. 42 (1970) pp. 752–61.
14. A. Santiago Aguilar Lara, *Tradición: ensayo histórico y social del legendario pueblo de Quetzalán*, 2nd edn (Puebla: Año 2100, 1988) p. 22.
15. Ibid., pp. 26, 109–10. Santiago is quoting from a letter of the viceroy, Luis de Velasco, written in 1557, citing Ramírez's report of his earlier visit. Ramírez's *visita* to the provinces of Vera Cruz and Pánuco lasted from October 1551 to August 1555, when he died in Otumba, Mexico. See W. V. Scholes, *The Diego Ramírez Visita* (Columbia, Mo.: University

of Missouri Studies, 1946); and M. J. Sarabia Viejo, *Don Luis de Velasco* (Seville: Escuela de Estudios Hispano-Americanos, 1978) pp. 366–83. I have been unable to trace a printed edition of the letter from which Santiago quotes and for which he gives as his source the library of *El Sol de Puebla*.

16. Santiago, *Tradición*, p. 26; D. Durán, *Book of the Gods and Rites and The Ancient Calendar*, trans. F. Horcasitas and D. Heyden (Norman, Okla: University of Oklahoma Press, 1971), pp. 238–47.
17. Santiago, *Tradición*, p. 90.
18. M. Leon-Portilla, *Aztec Thought and Culture*, trans. J. E. Davis (Norman, Okla: University of Oklahoma Press, 1963) p. 65.
19. Santiago, *Tradición*, p. 16. Cf. Toor, *Treasury*, pp. 317–23; H. Larsen, 'Notes on the *volador* and its Associated Ceremonies and Superstitions', *Ethnos*, vol. 4 (1937) pp. 179–92; L. Leal, 'Los Voladores: From Ritual to Game', *New Scholar*, vol. 8 (1982) pp. 129–42; M. G. Castro de DeLaRosa, 'Voladores and Hua-huas: Two Ritual Dances of the Region of Papantla', *UCLA Journal of Dance Ethnology*, vol. 9 (1985) pp. 46–64.
20. For the *quetzal* and *negritos* dances, see Santiago, *Tradición*, pp. 16–20; and Toor, *Treasury*, pp. 353–6, 361.
21. M. Stone, *At the Sign of Midnight* (Tucson, Ariz.: University of Arizona Press, 1975) p. 187, writing of the Dance of the Concheros, remarks, 'The baston, symbol of authority and depicted in the dance god's hands on sheet 88 of Codex Vaticanus 3773, is carried in a shortened version by all capitanes de mesa and by most dance chiefs'. Cordry and Cordry, *Costumes and Textiles*, p. 13, call the *Santiago caballero* 'the principal dancer' in *la danza de los santiagos*. He is the most picturesque but not, in the case of the Yohualichán troupe, the leader.
22. Cordry and Cordry, *Costumes and Textiles*, p. 16, provide a detailed drawing of the drum.
23. The dancer's name is Leonardo Galindo. He guided four of us to the ruins of Yohualichán, as well as introducing us to the mask-maker for his group, Sr Ernesto Toval Cruz, whom we were able to watch at work. Afterwards, Leonardo kindly invited us to his parents' home in San Miguel Tzinacapán, where we were able to photograph his costume. For a photograph of the shield, see Toor, *Treasury* pl. 68.
24. Cf. the masks worn by 'Christians' in V. J. Maya Rubio, *Máscaras: la otra cara de México* (Mexico: Universidad Nacional Autónoma de México, 1978) pls 41, 51, 52; and Wachtel, *Vision of the Vanquished*, facing p. 40, pl. 3.
25. J. H. Towsen, *Clowns* (New York: Hawthorn, 1976) pp. 3–21.
26. M. Díaz Roig, 'La Danza de la Conquista', *Nueva Revista de Filología Hispánica*, vol. 32 (1983) p. 194.
27. Santiago, *Tradición*, p. 24.
28. For a photograph of the parade of the *huipil* queen, see *Fiestas in Mexico*, ed. F. Santiago E. (Mexico: Lara, 1978) p. 143. Do beware of the information provided in this guidebook, however, as much of it is outdated or erroneous.

29. Santiago, *Tradición*, p. 25.
30. B. C. Brundage, *The Fifth Sun: Aztec Gods, Aztec World* (Austin, Tx.: University of Texas Press, 1979) p. 159–60.
31. Cf. Stone, *At the Sign of Midnight*, p. 44: 'Often that spring, as the danzantes talked of velaciones, funerals, and Masses for the dead, I heard them say, "It is the custom." '

Notes to Chapter 8: Hidden Aztecs and Absent Spaniards

1. B. Díaz del Castillo, *Historia verdadera de la conquista de la Nueva, España*, cap. 86, ed. J. Ramírez Cabañas (Mexico: Espasa-Calpe Mexicana, 1950) vol. 2, pp. 28–9; P. Gerhard, *A Guide to the Historical Geography of New Spain* (Cambridge: Cambridge University Press, 1972) pp. 141–2; R. García Granados and L. MacGregor, *Huejotzingo: la ciudad y el convento franciscano* (Mexico: Talleres Gráficos de la Nación, 1934) pp. 23–61.
2. F. Toor, 'Carnavales en los pueblos', *Mexican Folkways*, vol. 5, no. 1 (1929) p. 15, notes that 'about a thousand men took part' in 1928. The number of participants has therefore more than doubled in the last 60 years. Carnival is a movable feast, immediately preceding Ash Wednesday, the first day of Lent. In 1989 Carnival Tuesday fell on February 7.
3. García Granados and MacGregor, *Huejotzingo*, p. 346. A fairly full description of the carnival play, with a number of black and white photographs, is included in this work, pp. 326–46.
4. F. Toor, *A Treasury of Mexican Folkways* (Mexico: Mexico Press, 1947) p. 194. For a more complete account of the carnival, with a number of black and white photographs, see Toor, 'Carnavales', pp. 10–27. For two colour photographs, see M. Sutherland, 'Mexico's Booming Capital', *National Geographic*, vol. 100 (1951) pp. 818–19.
5. V. J. Maya Rubio, *Máscaras: la otra cara de México* (Mexico: Universidad Nacional Autónoma de México, 1978) p. 195. For a brief account of the historical events leading up to and including the defence of Puebla, see H. B. Parkes, *A History of Mexico* (Boston, Mass.: Houghton Mifflin, 1938) pp. 251–6; or J. Haslip, *The Crown of Mexico* (New York: Holt, 1971) pp. 162–80.
6. I. A. Leonard, *Baroque Times in Old Mexico* (1959; Westport, Conn.: Greenwood, 1981) pp. 117–29.
7. A. Toro, 'The Morismas', *Mexican Folkways*, vol. 1, no. 2 (1925) pp. 8–10. Calling the *morisma* a 'very ancient . . . custom', Toro cites the *Conquest of Rhodes* described by Bernal Díaz as its predecessor.
8. A. Salas, 'La batalla del 5 de Mayo en el Peñon', *Mexican Folkways*, vol. 8, no. 2 (1933) pp. 56–76. Salas does not specify the date on which the play was performed. I assume it was 5 May, the anniversary of the battle it commemorated. A paraphrase of Salas's article can be found in Toor, *Treasury*, pp. 225–9. Toor adds (p. 225) that the play had been performed at El Peñon 'since 1920 or thereabouts', and (p. 229) that the last time she saw it was in 1945.

9. Salas, 'La batalla', p. 60.
10. C.-A. Julien, *Histoire de l'Algérie contemporaine* (Paris: Presses Universitaires de France, 1964–79) vol. 1, pp. 66–7.
11. For a more detailed description of the costumes, which have not changed in the interim, see Toor, 'Carnavales', pp. 19–20; or Toor, *Treasury*, pp. 194–5. In Toor's description the Indios are called Serranos by way of reference to their home in the Sierra.
12. According to a programme quoted by Toor, 'Carnavales', p. 16, Saturday afternoon had begun in the 1920s with the plaza in possession of the French and Turks. It had then been taken by 'the forces of the General-in-Chief, making prisoners of all the enemy soldiers'. This had been followed by a parade. While this may have happened in 1989 before I arrived, nobody I questioned made mention of such an enactment. It would appear that this part of the play has now lost its narrative content and has become mere spectacle.
13. Toor, 'Carnavales', p. 18.
14. M. L. Moorhead, *The Apache Frontier* (Norman, Okla: University of Oklahoma Press, 1968) p. vii.
15. Toro, 'The Morismas', p. 9.
16. M. M. Bakhtin, *Rabelais and his World*, trans. H. Islowsky (Bloomington, Ind.: Indiana University Press, 1984) p. 92.
17. A. Artaud, *The Theater and its Double*, trans. M. C. Richards (New York: Grove, 1958) p. 124.
18. Toor, 'Carnavales', p. 27.
19. Ibid., p. 20.
20. García Granados and MacGregor, *Huejotzingo*, pp. 327–31, cite an old informant who claimed to have read a manuscript account, then lost, of the life of Agustín Lorenzo. According to the manuscript, 'El Meco' had been the member of the gang closest to Lorenzo and the one ordinarily entrusted with the most difficult and daring operations. It was he who used to carry love-letters between Lorenzo and the daughter of the *corregidor*. *Meco*, in Mexican, is derived from Chichimeca and means loosely 'wild Indian'.
21. According to F. Toor, 'Agustín Lorenzo: héroe de los juegos carnavalescos', *Mexican Folkways*, vol. 8, no. 1 (1933) p. 35, the bride and her abductor used to slide down a rope.
22. Toor, 'Carnavales', p. 22. George Mentore, Assistant Professor of Anthropology at the University of Virginia, has suggested to me that the donkey, a popular phallic symbol in the Caribbean, may have a similar significance here.
23. Ibid., pp. 23–4.
24. Artaud, *Theater*, pp. 27, 30–1.
25. Ibid., p. 124.
26. I had been told that Lorenzo used to descend from the mountain caves near Río Frío to rob the wealthy and help the poor. Toor, 'Agustín Lorenzo', p. 35, admits to having been unable to find any historical or literary confirmation of such legends. W. P. Sprattling, 'Agustín Lorenzo', *Mexican Folkways*, vol. 8, no. 1 (1933) pp. 36–45, suggests that Lorenzo hailed from Tlamacazupa, Guerrero, and that he was for

many years 'a great bandit' in the central states of Guerrero, Michoacán, Morelos and Puebla. Sprattling also mentions (p. 38) the performance in San Juan de Dios, Guerrero, of *El reto* [The Challenge], a confused festival drama of charging horsemen involving 'several principal characters . . . who had aztec [*sic*] names' and Agustín Lorenzo. D. C. Moreno, 'El bandido Agustín Lorenzo', *Mexican Folkways*, vol. 5, no. 2 (1929) pp. 86–8, writes that Lorenzo abandoned his banditry to fight against the French Imperial forces during the 1860s, and that when he abducted the daughter of the Chief of the Imperial Garrison in Huejotzingo, it was an act of political as well as romantic daring.

27. Julien, *Histoire de l'Algérie*, vol. 1, pp. 385–7, 393–5.
28. Cf. Maya Rubio, *Mascaras*, pl. 115, the photograph of a mask worn by the *rey moro* in the *danza de moros y cristianos* at Apaxtla, Guerrero; and García Granados and MacGregor, *Huejotzingo*, p. 27, the photograph of a fragment of prehispanic sculpture found by the authors at Nepopualco, some five miles from Huejotzingo.
29. D. Durán, *Book of the Gods and Rites and the Ancient Calendar*, trans. F. Horcasitas and D. Heyden (Norman, Okla: University of Oklahoma Press, 1971) pp. 248–60.
30. Toor, *Treasury*, pp. 535–6.
31. Bakhtin, *Rabelais*, pp. 279, 281, 283.
32. Leonard, *Baroque Times*, p. 125–6. The Chichimeca's banner, at Huejotzingo, proclaimed, '*Grupo de cánibales. Pies negros*'. The announcer named them '*africanos cánibales*'. But a spectator next to me called them '*mecos*', and most were dressed like Lorenzo's Chichimeca messenger.
33. Toor, 'A Glimpse of Oaxaca', pp. 5–6. *La danza de las plumas* is still widely performed in the villages of Oaxaca.
34. V. R. Bricker, *The Indian Christ, the Indian King* (Austin, Tx: University of Texas Press, 1981) p. 133.
35. M. Leon-Portilla, *Visión de los vencidos* (México: Universidad Nacional Autónoma de México, 1959). T. Todorov, *The Conquest of America: The Question of the Other*, trans. R. Howard (New York: Harper & Row, 1984) pp. 54, 232–3, draws attention to the way in which these indigenous accounts were filtered through the mindset of their European chroniclers.
36. M. Díaz Roig, 'La Danza de la Conquista', *Nueva Revista de Filología Hispánica*, vol. 32 (1983) p. 194.

Notes to Chapter 9: Barbarians and Other Neighbours

1. T. Todorov, *The Conquest of America: The Question of the Other*, trans. R. Howard (New York: Harper & Row, 1984) p. 241.
2. A. Pagden, *The Fall of Natural Man* (Cambridge: Cambridge University Press, 1982) p. 16. Pagden provides (pp. 15–19) a succinct account of the Greek 'image of the barbarian'.
3. Aristotle, *The Politics*, 1277b–1278a, 1328b–1329a, trans. T. A. Sinclair,

rev. T. J. Saunders (Harmondsworth, Middx.: Penguin, 1981) pp. 183–5, 414–15.

4. Ibid., 1253b, p. 62.

5. Ibid., 12601, p. 95. Aristotle, *Nichomachean Ethics*, 1162a, trans. M. Ostwald (New York: Macmillan, 1986) p. 239, does make one small concession to women, allowing the possibility that 'friendship' between husband and wife can transcend innate sexual inequality and, 'if the partners are good, may even be based on [shared] virtue and excellence'.

6. Aristotle, *Politics*, 1254b–1255a, p. 69. For a summary of Aristotle's position on slavery, see Pagden, *Fall*, pp. 41–7.

7. Aristotle, *Politics*, 1252b, p. 57.

8. Pagden, *Fall*, p. 47.

9. Aristotle, *Politics*, 1255a, p. 69.

10. O. H. Green, 'A Note on Spanish Humanism: Sepúlveda and His Translation of Aristotle's *Politics*', *Hispanic Review*, vol. 8 (1940) pp. 339–42.

11. J. G. de Sepúlveda, *Demócrates segundo o de las justas causas de la guerra contra los indios*, ed. and trans. A. Losada, 2nd edn (Madrid: Consejo Superior de Investigaciones Cientificos, 1984); cf. A. Losada, *Juan Ginés de Sepúlveda a través de su 'Epistolario' y nuevos documentos* (1949; Madrid: Consejo Superior de Investigaciones Cientificos, 1973) pp. 96–102, 189–229; Todorov, *Conquest*, pp. 152–61; Pagden, *Fall*, pp. 41–118. For a brief account in English of Sepúlveda's life and work, see A. F. G. Bell, *Juan Ginés de Sepúlveda* (Oxford: Oxford University Press, 1925).

12. L. Hanke, *Aristotle and the American Indians* (Bloomington, Ind.: Indiana University Press, 1959) p. 78.

13. A. López Austin, *The Human Body of Ideology: Concepts of the Ancient Nahuas*, trans. T. and B. Ortiz de Montellano (Salt Lake City, Utah: University of Utah Press, 1988) vol. 1, pp. 388–90. Cf. R. C. Padden, *The Hummingbird and the Hawk* (Columbus, Ohio: Ohio State University Press, 1967) pp. 14–48, 92–9.

14. Lopéz Austin, *Human Body*, pp. 387, 292. Cf. Todorov, *Conquest*, pp. 91–2; W. H. Prescott, *The Conquest of Mexico* (1843; New York: Random House, n.d.) p. 422; and B. Díaz del Castillo, *Historia verdadera de la conquista de la Nueva España*, cap. 141, ed. J. Ramírez Cabañas (Mexico: Espase-Calpe Mexicana, 1950) vol. 2, p. 169.

15. Todorov, *Conquest*, p. 76; D. Durán, *Historia de las indias de Nueva España*, tom. 2, cap. 28 (Mexico: Porrua, 1967–71) vol. 2, p. 233. Padden, *Hummingbird*, p. 39, suggests that Tlacaelel's argument was grounded more in military realism than in religious insight: 'The truth of the matter was that the Chichimeca were too hard to defeat; the Mexica [Aztecs] never succeeded in breaking their frontiers'.

16. M. Leon-Portilla (ed.), *The Broken Spears*, trans. L. Kemp (Boston, Mass.: Beacon Press, 1962) pp. 51–2; B. de Sahagún, *General History of New Spain, Florentine Codex* ed. and trans. A. J. O. Anderson and C. E. Dibble, 13 vols (Santa Fe, N. M.: School of American Research, 1950–82) vol. 13, p. 31.

17. B. de Las Casas, *Apologética historia sumaria*, lib. 3, cap. 4 (Mexico: Universidad Nacional Autónoma de México, 1967) vol. 2, p. 385; *History of the Indies*, trans. A. Collard (New York: Harper & Row, 1971) p. 184.

18. B. de Sahagún, *Historia general de las cosas de Nueva España*, lib. 1, prol. (Mexico: Pedro Robredo, 1938) vol. 1, p. 10; quoted in Todorov, *Conquest*, p. 239.

19. B. de Las Casas, *In Defense of the Indians*, ch. 3, trans. S. Poole (DeKalb, Ill.: Northern Illinois University Press, 1974) p. 39.

20. E. Dussel, *A History of the Church in Latin America*, trans. A. Neely (Grand Rapids, Mich.: Eerdmans, 1981) p. 6; Aristotle, *Nichomachean Ethics*, 1161b.

21. Todorov, *Conquest*, p. 168.

22. Ibid., pp. 42–3.

23. Ibid., pp. 44–6.

24. F. de Vitoria, *De Indis et De Jure Belli*, ed. E. Nys, trans. J. P. Bate (Washington, D. C.: Carnegie Institute, 1917). Since the first series of lectures (*De Indis*) deals specifically with the question of just conquest of the New World and the second (*De Jure Belli*) more generally with the principles of just war, I will confine my comments to the first and longer of the two.

25. *The Conquest of Jerusalem* was performed 5 June 1539 (see above, ch. 6, n. 31). For biographical data on Vitoria, see B. Hamilton, *Political Thought in Sixteenth Century Spain* (Oxford: Clarendon Press, 1963) pp. 171–6. For a discussion of the dates of the lectures' preparation and delivery, see L. G. Alonso Getino, *El Maestro Fr Francisco de Vitoria* (Madrid: Imprenta Católica, 1930) pp. 141–51, but beware of the misprint (1549 for 1539) at the foot of p. 148. For confirmation of the June 1539 delivery date, see *Gran enciclopedia Rialp* (Madrid: Rialp, 1975) vol. 23, p. 634.

26. Vitoria, *De Indis*, p. 120.

27. Ibid., pp. 125–9.

28. Ibid., pp. 138–49.

29. For the text of the papal bulls of donation, see M. Gímenez Fernández, *Nuevas consideraciones sobre la historia, sentido y valor de las bulas alejandrinas de 1493 referentes a las indias* (Seville: Escuela de Estudios Hispano-Americanos de la Universidad de Sevilla, 1944) pp. 165–211. For an English translation of the *Requerimiento*, see L. Hanke (ed.), *History of Latin American Civilization*, 2nd edn (Boston, Mass.: Little, Brown, 1973) vol. 1, pp. 94–5.

30. Todorov, *Conquest*, pp. 147–8. Lest we be tempted, in our own ethnocentrism, to assume that these kinds of bias were peculiar to the sixteenth-century, we would do well to remember the annexation by the United States of vast areas of territory, much of it already occupied by Mexicans and native Americans, in the name of Manifest Destiny. This singularly ethnocentric doctrine was founded not on papal authority but on the supposition of direct divine election.

31. Vitoria, *De Indis*, pp. 134–7.

32. Ibid., p. 151.

33. Ibid., pp. 155–7.
34. The phrase is taken from E. Broun, 'Foreword', in *The West as America: Reinterpreting Images of the Frontier*, ed. W. H. Truettner (Washington, D.C.: Smithsonian Institution, 1991) p. viii.
35. Vitoria, *De Indis*, pp. 158–61.
36. Todorov, *Conquest*, p. 149.
37. Vitoria, *De Indis*, p. 257: '*Primus titulus potest vocari naturalis societatis et communicationis*', cited in translation in Todorov, *Conquest*, p. 149.
38. Todorov, *Conquest*, pp. 149–50.
39. Ibid., p. 250.
40. Ibid., p. 202; cf. p. 222.
41. Ibid., p. 223.
42. A. López Austin, 'The Research Method of Fray Bernardino de Sahagun: The Questionnaires', in *Sixteenth-Century Mexico: The Work of Sahagún*, ed. M. S. Edmonson (Albuquerque, N.M.: University of New Mexico Press, 1974) p. 118.
43. Todorov, *Conquest*, p. 227.
44. M. S. Edmonson, 'Introduction,' in *Sixteenth-Century Mexico*, pp. 4–5.
45. Todorov, *Conquest*, p. 226.
46. López Austin, 'Research Method', p. 120.
47. Ibid., pp. 135–6.
48. Sahagún, *General History*, vol. 13, p. 54.
49. Todorov, *Conquest*, pp. 231–2.
50. Sahagún, *Historia*, vol. 1, pp. 53–75.
51. Todorov, *Conquest*, pp. 237–41.
52. Ibid., p. 202. For further biographical data on Durán, see F. Horcasitas and D. Heyden, 'Fray Diego Durán: His Life and Works', in their edition of D. Durán, *Book of the Gods and Rites and the Ancient Calendar* (Norman, Okla: University of Oklahoma Press, 1971) pp. 3–47.
53. Durán, *Historia*, lib. 3, cap. 74 (vol. 2, p. 539), cited in translation in Todorov, *Conquest*, p. 213.
54. Todorov, *Conquest*, pp. 213–8; Durán, *Historia*, lib. 2, cap. 1 (vol. 1, p. 224).
55. T. Todorov, 'Les Récits de la conquête', in *Récits aztèques de la conquête*, ed. G. Baudot and T. Todorov (Paris: Seuil, 1983) p. 361.
56. Todorov, *Conquest*, p. 225.
57. For the history of Durán's manuscript, see F. Horcasitas and D. Heyden's 'Bibliographical Note' in their edition of Durán, *Book of the Gods*, pp. xvii–xxiv. Durán was all but forgotten for almost 300 years after his death in 1588. His manuscript was discovered in the National Library of Madrid in the early 1850s and finally published in Mexico between 1867 and 1880. For the history of Sahagún's manuscript, see C. E. Dibble, 'Sahagún's *Historia*', in Sahagún, *General History*, pp. 9–23. Sahagún's papers were confiscated and sent to Spain in 1577, by order of Philip II, and were not rediscovered until 1779 in the Franciscan monastery of Tolosa in northern Spain. They were published in Mexico 1829–30.
58. Todorov, *Conquest*, p. 241.
59. S. J. Samartha, *Courage for Dialogue* (Maryknoll, N. Y.: Orbis Books,

1982) p. viii; R. C. Bassham, *Mission Theology* (Pasadena, Calif.: William Carey Library, 1979) pp. 84–91.

Notes to Chapter 10: Performing the Scriptures

1. T. Todorov, *The Conquest of America: The Question of the Other*, trans. R. Howard (New York: Harper & Row, 1984) p. 239.
2. Ibid., p. 179.
3. E. Broun, 'Foreword', in *The West as America: Reinterpreting Images of the Frontier*, ed. W. H. Truettner (Washington, D.C.: Smithsonian Institution, 1991) p. viii.
4. W. H. Truettner, 'Prelude to Expansion: Repainting the Past', in *The West as America*, p. 62. Leutze's painting is reproduced, ibid., p. 60. R. Hughes, 'How the West Was Spun', *Time*, 31 May 1991, pp. 79–80, argues that Leutze's painting is more 'ambiguous'. 'The Spanish conquistadors', he writes, 'are presented as brutes, one flinging a baby from the temple top, another tearing loot from a corpse; and Leutze's intent to provoke pity for the Aztecs is summed up in an upside-down torch, nearly out, which lies on the steps in the foreground, an adaptation of the classic funerary image of the reversed torch of extinguished genius'. Leutze's historical paintings, in general, tend to celebrate the European discovery of America and the founding and westward expansion of the United States. See B. S. Groseclose, *Emmanuel Leutz, 1816–1868: Freedom is the Only King* (Washington, D.C.: Smithsonian Institution, 1975).
5. A. P. Blaustein, *The Influence of the United States Constitution Abroad* (Washington, D.C.: Washington Institute for Values in Public Policy, 1986) p. 12.
6. Ibid., p. 1.
7. J. H. Yoder, *When War is Unjust* (Minneapolis, Minn.: Augsburg, 1984) p. 27.
8. N. Lash, *Theology on the Way to Emmaus* (London: SCM Press, 1986) pp. 37–46.
9. J. L. Esposito, *Islam: The Straight Path*, 2nd edn (New York: Oxford University Press, 1991) pp. 20–1.
10. G. S. Morson and C. Emerson, *Mikhail Bakhtin: Creation of a Prosaics* (Stanford, Cal.: Stanford University Press, 1990) p. 239; M. M. Bakhtin, *Problems of Dostoevsky's Poetics*, trans. C. Emerson (Minneapolis, Minn.: University of Minneapolis Press, 1984) p. 7.
11. B. B. Warfield, *Selected Shorter Writings of Benjamin B. Warfield*, ed. J. E. Meeter (Nutley, N.J.: Presbyterian & Reformed, 1973) vol. 2, p. 547.
12. Morson and Emerson, *Bakhtin*, p. 267.
13. Lash, *Theology*, p. 25.
14. A Shorter, *Toward a Theology of Inculturation* (Maryknoll, N.Y.: Orbis Books, 1988) p. 18.
15. B. Lonergan, *Method in Theology* (London: Darton, Longman & Todd, 1972) pp. 300–2, 326–7; Lash, *Theology*, p. 20; Shorter, *Theology of Inculturation*, pp. 19–20.

16. A. Kuyper, *Principles of Sacred Theology*, trans. J. H. de Vries (1898; Grand Rapids, Mich.: Baker, 1980) p. 658.
17. Ibid., p. 664.
18. G. C. Berkouwer, *The Church*, trans. J. E. Davison (Grand Rapids, Mich.: Eerdmans, 1976) p. 57.
19. Lonergan, *Method in Theology*, pp. 362–3.
20. G. Delling, '[τέλειος]', in *Theological Dictionary of the New Testament*, ed. G. Kittel and G. Friedrich, trans. G. W. Bromiley, 10 vols (Grand Rapids, Mich.: Eerdmans, 1964–76) vol. 8, pp. 67–78.
21. K. Barth, *Church Dogmatics*, trans. G. W. Bromiley *et al.*, (Edinburgh: T. & T. Clark, 1956–75) vol. 1, pt 2, pp. 418–19.
22. M. M. Bakhtin, *Art and Answerability*, ed. M. Holquist and V. Liapunov, trans. V. Liapunov (Austin, Tx.: University of Texas Press, 1990) p. 128.

Notes to Chapter 11: Incarnation and Other Dialogues

1. M. Buber, 'The History of the Dialogical Principle', trans. M. Friedman, in M. Buber, *Between Man and Man*, trans. R. G. Smith (New York: Macmillan, 1965) pp. 209–24.
2. Ibid., p. 210.
3. J.-P. Sartre, *Being and Nothingness*, trans. H. E. Barnes (New York: Washington Square, 1966) p. 355.
4. Ibid., pp. 302, 347.
5. K. Clark and M. Holquist, *Mikhail Bakhtin* (Cambridge, Mass.: Harvard University Press, 1984) p. 65.
6. M. M. Bakhtin, *Art and Answerability*, ed. M. Holquist and V. Liapunov, trans. V. Liapunov (Austin, Tx.: University of Texas Press, 1990) pp. 22–3.
7. Clark and Holquist, *Bakhtin*, p. 70.
8. G. S. Morson and C. Emerson, *Mikhail Bakhtin: Creation of a Prosaics* (Stanford, Cal.: Stanford University Press, 1990) pp. 52–6.
9. Bakhtin, *Art*, pp. 25–6.
10. Ibid., pp. 73–8.
11. Clark and Holquist, *Bakhtin*, p. 9.
12. Bakhtin, *Art*, p. 27.
13. G. S. Morson and C. Emerson (eds), *Rethinking Bakhtin* (Evanston, Ill.: Northwestern University Press, 1989) p. 11. The editors provide (pp. 5–29) a lengthy summary, with quotations, of Bakhtin's still-untranslated essay, 'Toward a Philosophy of the Act'.
14. Clark and Holquist, *Bakhtin*, p. 68.
15. M. M. Bakhtin, 'Response to a Question from the *Novy Mir* Editorial Staff', in M. M. Bakhtin *Speech Genres and Other Late Essays*, ed. C. Emerson and M. Holquist, trans. V. W. McGee (Austin, Tx.: University of Texas Press, 1986) pp. 6–7.
16. Ibid., p. 4.
17. Ibid., p. 7.
18. Morson and Emerson (eds), *Rethinking Bakhtin*, p. 12.

19.   I am indebted to Gary Saul Morson for providing me with a transla-
       tion of this sentence over the telephone, 18 April 1991.
20.   Morson and Emerson (eds), *Rethinking Bakhtin*, p. 12.
21.   Ibid., pp. 6, 263.
22.   P. Schaff (ed.), *The Creeds of Christendom* (New York: Harper, 1877)
       vol. 2, p. 69.
23.   K. Barth, *Church Dogmatics*, trans. G. W. Bromiley *et al.*, (Edinburgh:
       T. & T. Clark, 1956–75) vol. 1, pt. 2, p. 161.
24.   K. Barth, *The Humanity of God*, trans. J. N. Thomas and T. Wieser
       (Richmond, Va.: John Knox, 1960) p. 45.
25.   A. Shorter, *Toward a Theology of Inculturation* (Maryknoll, N.Y.: Orbis
       Books, 1988) p. 83.
26.   Barth, *Humanity*, p. 51.
27.   Barth, *Church Dogmatics*, vol. 1, pt 2, pp. 160–1.
28.   Shorter, *Theology of Inculturation*, pp. 157–61.
29.   Ibid., pp. 82–4.
30.   T. Todorov, *The Conquest of America: The Question of the Other*, trans.
       R. Howard (New York: Harper & Row, 1984) p. 177.
31.   T. Todorov, ' "Race," Writing, and Culture', trans. L. Mack, *Critical
       Inquiry*, vol. 13 (1986) p. 175.
32.   Ibid., p. 181.
33.   Todorov, *Conquest*, p. 251. For a summary of Bakhtin's view of ethics
       and relativism, see Morson and Emerson, *Bakhtin*, p. 26.
34.   Shorter, *Theology of Inculturation*, p. 14.
35.   D. J. Goldberg and J. D. Raynor, *The Jewish People: Their History of
       Religion* (Harmondsworth, Middx: Viking, 1987) p. 282, remark on 'a
       strong tendency on the part of Diaspora Jews to integrate themselves
       – when permitted to do so – into the political, social and cultural life
       of their countries of domicile, and yet to preserve their own identity'.
36.   N. Lash, *Theology on the Way to Emmaus* (London: SCM Press, 1986)
       p. 21.
37.   L. Fischer, *The Life of Mahatma Gandhi* (New York: Harper & Row,
       1983) p. 268, remarks that the salt march 'required . . . the sense of
       showmanship of a great artist'.

Index